EVERYDAY EVALUATION
ON THE RUN

THIRD EDITION

EVERYDAY EVALUATION ON THE RUN

THIRD EDITION

Yoland Wadsworth

Left Coast
Press Inc.

Walnut Creek, CA

This book is dedicated to the former Premier of Victoria and Ministers for Education, Community Services, and Health—the Honourable Joan Kirner, Kaye Setches, the late Pauline Toner and Caroline Hogg—for originally supporting this cross-portfolio work, and for believing in the importance of hearing the voice of those for whom social justice has not yet been achieved.

LEFT COAST PRESS, INC.
1630 North Main Street, #400
Walnut Creek, CA 94596
http://LCoastPress.com

Cartoons by Simon Kneebone.

FOREWORD TO THE FIRST EDITION

'Evaluation' has become something of a popular incantation, regularly invoked to ensure that the bad spirits of inefficiency, ineffectiveness and inappropriateness do not characterise our human service efforts!

Yet, like 'research' and 'science', it has become a technical specialty with its own language and high priests. This often makes it difficult for those who use or provide the services to feel confident evaluating their own services. We want this guide not only to make evaluation understandable, but also to give readers a sense of the satisfaction that can come from this kind of activity. There can be a real feeling of achievement and purpose from a self-directed learning effort that leads to services that are more spot-on and responsive to users.

Evaluation continues to be used as a reporting and accountability strategy by funders and other authorities. Yet their purpose of providing value for money is not served well if the evaluation either fails to 'get at' the qualitative nature of people's experience, or if it counts the wrong things, does so at the wrong times, or is done for the wrong reasons. This book attempts to outline ways of evaluating that provide meaningful and useful accounts of situations.

As with *Do It Yourself Social Research* (Wadsworth, 1st ed. 1984; 3rd ed. 2011), to which this book is a sequel, the assumption is that readers are best served not so much by a 'cookbook', but rather by describing some of the underlying concepts and principles. Given an understanding of 'why', we have found that people are able to apply the 'how' in flexible ways to their own varied situations.

v

Not a "cookbook" but an explanation of underlying concepts.

We would like to thank all those who have contributed to the various reference groups in which the ideas in this book were developed, debated and tested. We look forward to your feedback for our own further evaluation!

We would like to thank Yoland Wadsworth for her inspiration, rigour and untiring efforts to articulate new and better ways of grasping the business of evaluation and research. We know she considers this book to represent a 'work in progress'. However we are aware that its ideas represent new ways of thinking about and dealing with problems that have already been seized on enthusiastically by those in the field. We hope that these ideas will be widely discussed over the coming years.

Finally, the vision and funding provided by the Victorian State Government Social Justice Strategy has allowed this project to be undertaken. The abiding 'achievement indicator' for the long-term evaluation of the project's success will be whether people find (or are assisted to find) a 'voice' with which they can speak more clearly and loudly about the conditions that are problematic to them, and about the human services that are intended to meet their needs. Under conditions of financial stringency, it is all the more critical to have evaluation approaches that enable us to focus clearly on the ultimate purpose of all our efforts.

—*Sue Kenny*
Action Research Issues Association (Incorporated)

GUIDE TO CONTENTS

WARNING!!
THIS BOOK CONTAINS SOME UNFAMILIAR AND THEORETICAL IDEAS
THAT MAY SOMETIMES SEEM LIKE HARD WORK. PERSEVERANCE WILL
BE REWARDED! PLEASE READ THIS PAGE.

CHAPTER 1: INTRODUCTION

This chapter explains why built-in 'naturalistic' everyday evaluation is so valuable, and introduces the familiarity of its process. It sketches the ideas contained throughout the rest of the book by the example of an evaluation of a humble coffee mug.

CHAPTER 2: A CONCEPTUAL FRAMEWORK

This chapter tracks around a cycle of the evaluation research process—from observation, to designing further fieldwork, to reflections and conclusions, and assessment of future options for new practices, and finally to their planning and enactment. includes a comprehensive discussion of who the evaluation is for, and also of the pros and cons of 'insider' and 'outsider' evaluation.

CHAPTER 3: TWO APPROACHES TO EVALUATION

This chapter commences by asking whether we need to do more evaluating or whether we already know enough to report to those who might have a need to know. When we need new evaluation, two different approaches to evaluation are then contrasted: an 'open inquiry' approach that asks 'Is it working?' and 'Why?', and an audit review approach that asks 'Did we do what we set out to do?' This is a little heavy going, but attempts to dispel the myth that evaluation can only start from formal written objectives. Evaluation should also proceed from observing and reflecting on our large mental store of experiences, intentions and purposes.

CHAPTER 4: DOING EVALUATION

Phew! Now with all that theory behind us it is hoped that we can see how to actually 'build in' evaluation as part of our everyday lives. This chapter proposes the idea of a 'culture of evaluation', ranging from the most micro and short-term to the more macro and long-term—reflecting the different scale of our activities and alignment with our purposes, from over-arching philosophy right down to whether we should, for example, change the phone answering machine message this morning—what we now call 'program logic'.

CHAPTER 5: THE EVALUATION INDUSTRY'S TOOLBOX

Do not sit down and read this chapter from start to finish! Instead, we suggest skimming its index and picking and choosing. The Further Useful Reading at the end is also for the enthusiast. Everyday evaluators can almost certainly get by without knowing all this (however, bits of it might be very useful).

WHAT'S IN
THIS BOOK

CONTENTS

SOME READING

LIST OF GUIDES, DIAGRAMS AND TABLES

GUIDES

DIAGRAMS

TABLES

PREFACE TO THE FIRST EDITION

While 'research' and 'evaluation' are commonly thought to be separate activities, this book describes evaluation as a process of assessing the value of things around us, or things we do, using the same logic and sequence of steps utilised by the kind of research process described in *Do It Yourself Social Research* (3rd ed., 2011).

What this book does as a sequel to *Do It Yourself Social Research* is to examine in far greater detail the evaluative elements of research that become uppermost in our minds when we call our research 'evaluation'. Matters dealt with more fully in the previous book—such as descriptions of techniques, questionnaires and interviews, other resources available, and so on—are touched on only lightly here.

To focus separately on research and evaluation is to focus on different elements of an integrated process. If the previous book looked through the windows of a house, then this book provides some ideas for looking up the front path, through the front and back doors, and down the chimney!

It has been interesting to find that the subject of evaluation has seemed even harder to tackle than that of research in general. It seems that as soon as we move closer to talking explicitly about 'values', there is both more at stake and less that is certain. Many people feel uncomfortable about the loss of certainty and apparent objectivity. In an attempt to reduce this discomfort, there has been a tendency to reach immediately for formal written statements of objectives and specific targets against which activities or practices can then be measured. However, this does not necessarily provide us with the fullest way of evaluating, for reasons that are made clearer in the book. Some of this is difficult terrain. However, while this book is more dense than its precursor, it carries three simple overall messages:

1   Evaluation is a more or less easily accomplished facet of our daily life. Grasping how we do this equips us with exactly the conceptual framework for larger and more conscious efforts.

2   The more we engage in regular, simple, small-scale, theory-building evaluations, the more we will stay 'on track' and the less we will need to resort to large formal and sometimes crisis-provoked theory-testing evaluations.

3   The key to keeping all parties to an evaluation focused on the relevant criteria for judging value (merit, worth or significance) lies in increasing our capacity to hear and voice consumer (or other end-beneficiary) experiences, issues and concerns.

—Yoland Wadsworth
December 1990

3RD PREFACE

PREFACE TO THIS EDITION

Over the past decade, the idea of a 'culture of evaluation' or of research has become widespread. Where once it had to be argued that people's everyday evaluative thinking and feeling rationality had legitimacy, this is now largely considered unremarkable. And where once people's input was seen as essentially 'biased', stakeholder involvement is now considered essential, both as a source of experiential 'data' as well as for its users' own successfully reflexive practice. Indeed, the codes of conduct of the world's evaluation societies now mandate it as part of fully professional practice. The sequel to this book, *Building in Research and Evaluation: Human Inquiry for Living Systems*, describes a deep rationale for why this should be so. This third edition of *Everyday Evaluation on the Run* touches on this deeper articulation of evaluative inquiry as the dynamic of any (truly) living system, but tries not to duplicate that book's content too much.

Questions of value, as well as their articulation as more general principles, have moved to centre stage in recent times. Given the current global trajectory charted by the values that have guided our human decision-making to the precipice of catastrophic climate change, urgent attention has refocused on how matters of values and valuing might more deeply govern action rather than all too easily give way to pragmatic modification and 'mere appearances' without substance.

To achieve this, we are seeing a shift towards balancing the heavy focus of the past on after-the-event, audit-style evaluation that can often only rather helplessly describe *retrospectively* what has already happened to integrating this with more *prospective* open inquiry-style evaluation that can ask the questions about what might be of more value in *future practice* and why. In this way, evaluation's necessary admission of the act of *valuing* promises to 'join the circle' from inductive to abductive to deductive evaluative inquiry (Wadsworth, 2008b; Barton et al., 2009), putting an end to the paradigm wars, and reintegrating 'human systemicity' at any scale.

However, despite much progress, there continues to be a gap between the elaborate and sophisticated activities of evaluation professionals and the small-scale but essential everyday evaluative activity of all those others engaged in human activities, efforts and services.

Yet the need to build on the capacity for thoughtful, reflective, evaluative practice of the latter group, and to decrease their loss of confidence in their abilities to do this, has never been more urgent.

When professional evaluators share 'war stories' of the wastage of their efforts, what I suspect is really at issue is the dearth of built-in ways for people throughout the social systems that have engaged their services to stop and think about what they are doing, to inquire into the effects, to discuss this among themselves, and then narrow the distance between the desired and the actual. I hope this book makes a modest contribution towards continuing to build a broader culture of evaluation throughout human systems.

—*Yoland Wadsworth*

ACKNOWLEDGEMENTS

Many people have contributed to this project during its initial years of gestation and since, either directly or by participating in a more general evaluation culture.

Special thanks go to:

- the original Social Justice Partnership Project Steering Committee members, for their support and for their intellectual contribution, with:
- Lynton Brown, Nominee of the Minister of Education
- Sue Kenny, Action Research Issues Association
- Des Lavery, Nominee of the Minister for Community Services
- Helen Lee, Brunswick resident—co-opted member
- David Legge, Nominee of the Minister of Health, and Manager of the Partnership Project, Health Department Victoria—until January 1990
- Onella Stagoll, Deputee of the Manager of the Partnership Project, Health Department Victoria, February–March 1990
- George Preston, Deputee of the Manager of the Partnership Project, Health Department Victoria—from April 1990
- Veronica Spillane, Social Justice Strategy Unit, Department of Premier and Cabinet—until December 1989
- Ros Johnson, as above—from January 1990–April 1990
- Mary Baker, as above—from May 1990
- Gai Wilson, seconded project worker from Melbourne District Health Council—until September 1990
- Jane Wexler, Project worker—from October 1990, and
- Ros Wood, Nominee of the Collective of Self-Help Groups

The original Readers' Sounding Board and their then-auspicing organisations, including Ann Barry (Low Income People's Network), Jacques Boulet (Phillip Institute), Raewyn Connell (Macquarie University), Joan Chan (Broadmeadows Community Health Centre), Linette Hawkins (ARIA), Stephen Kemmis (Deakin University), Fiona McDermott (University of Melbourne), Rick Mohr (evaluation consultant, Sydney), Barbara Potter (Alzheimer Society), Stuart Rees (Sydney University), Gavan Thomson (Friends of the Earth), Jenny Trethewey (Brotherhood of St Laurence), the late Robyn Walker (Springvale Community Health Centre) and members of the Steering Committee.

Those associated with the Alzheimer Society 'Carers as Researchers' and 'Professional Carers' Seminars' evaluation project—Barbara Potter, Margaret McLaren, and the carers who met at Kerang; those associated with the Royal Women's Hospital midwifery consumer study, including Margaret Mabbit and Lynne Maggs; those associated with the Community Development in Health/District Health Councils 'Deep Thought' project, and later, the Researchers in Community Health (RICH) Network including Fiona Gardner, Janice Jessen, Catriona Knothe, Demos Krouskos, Erica Moulang, the late Marjorie Oke, Gavan Thomson and the late Robyn Walker; Joan Byrne of the Women's Arthritic Task Force; the 1989 third-year Phillip Institute of Technology Social Work research course students; those associated with the North Richmond Community Health Centre and its 'Positive Visions' project, including Colleen Pearce, Ian Sharpe, Julie Shiels and Annie Sprague; Kate Sommerville and those who attended the Richmond Fellowship Service Agreement Workshop; those who took part in the Consumers' Health Forum Grants Program Group Self-Evaluation; Gaylene Kyrgiou, Mary Furman and Lou Iaquinto of the Colanda deinstitutionalisation research project; Susanne Baxandall and Pat Dodson from the self-help/ support groups evaluation project, Anti-Cancer Council of Victoria; and Lyndal Grimshaw, Di Otto, the late Joan Roberts, Maggie McGuiness and Terry Melbourne, involved in two projects of the Victorian Mental Illness Awareness Council designed to introduce the direct participation of psychiatric service-users in evaluating, influencing and making decisions about these services.

Members of the Melbourne Evaluation and Research Group, etc. (MERGe), especially those participating in the discussions on standards manuals, service agreements, performance indicators, and internal and external evaluations, also in particular Inez Dussuyer, Jerry Winston, Mary Crooks, and Marie Brennan; Lucinda Aberdeen, David Green, Meg Montague, and the late Wendy Weeks of the Action Research Issues Association; members of tenant groups at Ross House, in particular Robyn Tumelty (VICRAID), Lesley Holton (Caravan Parks) and Lyn Romeo (formerly of Shelter Intellectual Disability Linkages project); those involved in the development of the *Notes on Running An Introductory Workshop* on Evaluation, in particular Rhona Miller and the ten trial workshops' participants; and Jacqui Robinson and the volunteers coordinators associated with the Volunteers Centre for Victoria who first trialled it successfully as a 'train the trainer' approach.

Simon Kneebone, cartoonist, for his always-wonderful illustrations.

For permission to use other material and illustrations: Marcia Plummer; Ian Sharpe; Michael Quinn Patton and the Public Health Association of Australia (for themes of qualitative inquiry); Denise Fry and the Australian Community Health Association (for CHASP example); Combined Pensioners Association of NSW Inc. (for *Consumers' Fair Go! Kit* feedback sheet and cartoon); Robin McTaggart (seventeen characteristics of action research); Margaret McLaren and the Alzheimer Society of Victoria (seminar evaluation form); Hugh Guthrie, TAFE National Centre for R&D (cartoon from *Making Changes*); Victorian Association of Citizens Advice Bureaus (self-evaluation kit cartoon); the late Patricia Morrigan (Neuro Linguistic Programming definition); Southern Community Health Services Research Unit, South Australia cartoon; Ministry of Education (*Group Self-Evaluation Reader* and *Destination: Decisions* illustrations); Stephen Kemmis (Barry McDonald commentary); the late Egon Guba ('forms of inquiry' table); Consumers Health Forum (program evaluation material); and Susanne Baxandall and Pat Dodson of the Anti-Cancer Council of Victoria (self-help groups' evaluation).

PREAMBLE

WHO AND WHAT THIS BOOK IS FOR

THE VALUE OF DOING EVERYDAY EVALUATION—AND WHY WE DON'T DO IT

You're already flat out just getting through the day. And then—on top of it all—an evaluation?! Perhaps you want to do it, but it keeps getting put off. Or maybe They want it, and now at last it has to be done. Maybe committee and staff meetings always seem too full of other items. Maybe it's been delegated to the one more or less enthusiastic 'volunteer'. Maybe that 'volunteer' is you! Or maybe last time it got cobbled together rather unsatisfactorily, or got farmed out to an external consultant who came and went and left behind a report that didn't seem to change things much, or changed things in ways you didn't particularly like!

These kinds of repeated experiences suggest to us that one of the most pressing needs is for evaluation to be practised as an *ordinary everyday part* of what we do—rather than saved up until later when things have settled down, or when there is more to show for what we've done, or when we can afford the time, or when it seems easier. But when do things ever settle down? When is it ever easier? When is there ever time?! And meanwhile, can we risk going on thinking we're getting it right—but perhaps not? Or suspecting we're not, but preferring 'not to go there'?

There is a lot of talk about needing to build in evaluation, but we still seem stumped about how to go about this—apart, perhaps, from having a computerised statistical database, feedback sheets after course sessions or an annual 'planning and review day'. Yet it is also obvious that people must be able to do their own ongoing evaluation. The idea of bringing in an external evaluator to every one of thousands upon thousands of human services presents a financial nightmare when we think about the sheer volume of such expensive specialist services we'd be needing.

Not only is it impractical and costly for people not to do their own evaluation, but it is also wasteful of insiders' vast store of practical wisdom and experience, on which we all act daily anyway. In a later discussion about the pros and cons of internal and external evaluation, it will be seen that the insider's evaluation stands a better chance of being more practically fruitful. However, the outsider can, among other things, contribute a perspective that can assist insiders to be more self-critical or see things in a fresh and different way. But, rather than insiders being assistants to outsiders, it would seem to be less costly and more effective for outsiders to be the occasional assistants to insiders.

In moving towards a situation where every user and provider of a service can confidently self-evaluate, there are a number of hurdles to be leapt over—not least of which are the ideas that evaluation is difficult, uncomfortable, time-consuming, technically mysterious and requires specialist expertise. It is hoped that Chapter 1 of this book will show that evaluation is easy and very do-able (actually, we do it all the time without even being asked!) and should more often be experienced as a great relief. The view of evaluation as a hard, disempowering and unwelcome torment relates to an important set of very ingrained assumptions that lead us to think evaluation has to be done in a particular and rather unnatural way.

First of all, evaluation is commonly experienced as something done 'to', 'at' or 'on' us. This is often justified by saying we are too biased and value-laden to do it ourselves (and expert specialist 'Others' somehow don't have biases and values!). When we have it done to, at or on us, it can make us feel very powerless. This can also be very threatening—especially if we are trying to do things we are not sure everyone likes (whether fellow group members, managers or service-users), or if we would like to have something exposed that Some Other People don't want exposed. There is no point in anyone just insisting that evaluation won't hurt us. The way around this is for evaluation to be self-directed for our own learning—for all of us involved (service-users, providers, administrators, funders, and so on).

WHOSE VALUES?

Ultimately, it is up to us to examine our own practices and act to improve them. Then we will have trust and confidence in the process and feel strengthened by it. This goes for both service providers and service-users. However, while service providers must be able to do their own evaluation, they are not, in the final analysis, doing it directly for themselves. The crucial point of logic relating to all the possible stakeholders or audiences for evaluation is that, in the final analysis, evaluation is for those whose unmet life needs provide the benchmark and driving values for checking whether a program, service, campaign or activity actually works. Thus we must effectively point evaluation in the direction of always seeking to identify 'who' or 'what' it is all *for*.

This also indicates to us who must be most importantly involved in evaluation. Conventionally, human services delivery funded by Western governments might be illustrated as a pyramid whereby the Westminster system of government assumes that the minister, elected by those for whom the government services all exist, identifies problems remotely and directs from above what will be done about them for citizens.

However, this can result in solutions that don't 'gel' with people's actual lives, and can leave people waiting for what they need and for others to do things, becoming less and less able to take initiative together themselves. Perhaps human services may be better conceptualised as the people—those who have the needs to be met—being surrounded by various networks of resourcing arrangements, some close and providing daily sustenance and support, and others—including those of the funded services—at more of a distance. In all cases, though, the organising focus of the evaluation is those the services are intended to resource.

In evaluation, it is critical to retain this perspective throughout because it is the decisions about the user's or consumer's needs—expressed as values—that provide the ultimate benchmarks for all evaluative judgements about whether or not a service or other effort is working. Even when we are part of the pyramidal bureaucracy or professional service provision, and have our own needs and values, or views about what users and consumers' needs and values are or should be, clarity of purpose and effort lie in keeping the direction of one's gaze firmly on the ultimate purpose of all our effort. This book is designed essentially for anyone who wants to evaluate an activity or human service from the perspective of who it is for—that is, the user, consumer, participant, resident, client, patient, taxpayer, claimant, customer, citizen, self-help group, community, and so on. There are complexities involved in identifying these groups and hearing their voices, but the effort must continuously be undertaken. Chapter 2 provides a full discussion of this matter, as well as an exploration of how best to assist consumers or users (or critical reference groups)—as well as all other parties to evaluation—to raise their questions, explore them, reach conclusions and then go on to improve their activities or services.

Administrators, funders, businesses and managers who are remote from the ground have a huge stake in this kind of evaluation being done, as their own success and ultimate reason for being stem from and back to those same critical reference groups, and the kinds of lives they are resourced to lead.

BUT HOW ON EARTH CAN WE MAKE TIME FOR IT?

Even if we see ourselves as able to do our own evaluation, why do we never seem to have time to devote to it? Why is it that thinking about what we do and why we do it so easily gets swamped by the doing itself? Why do we quickly pick up the ringing phone, feel compelled to open the mail, meet that deadline, feel driven to take on that extra task, squeeze in another appointment or meeting, or just find ourselves doing the same-as-usual, even though we might have growing feelings of unease? Why do we prioritise all these other things, but not prioritise reflecting on whether they are worth doing? Why do we go on doing all sorts of things when we may not have thought consciously about their value? Perhaps it's because it feels easier to do what we've always done; perhaps it's because it seems to work well enough. Perhaps stopping to think doesn't feel legitimate. Perhaps it doesn't seem that doing so will make enough of a difference anyway. Maybe we feel uncomfortable at the thought of checking what we are doing with our end-user populations.

For most of us, everyday evaluation won't be done regularly 'on the run' unless we are able to change the initial value we place on spending all our time *doing* rather than setting aside some of our time for *thinking* about the value of what we are doing. To successfully blend evaluation into our everyday lives requires us to deliberately set aside time—a minute at the start of that activity or end of that discussion, a few moments at the end of each meeting, an hour a week, a day during a month's campaign, or a week each year—to reflect on the value of what we are doing or planning to do. This time needs to be collectively agreed upon as valuable, labelled legitimate and treated as precious. It needs to become part of our work plans and diaries, as only then will we have time to stop and think, collect more information where we need to, and reflect more deeply on its implications and generate what might be better. Only in this way will we gradually get the evidence we need that will guide and strengthen our practice and reduce any fears and anxieties about what we are doing, *and* enable us to feel comfortable that we are routinely questioning and checking even the most taken-for-granted aspects of our practice and certainly regularly lifting the rocks on the bits that we fear might be dodgy!

INTRODUCTION

chapter 1

WHAT IS EVALUATION?

A FAMILIAR EVERYDAY PROCESS

When did you last conduct an evaluation? Last year? Never? This is evaluation with a capital 'E'. However, in practice we are evaluating all the time.

Consider last night's community committee of management meeting:

Leanda: *'I quite like going to our Centre committee meetings—I get to feel more in touch with what's going on.'*

Carolyn: 'Heavens, how can you tell?!! I'd rather be home watching *Pride and Prejudice*.'

Leanda: *'Well, yes, I know what you mean—they can be a bit tedious: all that stuff about risk-management procedures and that. But at least you and I and some of the old crowd get to catch up!'*

Carolyn: 'Yep, that's great!'

This is evaluative talk! It is talk that reflects upon the value, merit, worth or significance of the thing in question—in this case, committee meetings (and risk-management procedures, television series that reflect current human issues, and supportive social relationships!). We could easily extract from this exchange at least four 'performance criteria' for committee meetings—including two that might be breaking new ground in relation to currently more familiar formal indicators. (Answers at the end of this chapter!)

Actually, you may have done half a dozen evaluations since you got up this morning—perhaps even before getting out of bed! First, you made a judgement about the weather conditions, followed quickly by an evaluation of the clockface, then a brief review of the previous day's events, before yet again noticing those irritating cobwebs in the corner of the ceiling, then an evaluation of what the baby did to the cat's fur yesterday, an anticipatory assessment of today's tasks and tonight's school reunion, and finally a groan about the house loan payment due on Wednesday. Later you might have made a series of deft judgements about the best route to your first destination for the day, the state of a friend's or partner's mind, the lunch you bought from a new shop, and so on.

We evaluate all the time. From the minute we meet someone new, or sift through the day's mail, or walk into a shop or office, or decide on the week's activities, we are evaluating. We decide whether things are valuable or unimportant, worthwhile or not 'worth it'; whether things are good or bad, right or wrong, are going OK or 'off the rails'; are attractive, difficult, exciting, off-putting, useful, undesirable, important, functional, effective, boring, expensive, too much, too little, just right, interesting, too simple, much too complex or a disaster! Every time we choose, decide, accept or reject, we have made an evaluation. And if pushed, we can even measure, rate or scale many of our judgements, describe them in word-pictures, or tell a story to illuminate them.

You have evaluated the possibility of buying or reading this book. You have evaluated, even if only in a preliminary fashion, what you have read so far!

Let's look a little more closely at what is involved in the act of evaluation.

WHAT ARE WE DOING WHEN WE EVALUATE?

We find we are suddenly evaluating when we are busy going about our everyday business, and then, for some reason, we notice something.

We notice a discrepancy or a split between what we expected or didn't expect, what we wanted and didn't want, what we planned and what actually occurred. A difference between an 'is' and an 'ought' (or an 'ought not'). Or, more accurately, the difference between a valued (or it might be an unvalued) 'is' and a valued (or unvalued) 'ought' or expectation. And the reason why we notice anything is because we have already stored in our heads images or descriptions of the world on which we have placed a value—descriptions we sometimes term our 'values' or 'interests'. When these 'fail to compute' with what we are seeing or experiencing in front of us, that sense of discrepancy is felt by us to be problematic. Initially this may quite literally be sensed as an embodied feeling, or as an image not yet put into words, but given time it can be articulated and thought through.

Essentially, we are taking a piece of the world and comparing and contrasting it by holding it up against something that we already think and know, and have decided the value of—whether good or bad, useful or not, high, medium or worthwhile, right or wrong. These

existing 'descriptions of the world' against which we compare and contrast the piece of the world we are evaluating provide our benchmark, criterion or standard, as a kind of template (a bit like those little plastic maps some of us had at primary school and traced around to make a shape we knew was our country). We carry all these around in our heads (including elaborate descriptions of indicators and objectives) and pull them out when we want to check or assess new things. And then, when we decide on the value of something new, we store that away for future reference as well.

Thus, when we wake up and glance at the clock, we evaluate it in relation to a mental picture of 'the time'. This mental picture might be of the time at which we had already decided we wanted to get up, or perhaps of the time we hoped it would be, or perhaps of the time we feared it would be! Or the weather strikes us as pleasant or unpleasant depending on how discrepant it is with the picture of the weather we had expected or wanted. Our previous day went well or not, depending on what we had hoped or anticipated. The cobwebs are irritating because they are not valued in relation to a mental image of a clean (cared for) house minus cobwebs—or they *are* valued as a sign a spider finds our house conducive for life (or they tell us it is going to rain when we've been experiencing drought!). And so on.

We evaluate like this constantly, effortlessly, as a natural built-in part of our everyday lives. And when we examine a little more closely what we actually do every time we accomplish such an everyday evaluation, we find we are doing in microcosm exactly what we need to do on a larger scale when we 'do' a Proper Evaluation. Let's take an example.

AN EXAMPLE: YOUR TEA OR COFFEE MUG

Let's magnify one of these little microcosm evaluations and see what it consists of. Take something close to hand. It doesn't matter much what it is, because the technique will reveal pretty much all the basics about evaluation in a nutshell! For example, take your

tea or coffee mug. Bring it closer and examine it carefully. You will need a context (as no evaluation can be context free, since it depends on comparison). Say you are at your community service, in the kitchen. You open the cupboard door to take out a mug to have a cup of tea or coffee. Now evaluate it by asking whether you would use it (to get quantitative 'yes or no' answers), and why (to get qualitative interpretive answers).

You might say: 'Um, well, I like it. I like it a lot. I always choose it.' (Q. Why?) 'Well, because it's lightweight, fine bone china. And it's nice and bright because it's white with a glaze so I can get it clean, and it has those pretty little yellow flowers round the top, and there's a really thin lip with a gold rim which makes it nice to drink from.'

Or, if it was an old brown 1970s work mug, and somebody else had made you a drink and brought it to you, you might have said: 'Well, this one is OK. It's functional. But it's a bit "clunky" and not quite big enough. The colours are nice but the pattern is yukky. The handle doesn't feel quite right either. I wouldn't fight anyone for it!'

In each case:

- You have questioned yourself more closely: 'Well what do I think of it—and why?'
- You immediately noticed the things that are most noticeable for you—whether positively appreciated or negatively problematic—and these were in relation to the guiding *purpose* you had for the mug.
- You have either resorted to 'historical' (memorised!) records of 'fieldwork' of having used it and drunk from it previously or, if it was a new mug to you, you did some new 'fieldwork': touched it or picked it up, felt its weight and shape, and assessed associated memories to guide you. If asked about them, you might be able to explain that the gold rim and flowers remind you of your grandmother's enjoyable afternoon teas and teacups for special occasions; or that the brown pottery mug reminds you of your parents' 1970s kitchen, and so on.
- You have 'analysed the data' and drawn a conclusion about its value to you.
- If I asked you to, you could tell me your recommendations regarding whether you'd choose it again, or would prefer something else—and why. You might by now have so raised your consciousness about mug selection that you become very discriminating!
- We could then see what you next did in practice, and either confirm your conclusions or raise new questions if you didn't do as predicted!

In microcosm, you would have just done a little piece of evaluation research—or rather, gone round one more cycle in an ongoing process of acting and evaluating, acting and evaluating.

This cycle is explored in much greater detail in Chapter 2, and is illustrated too in the Action Evaluation Research Process wall chart located on the page for this book on the Allen & Unwin website. Search for 'Everyday Evaluation on the Run 3rd edition' at www.allenandunwin.com.

Just before we leave our mug-evaluation-in-microcosm, let's make some further observations of what we did (and didn't do) in order to throw some more light on the process of evaluation, and on some of its paradoxes explored further in later chapters of this book:

- You may never have actually stopped and evaluated your mug in this very conscious way—yet it turns out that you had already repeatedly evaluated numerous previous mugs, and stored away the valued and unvalued images and memories for later use. The finely detailed descriptions of the world that we carry about in our heads may literally only be in our heads! Some of the most fruitful, rich, extensive, imaginative, creative and valuable 'evaluation criteria' that we have may not be written down, much less formalised as measurable service objectives. Maybe they never will be. Maybe if they were, we would find ourselves using such a tightly constricted and over-elaborated set of objectives, translated into standards, that we may set our expectations and rules so rigidly in concrete that change would become difficult.

  But had we, for example, drawn out from practice what the implied specific or targeted characteristics would be for our mug evaluation (to be lightweight, to be made of fine bone china, to be white, fluted, have a traditional delicate flower design, thin lip with gold rim), and then evaluated all other mugs against such a tight specification, we may have found ourselves wanting to say, 'Oh, but this one's nice too. I don't mind it being a bit clumsier because the design is such fun', or 'Well, I'd prefer that melamine one today because it's for a picnic', or whatever. Often we find ourselves resorting to more abstract generalities when we try to express our evaluative criteria: 'To be appropriately designed', 'To be functional', 'To be visually attractive', 'To be an appropriate cost'. These are helpful because they give broad guidelines, and are grounded in the pooled insights that can be accrued from many efforts at 'evaluating' mugs. But they leave out the deeply refined qualitative detail that operationalises the abstract generalities in actual practice (and thus we can also spend a lot of time discussing what 'appropriate' or 'relevant' might mean!)

- Evaluation against formalised, written-down, clearly articulated, passed-on and inherited criteria and principles will generally be extraordinarily helpful, but may never be the full answer. It may always need to be complemented by the in-depth, richly qualitative experience that generated the abstractions in the first place. And it may always also need to remain open to as-yet unnamed, unarticulated and even unthought-of criteria. Broad criteria thus are put into actual practice in highly specific ways, which then are subject to change. So it is often best to keep these highly specified targets provisional or flexible. The art of both these kinds of evaluation is discussed in Chapter 3.

- If the mug was well known to you, you may have found the exercise more difficult or more tedious—or literally pointless. It is hard to problematise and notice (and thus evaluate) the taken-for-granted in a familiar context. The drive to evaluate lies essentially in values that express our interests that give us a *purpose* and our guiding frame of reference. In the coffee mug example, everything about our evaluation changes if the purposes shift from 'drinking coffee at work', to 'drinking coffee at a friend's' to 'drinking beer in a pub' or 'going on a picnic'. We might not trouble too much about the differing purposes that attach a slightly different set of values to a mug for work compared to a mug at a friend's, but seeking a mug to drink beer from at the pub or to take on a picnic might suddenly illuminate a problem if we only had bone china in our cupboard!

Thus, depending on how much a discrepancy relates to our already stored 'descriptions', 'templates' or 'values', we will either return to our taken-for-granted existence (if the discrepancy is insignificant), or we will be propelled to a sense of unease (or elation!) or find it a downright problem—particularly if the discrepancy is significant.

Sometimes it is helpful to actually try to see whether there is 'a problem' of which you hadn't been aware. Some people find that kind of review exercise more enjoyable while others find it tedious. For example, you might ask 'Is this mug really good enough for my purposes?' or 'Could there be a better alternative?'—even though it doesn't seem to be problematic. Sometimes this alerts us to situations we tolerate without realising they are less than ideal. Focusing on instances of when things have been particularly *good* can highlight more life-giving criteria than may initially seem available, and this may be even more so if we do it with others—always a source of more ideas to resource evaluative journeys.

- You found the fieldwork to evaluate the mug more or less effortless because you had no trouble doing the 'interviewing' and knowing what to ask—because the whole exercise was for your tea- or coffee-drinking pleasure! You naturally made observations that were directly relevant to the intended purposes and desired outcomes: an efficient and effective tea- or coffee-drinking experience for yourself. If, however, you were evaluating a mug to be used by someone else, you might immediately have needed to plan some other fieldwork. In Chapter 2, there is an extended discussion of how to orient evaluation to those who it is all for—what I have called the *critical reference group* (in this instance you, if the mug is for your own use, or another person or group, if it is for them). When there are so many well-meaning and highly qualified people around who are there to help you with your tea-or-coffee-drinking experience and advise on (and make policy about) optimal tea-or-coffee-drinking apparatus, you may well find that the seeking of your own opinion sometimes gets forgotten!

- Thus the best data will be that which makes it clear what *your* evaluation of the mug is—*for you*. For example, if you say 'It is durable', this looks like a positive evaluative statement, but further exploration may reveal you saying, 'My mother would always have wanted me to ask if it is durable, but to be honest, that always conjures up hotel-standard thick-ware, and I'd rather buy a supply of fragile, flowered bone china.' The most important clarifying question you can ask in evaluation is 'Why'—'Why is that?', 'Why did you choose that?', 'Why did you say that?' The 'why' questions (or associated questions like 'Can you say a bit more about that?') will get at the all-important context for your reasoning. Context gives meaning. And meaning is essential to understanding value. 'I like the colours' becomes less trivial if it turns out that the colours are the purple, green and white of the women's movement. The meaning of the colours is 'constructed' by those who give them that meaning. It is literally not the same coloured mug for different observers with different purposes, meanings and values.

- As noted at the outset, we could become more conscious of the reasons and purposes behind our evaluation of the mug, and more consciously draw on these next time we go to choose a mug to drink from. Provided we do that sensibly, in proportion to the task, and with openness to the possibility that our conscious inventory of 'objectives', 'standards', 'performance indicators' and 'targets' might need to change, then we may find that a valuable exercise. We may find it speeds up our discriminating powers ('Ah! Now I know why I feel dissatisfied every time I look in this kitchen cupboard—all the mugs are too clunky! I'll go out and buy a more delicate one!').

- Say you now go out and buy a satisfying-feeling fine bone china mug. Everybody promptly chooses it and you can never lay your hands on it! You have another discrepancy to resolve! You embark on another piece of action evaluation. Or perhaps you go out and buy a satisfying-feeling fine bone china mug and you use it constantly. For a while, you lovingly evaluate it against its objectives. After a while, you cease to bother; life goes on, the mug is taken for granted! . . . until something leads you to 'problematise' it again.

There are several final points that can usefully be made while we are thinking of the coffee mug evaluation. First, this has been a straightforward self-evaluation exercise; however:

- Say that, instead of it being in the context of going to a cupboard and choosing a mug for your own personal use, it was a group of staff volunteering their evaluations with a view to one of them going out and buying a set of mugs for the other staff. This may seem a little presumptuous—why not let the group choose their own mugs?—but it is a common scenario in the human services area. It becomes clear that the group doing the buying (or making the policy about the buying) must primarily not merely consult the mug-using group, but provide the conditions for that group to clarify and build their own consensus about what are their evaluations and what they want in the way of mugs.

- Or say that part of the group is going to go out and buy the mugs *for others* in the group. Now it becomes clear that we would be in an evaluation consensus-building exercise around what evaluation criteria or characteristics would form the basis for their selection. People would need to start with 'fieldwork' that gave clarity about each other's likes and dislikes. Indeed, the bulk of the 'evaluation' will comprise a free exchange of perceptions, and the reaching of increasingly refined and possibly imaginative conclusions about what most-valued action to take. (For example, if people can't agree on the value of one design or 'one size to fit all', people may choose to be reimbursed for the purchase of their own. Or three designs may be chosen with at least one suiting each. No wonder dialogue has become such a critical evaluation method in a post-modern, post-colonial world! As Robin McTaggart has put it:

  > Action research [or evaluation] is the way groups of people can organise
  > the conditions under which they can learn from their own experience . . .
  > (Nicaragua, 1989)

- As with most everyday evaluation, the kinds of discrepancies perceived are generally of a 'Yes' or 'No' nature. That is, things are either OK or not OK, better or worse, acceptable or not good enough. Questions of extent (How OK?, How much worse?) are frequently of less concern to everyday evaluators. But when finer amounts of discrimination are called for, then some kind of measurement may become necessary. This is one way in which 'quantification' may enter the area of evaluation. It can generally be kept very simple and straightforward by using everyday ways of comparing and contrasting, such as along a simple scale (a lot, some, not much, none) or by ranking (most, less, least).

The major need for exactitude in quantifying and measuring is often nothing to do with evaluation *per se*—but is rather about convincing others who do not share the same views or values.

- The other main way 'quantification' may enter evaluation is if the question is one of 'how many' people think that such and such is of a particular value, merit or worth or 'how often' such and such happens. Again—and as with all survey research—the questions and interests of the research or evaluation should drive whether the questions call for answers that are 'how many' or 'how much', or whether they are more questions of 'who, which, what, when, whether, where, why or how'.

There is a further discussion of numbers and quantification in Chapter 3. Evaluation and research do not equal surveys, questionnaires and statistical and mathematical computation. These are merely tools, and often tools that are over-used and quite often badly used. They are techniques for particular purposes, and their use is not automatically warranted, even while they retain an important place in assisting some people to see what is going on and as a contribution to reflexivity: analysis, reflection, dialogue and new synthesis.

'That's all very well,' I hear you say, 'but don't you start an evaluation by asking what were the objectives?' Well you can, and many of us do. But it turns out you don't actually need to know the objectives of something to evaluate it. Indeed, if ever you are to change to improve something, and you only ask whether its objectives were being met or not, you may never actually know whether it *was* still a good thing if they were met—or whether things had changed (or the objectives were wrong in the first place) and it was a good thing that the objectives were *not* met! Or great that they *were* met, but *greater still* if there could be some new objectives developed. Or even where they were met, and that was good, and nothing more needs to be done for the time being. Each of these scenarios needs a bigger context for sense-making than the one in which the existing practice is taking place.

CONCLUDING REMARKS

This chapter has used the simple everyday-type evaluation we might do of our tea or coffee mug as a microcosmic example of the full evaluation research process explored in Chapter 2. It has also shown the simple process of inquiry ('What do we think of this mug?') that characterises the kind of evaluation that is most effective in drawing out an understanding of what is problematic, with a view to developing or improving a situation, service or practice. It has illustrated, in a very rudimentary form, how this kind of inductive, value-identifying, open-inquiry theory-building exercise can result in an account of implicit values, intentions and purposes ('What are we looking for in a mug?'). When these are consciously written down as a formal statement of goals and objectives, and the logical outcomes expected, they can then be used to 'audit' or review any subsequent situation or future service or practice ('Does this mug accord with our previously identified objectives for mugs?', 'Did we get the outcomes we sought?'). These two key approaches to evaluation are explored in Chapter 3.

Finally, this introductory chapter has tried to show that evaluation is a process that happens naturally on a very tiny scale throughout everyday life. I hope to show in Chapter 4 how this process can be 'scaled up' through a range of different levels, and in this way can become a more truly built-in and naturalistic element of any situation or service.

ANSWERS TO EVALUATION OF COMMITTEE MEETINGS QUIZ

1   The first comment reveals a traditional criterion—that of ensuring communications and information-dissemination.

2   The response to the first comment suggests a new criterion—either ensuring liveliness or a capacity to give pleasure or (if this is a community health centre committee or neighbourhood learning centre) whether the television program *Pride and Prejudice* presents images and exemplary family practice as a clue to what the service could be doing (e.g. a participatory study by the parenting group on what is exemplary/reassuring about this popular TV series about adult offspring leaving home only to return to the roost soon after due to a complex range of social and economic factors).

3   The second comment suggests that risk-management procedures may be seen by committee members as problematic and that 'tedium' could be either a useful indicator of when these interests are prevailing over those of service-users (and hence spark a search for more creative solutions), or of where staff need to convey things differently, or of where funding bodies need to realign their demands more to the needs of service-users.

4   The second part of the second comment suggests another possible new criterion—that of ensuring conviviality or a sense of community.

A CONCEPTUAL FRAMEWORK

chapter 2

THE EVALUATIVE RESEARCH CYCLE

INTRODUCTION

This chapter explores in more detail the elements or steps that make up a cycle of evaluative research. It is illustrated by the wall chart on the Allen & Unwin website. If you lose your place, just check the heading for the section you are reading and relocate it on the wall chart.

To 'do an evaluation' is actually to do a piece of research or inquiry—but with the focus or emphasis on finding out what *value* people place on things. Doing an evaluation may be thought of as doing a piece of research about people's evaluations of things. There is value in knowing what people think of things, but even more value in knowing *why* (whether to illuminate *past* practice logic or to illuminate what they would *prefer in future*). People's preferences or possible future options can then also be evaluated by them and the agreed 'best way to go' subsequently enacted. (As new 'enacting' will rely on those very same people, this is all the more reason for their participation throughout the evaluation.)

So evaluation can help people to look back at things *retrospectively* as well as forward at things *prospectively*.

Thus ideally, while any evaluation will follow the steps described below, it is also setting in place processes which enable others (who are making value judgements) to effectively follow the same steps for their own evaluations:

- reflecting on their observations and felt discrepancies

- seeking more answers to questions about what has been of value or not
- reaching conclusions about what they and others think about things and why they value things or not, and what they would prefer next
- thinking through the consequences in terms of considering future actions
- then acting to plan and implement them
- and then observing and reflecting again.

This is the meaning of do-it-yourself action evaluation, or what Michael Patton (1994, 2010) calls **developmental evaluation**, now also known as MERI (monitoring, evaluation, research and improvement). It is not research or evaluation done by some people and (it is hoped) followed by action by some other people—it is action that is evaluated and researched with a view to identifying both where it has 'worked' and what to do if it can be improved by those who are parties to that action. This kind of evaluative research therefore starts with action and reflects on its value.

Now if you take the wall chart on the Allen & Unwin website, you may in practice be at any point—perhaps in the middle of theorising why you are seeing what you are seeing, perhaps weighing options for future action, or perhaps at the point of implementing a new action based on an identified logic. However, in order to begin the discussion in this chapter, the part of the diagram that marks a 'natural' point of an evaluative narrative—both an end and simultaneously a beginning, is when we stop and metaphorically look back over our shoulder at what we are doing right now . . .

REFLECTION: NOTICING DISCREPANCY

We have seen that any piece of evaluative research commences with observing (or noticing) a discrepancy between an 'is' and an 'expectation'—a 'problematising' of experience, where you hold an image of the world (about which you have already decided the value) up against a description of the world-as-it-is-here-and-now.

We find ourselves doing this when our taken-for-granted world strikes us as being too different from what we expected, or whenever we consciously pause for a moment

and ask ourselves, 'How are we going?' or 'What do I think of this?' Sometimes we've already been stopped in our tracks and we can't proceed until we deal with it. At other times we may feel surprised, confused, uncertain, puzzled, troubled or just have an uneasy sense that all is not well. At yet other times, everything may seem routine and unproblematic to us.

'Problematising' here does not, however, always mean noticing 'a problem'.

It is more about critically questioning—that is, making a judgement ('critical' from the Greek *kritikos* meaning 'judge, decide'). It can also happen when things are going so well we notice and appreciate them! Most of our experience of noticing discrepancies or problematising occurs when we have descriptions or images of a desirable or valued world in our heads, against which we determine that what is happening in the world is *not* so valued and may even be undesirable— propelling us to want to fix things or change them for the better. However, it is possible also to have not expected much (or even expected the worst) and done better—or expected a good outcome and noticed an even better one!

This latter approach is described briefly in Chapter 5 as the technique of 'positive evaluation', which may not necessarily be about everyone finding that they are doing a good job, but is instead about identifying the conditions under  which things went well for a change. 'Strengths-based' evaluation, narrative evaluation and appreciative inquiry are all new research approaches in this style (also annotated in Chapter 5).

If we raise our problematisation to the level of consciousness and notice what the discrepancy is, this can then drive us towards generating an answer to the question, 'How are we going?' The more sharply and clearly we experience the differences between the two sets of descriptions or valuations of the world, the easier will be the evaluation and the faster will be the impetus to resolve the split. Such comparative data can be qualitative (identifying a pattern or absence/presence) or quantitative (identifying extent), or a mixture of both.

The importance of the discrepancies we experience— and our awareness of them—is fundamental to evaluation that contributes to improving the value of things, and is illuminated by the following story. It concerns the possibly apocryphal science experiment in which a frog that is thrown into boiling water will promptly jump out, but a frog that is put into a pot of tepid water that is slowly heated to the boil will not 'notice'  the small increases in the temperature of the water, and will eventually boil to death!! (Peter Senge, *The Fifth Discipline*, Doubleday, New York, 1990)

The moral of the story might be: when we feel ourselves in 'merely' tepid water, we should notice and evaluate!!

This is not to say that we don't attach a value to those matters that remain taken for granted; it means only that, until we examine or review these matters consciously, we might not be able to really say what value we have or haven't attached. We might guess or assume—and guess at others' values or make assumptions about them—but it remains guesswork and untested presumption until we self-reflect or ask more explicitly, and in ways that effectively allow us to examine what we or others *really do* think and feel.

DESIGN

Planning to evaluate

No matter how small or how elaborate the evaluation, the 'design' involves deciding what is to be evaluated, for what purposes and by whom. These decisions in turn will determine what questions need answers, and of whom these questions should be asked.

This planning phase of working out exactly what the evaluation is of (and for) is probably the most important 'moment' of the whole process. Get this right and the rest will flow easily. Get it wrong and you may end up with the wrong answers to the wrong questions. Here's what typically can go wrong in planning an evaluation.

When we pose ourselves the question (or have it posed to us), 'How is it going?' or 'Is it working?' there can be a number of responses:

- We think it's going really well but have to pretend we don't know (or They'll say we're biased), so we have to set out to try to prove what we already know. We spend a lot of time rediscovering many wheels (but perhaps failing to address some really sticky questions that had never occurred to us). The report gets called biased anyway.
- We're not absolutely sure how it's going, but we know what They expect, or we fear They want to change us or close us down, so we propose to frantically collect all the positive material we can, and put our genuine questions on the back-burner. They change our program guidelines regardless.
- We think some things are going really badly or will look that way and we do a white-wash job in case They find out and cut our funds without giving us a chance to fix them. The report gets called biased and they cut our funds anyway.

- Some of us think others are Not Doing a Good Job so we want to try to work out ways for this to become obvious without us ever having to say so out loud. It either works, and those others get very angry and never change, or it doesn't work because those others sabotaged the evaluation! Nothing changes.
- Some of us think others are Not Doing a Good Job and we plan to tell them (or announce it to the local papers). All hell breaks loose and a lot of people get their backs up. Nothing changes for years until they've all moved on.
- Some of us are afraid we are not doing a good job and this will be found out or it will be made to look worse than it is and nobody really understood us—so we need to control it or undermine its legitimacy. Our good work is never given credit.

We need a way through all this, especially when it comes to all the different interpretations of 'value' or 'worth' of an effort, and it is at the planning stage that we can find it. The primary task is to focus on the ultimate purposes of the evaluation, and to sort out who all the relevant parties to an evaluation will be and how they do (or don't) relate to these ultimate purposes.

Who the evaluation is for: The concept of the critical reference group

The best practical solution lies with orienting the evaluation towards common ground about 'what we're all here for'. And the 'what we're all here for' is essentially those who the effort, activity or service is all for—in the sense of being to help or assist overcome their problematic situation, resolve problems, overcome disadvantage or meet the group's needs.

The term *critical reference group* will be used throughout this book as a general term referring to all these kinds of groups that human services, health and well-being, community and self-help group efforts are *for*. If the term critical reference group sounds clumsy, please suggest an alternative!!*

---

* Some of the language used in this book may sound a little unfamiliar. This is largely because we don't talk about these things a lot, and still haven't yet invented words for many 'problems without names'. As we become more familiar with the ideas, we might 'happen upon' better ways of naming things. Suggestions are welcome!

Do critical ref. groups = stakeholders.

Otherwise we would have to say every time 'who-it's-all-for'—that is, users, consumers, participants, residents, clients, citizens, patients, constituents, taxpayers, claimants, self-help groups, identifiable communities, the humans that human services serve, and so on!

Because those whose needs are unmet are those who are often getting 'the rough end of the pineapple'* words like 'powerless', 'excluded', 'disadvantaged' 'discriminated against' and 'oppressed' might also be terms useful for identifying critical reference groups. Additional descriptions might also imply disempowerment such as age (e.g. very young, elderly), gender (e.g. women), cultural background (e.g. Turkish, Egyptian) or Aboriginality (e.g. Koori, Murri). Other descriptors may refer to the nature of an injustice (e.g. violence, poverty, structural unemployment or discriminated sexuality), the kind of group being hurt (e.g. abused children, battered women); or the kind of disabling condition (e.g. physical, learning, height or weight).

However, the term also refers to all those who are simply intended to be the end-beneficiary of any evaluand—whether a kindergarten, hospital, an education system, a business, a community, a human right, or all of us affected by the climate change emergency.

The term *critical reference group* tries to capture the ideas that:
- this is the *group* whose 'members' values and practices stem from their shared interests and who are thus the source of the most decisive or critical questions
- this is the group to which services and providers (as well as the group itself) *refer* if they are to identify accurately what the group's needs are, and what are the best responses, solutions or generative developments
- this is the group whose members finally discern or determine ('*critical*' from the Greek meaning 'to judge' or 'decide') whether the services or actions 'got it right' and their needs are met, their hopes addressed, their issues resolved or problems overcome, and their lives improved as a result.

Target audience [handwritten marginal note]

The questions driving evaluative research are self-consciously value driven (although some evaluation tries to proceed as if it isn't!). This makes it both easier and also more difficult to sort out whose values are predominating. On the one hand, it is easier because it is clear—even just from the term 'evaluation'—that values are being used to judge practices. On the other hand, it can be more difficult because evaluation can try to appear always and only objective in the sense of being neutral or value-free (for purposes of legitimacy, or to try to indicate certainty or achieve agreement, for instance.). While there may be a time where a certain kind of intersubjective 'objectivity' is able to be achieved, this may make it more difficult to continue to realise that value is not inherent in what is being evaluated, but rather is ascribed by all those observing it (including by the evaluator *and* those whose actions, practices and beliefs are being evaluated). Sometimes this situation makes it more difficult for those who make up the critical reference group (who it's all ultimately for) to

---

* An 'Australianism' for not only not getting what you need but being dealt a painful lot in life as well.

have a say if their voice alone is identified (inaccurately) as the only one that is value-driven and subjective—possibly because it differs from the equally (and also) value-driven and subjective voices of more dominant others.

Yet in the final analysis it doesn't work for anyone else to decide *for* critical reference groups, as there is no way of knowing whether they 'got it right' for them except by reference to at least some kind of expression by critical reference groups of their situations, experiences, context and purposeful intentions. Sometimes this expression can be very clear and direct (such as where members of a well-organised and articulate self-help group analyse their experiences and make a request for what they require), or the signs of expression can be subtle and require great interpretive sensitivity (such as where someone with an intellectual disability or Alzheimer's disease is unable or unwilling to communicate their will except by non-verbal body language or their actions).

Thus effort must continually be made to seek out the expression of critical reference groups' will—and all possible barriers to this continuously dismantled.

Nor can we rest with the idea that a few representatives of critical reference groups can make everything go right by sitting on a committee of management for a couple of hours once a month, or by filling in a customer satisfaction survey, or contributing to a consultation once every few years. These are all very necessary but usually insufficient ways of hearing the voice of the critical reference group. We must look to constant everyday ways of doing this. Every time there is contact between service users and providers, for example, users must have channels for 'voicing' their experiences and needs, and providers must have—and show they have—'ears' and 'eyes' to hear and see. Providers need to go to consumers' worlds, not expect them to come to providers' offices, websites and formal meetings. Then there need to be ways for providers and users *together* to discuss the feedback and jointly plan consequent changes in practice, then monitor and revise them again.

Where there are diverse views within and among critical reference groups (and other stakeholder groups), this variety must also be able to be expressed and heard. And if lack of consensus is a problem, then ways must be found for communities of interest to work this out among themselves, such as through the use of formal dialogue methods.

This matter of ultimate orientation may run the risk of being glossed over by including parties to the evaluation in a kind of 'pluralist partnership' between service providers, managers, users, carers and other community members.

There is a sense in which such a pluralist partnership captures nicely how a piece of collaborative and dialogic evaluation must proceed to achieve practical change, but this ought not to be at the expense of obscuring the fact that the partnership is still primarily for one of the partners only: the critical reference group.

In the next section, there is a discussion of the other parties (or stakeholders) to evaluation, which points out that the same conditions that apply to critical reference groups (the stakeowners) must also apply to them—namely respect for their ideas, and time and safe space in which these ideas can be expressed and taken into account. As well, other parties to the evaluation may identify with the interests of the critical reference group. However, they are not the critical reference group *per se*, and many evaluations founder because they lack the guiding compass of a critical reference group perspective that can navigate a path through all the views and ideas, and eventually evaluate the evaluations and drive the effort to new and better ways of doing things.

It is important—if starting from a critical reference group's concerns—to identify the sorts of services that might be relevant to them, or—if starting from a service—to identify *their* critical reference groups. Some examples are shown in Guide 1.

Of course, these services may serve other interests besides those of the critical reference groups listed. For example, Citizens' Advice Bureaux might also be meaningful places for voluntary work by local women; general practices may also serve as training places for medical students or as small business ventures; women's refuges, community health centres, labour schemes, residential institutions and legal aid offices may provide valuable work opportunities for a range of non-professional and professional workers who are keen to make a contribution to creating a better society and also have paid jobs; a Poverty Action Program may also promote a government's image as supporting social justice; academic research may provide publications that are essential to an academic's job chances; psychiatric hospitals may indirectly provide respite care for family members suffering exhaustion or even physical injuries received from the distressed person who is hospitalised; and schools may serve the business community's and industry's need for a trained labour force and parents' needs for day care for their dependent children.

Some of these other instrumental interests may be able to be aligned with or related to those of critical reference groups, while some may be only remotely related, and some may even conflict with their life needs. For example, human services may also serve to provide data to reassure central managers, or they may provide well-paid jobs or professional social status, or they may provide a service in such a way as to perpetuate a person's loss of dignity or subordinate status.

The now-folkloric episode of the British comedy television series *Yes Minister*, in which a hygiene award-winning hospital functions entirely without patients, touches nicely on our understanding that such a travesty is funny because it is both 'impossible' in terms of what a hospital is for (treating sick and injured people) and possible in terms of what else a hospital is 'for' (providing work opportunities; being kept clean, administered, maintained and managed; legitimation of a government keen to be seen to be doing Good Things; keeping down the bed-day statistics, and so on).

It is terribly important that these other interests (both benign and not so benign) are understood and effectively incorporated as part of the evaluation effort; however, it is critical that they be recognised as secondary to and dependent on the existence of the life needs of the primary or critical reference groups. They should be assessed for their alignment and consistency with meeting the needs of the latter.

GUIDE 1

SOME EXAMPLES OF SERVICES TO BE EVALUATED AND THEIR POSSIBLE CRITICAL REFERENCE GROUPS

Service	Critical reference group
Citizens' Advice Bureaux	Local residents
Doctors	Patients
Women's refuge	Women experiencing violence
Poverty Action Program	Low income people
Academic research into Aboriginal health	Aboriginal people
Community health centres	Local populations
Skillshare	Unemployed young people
Residential institutions	People with disabilities
Psychiatric hospitals	Inpatients and outpatients
Schools	Students

Even where individuals or groups have the best interests of critical reference groups at heart, it is important to distinguish between primary and secondary (and even tertiary) interests. This is especially so in ambivalent cases where, for example, a 'secondary' interest group may become a primary or critical reference group in its own right—such as a group of carers of people with Alzheimer's disease forming a self-help group to deal with their own physical and emotional health issues; or where several prison warders or police officers form an association to create a death benefits scheme to insure their families against their loss while on active duty; or where a number of violent men from a 'Violence Anonymous' group meet to understand the why and how of *their* situation. Another example would be students doing vocational welfare courses. They would be the reference group of staff in relation to *learning* from the course, while staff would have their own industrial and emotional interests and would thus form another reference group of their own. However, the critical reference groups for *both* students and staff in terms of the course content would be the students' future clientele.

While it is important that secondary and tertiary reference groups organise around their own interests where it is relevant, the conceptual link with the primary reference groups (and logical distinction from them) should never be lost for two crucial reasons.

• Firstly, secondary and tertiary groups may not be able to make full sense of their own actions or difficulties, except by reference to the kind of problems suffered or desires and goals experienced by the primary reference group. A full understanding of one may throw important light on the other. However, it is the primary or critical reference group's experiences that provide the necessary compass point when it comes to the other groups' new actions in relation to them.

- Secondly, if this conceptual link is not retained, the resolution of the interests of the secondary or tertiary groups may be at the expense of those of the primary group—hence risking compounding the long-term resolution of all groups' interests anyway. In either case, the situation for both groups may remain problematic.

This is easier to see if it is the professional interests of workers that are beginning to take precedence over those of clients (for example, where staff health programs become a service goal rather than a means to an end for the primary group—such as housing for those who are homeless). However, there can be borderline cases where, for example, the needs of family members for tranquility and the preservation of their own health (and that of workers assisting them) can lead to the involuntary committal of their relatives experiencing mental and physical ill-health.

Here we enter an arena in which both reference groups need their own evaluations, advocacy and bases of strength from which observation, reflection, dialogue and negotiation can take place, and alternative solutions can be worked on that have the best outcome for both groups—while not forgetting that, as a class of people, those who are homeless in this case remain the primary disadvantaged or critical reference group (with the problems of the secondary group stemming from and depending on those of the primary group).

The other parties to the evaluation, in relation to the critical reference group

There is a discussion of all the various parties to research in Chapter 2 of *Do It Yourself Social Research*, that is worth reading or rereading. It notes that there are conceptually four kinds of potential parties or stakeholders (and stakeowners) to any evaluative research effort:

1   the evaluator or evaluators
2   the evaluated (also called 'the evaluand')
3   those the evaluation is *for* (to help meet their life needs, or help them address their interests or solve their own problems—the critical reference group)
4   those the evaluation is *also* for (in the sense of informing, inspiring, empowering, influencing or convincing them to act for the critical reference group or not to act against it, or to provide a service differently, or to fund it or not de-fund it, and so on.).

It is tremendously important that these four *conceptual* groups (together with identifying who belongs to which, including multiple memberships) are clarified at the planning stage of evaluative research. For example, even when evaluation is for an 'us' of the paid professional staff, or even an 'us' of the service administrators or funders, it remains ultimately and primarily for the relevant critical reference group or groups.

Conceptually, all four groups would overlap completely in, for example, an evaluation of, by and for a self-help disability group; and potentially not overlap at all in, for example, an evaluation by an external consultant for a funding body, and of a funded institution representing the interests of (but not run by) people with disabilities.

The different possible constellations of these four parties represent varying opportunities for enhancing or limiting the chances of successfully ensuring that the critical reference group perspective drives both the evaluation and consequential valued change (including potentially valued *no* change). The greater the overlap, the better the chances, while the least overlap presents the greatest risk of lack of common ground, not hearing clearly the voice of the critical reference group or not communicating effectively with the other parties.

Of course, an evaluation can be conducted entirely by and for parties other than the critical reference group—such as an external consultant employed by a government department to evaluate a service program on the basis of statistical returns and annual reports with neither the knowledge nor the participation of the service providers or users. The chances of such an evaluation 'getting it right' for consumers may be slim, however—especially if neither the consultant nor the department has much familiarity with the service as experienced in its local context. However, it is possible that such a 'remote-control' study might get it right. (Perhaps the evaluator did have such familiarity and was able to use a consumer perspective and the department was implementing a consumer rights policy and evaluating against this.) Perhaps, ironically, this may even have been the best way of bypassing one or two local 'gatekeeping' service providers who were themselves unable to adopt a user perspective.

However, such an outcome—while 'successful' in the short term—must be considered a long-term risk on both methodological and practical grounds. That is, a non-participatory, non-democratic process of evaluation cannot ensure a user-appropriate outcome. A participatory and democratic evaluation process is a better way to increase the chances that critical reference groups—through their active participation in the evaluation—both determine the 'descriptions of the world' that are used as the basis for evaluation, and also are able to judge the value of these images or descriptions if the evaluation is intended to contribute to improvement, change and development of services *for them*. These ways of participating go far beyond conventional notions of representation on evaluation committees, and penetrate deep into the everyday fabric of service provision—but more about this later. Furthermore, by involving the other parties in such a democratic or collaborative evaluation, the chances are increased of the contribution, understanding and enthusiasm of all.

Differences of interests must be seen as part of the contextual material of the evaluation. Nevertheless, when an evaluation comes down to a practical collaborative effort, it is only the ways in which interests overlap with and resource those of the critical reference group that can form an effective practical basis for proceeding.

Target group terminology

In the light of this discussion, we might pause to evaluate critically the common use of the term 'target group' by professionals and managers as a description of the critical reference group. The strong implications are that the professional or managerial group is planning to do something to or at the critical reference group, when the more appropriate approach would be partnership actions with and for the critical reference group. This latter resourcing approach would imply taking seriously the matter of involving members of the critical reference group in the planning and implementation of services or measures intended to benefit them. 'Target group' terminology may imply instead an almost militaristic paternalism towards a passive 'sitting duck' group, and an absence of that group's members actively determining together what is to be done and how in their own lives.

It might be more understandable if the critical reference group used the term 'target group' to refer to groups of professionals or managers or identified sources of their problems!

However, instead of either group 'targeting' the other, it is the *issues* that compound critical reference groups' problems—such as the unhelpful prevailing ideas, organisational structures, cultural expectations and material conditions that hold the problems in place—which need to be targeted. These issues can then be addressed by all parties from their differing perspectives *together* with critical reference groups—within a full discussion of those different perspectives and their rationales or contexts, always using the guiding criteria 'Is this good for the critical reference group?' or 'Is this best for the critical reference group?' These are important tasks of ethical fieldwork that should be planned for at the design stage.

Taking a critical reference group perspective

In relation to the above, service providers, policy-makers and managers must carefully search their own values for those that are congruent with working *for* and *with* their critical reference groups. Services that meet the needs of consumers cannot be designed and implemented without insightful understanding by providers of the needs and interests of consumers. These are achieved in evaluative dialogue *with* them in what amounts to a co-inquiry or co-evaluation. And such understanding cannot be gained without service providers grasping, through acts of empathetic and active understanding, the nature of critical reference groups' experiences, observations, interests, values, hopes, situations, wider contexts, perceptions and ideas. More than this, however, such empathetic understanding must continue to be driven by these values and interests if the service provider is to continuously 'get right' the design and implementation of a service.

In its deepest sense, collaboration by providers with consumers is the methodological route to both more effective service provision and more valid and trustworthy service evaluation.

This adoption of a critical reference group perspective involves a number of criteria being possessed or adopted by anyone who works to meet the needs of critical reference groups. These criteria are listed in Guide 2.

People whose purpose or job or role means they are not primarily there as a member of a critical reference group can have, or can acquire, such a perspective—and indeed must do so if their work is to assist the groups they intend to benefit. Furthermore, if paid service staff are part of a self-help group, or if the service administration includes user representatives on a management committee, then these all occupy dual (or multiple) positions in both the critical reference group and the advocacy group (which acts *for* the critical reference group). However, if they are service providers, they are not consumers or consumer representatives *per se*. They would instead *advocate* a consumer perspective. A strong test of identification with a consumer perspective is if this advocacy is at the expense of their other interests—for example, furthering their own professional status or career interests—or if they are prepared to concede that their own profession's (or service's or sector's) activities might be excluding, disadvantaging or otherwise damaging consumers or service-users.

Many service providers who advocate for a consumer perspective are acutely aware of how organisational pressures seem to work in favour of their being silent about consumer needs and perspectives. However, nearly twenty years of organisational interest in 'customer satisfaction' and 'client-driven' or 'client-centred' services—stemming in part from new management practices in the commercial sector—has connected with longer-standing human services traditions of community involvement, human rights, compassion and empowering the disadvantaged, as well as with more recent policies of self-management and inclusion.

For critical reference groups that are evaluating services they are receiving (or assessing other situations they are experiencing), the conditions for collaboration in an evaluation will include:

- a capacity to identify accurately the ways in, and extent to, which providers or others are prepared to be 'with them and for them' (without either over-estimating this and risking disappointment, or under-estimating this and risking staying 'backs to the wall')
- an ability to identify accurately whether there are real opportunities to participate, and to give feedback and engage in dialogue about it, and what these are
- retaining confidence that they have essential insights and observations that service providers can't manage without, and can continue to put them forward

GUIDE 2
WHAT IS A CRITICAL REFERENCE GROUP PERSPECTIVE IN EVALUATION RESEARCH?

- A capacity to identify the interests of those who are meant to be served by the services or actions being planned, provided, evaluated or otherwise researched, and who may currently be suffering disadvantage, discrimination, deprivation or injustice, or otherwise identifiably unmet needs (the primary or critical reference group).

- A capacity to identify with these interests—either because you are part of the critical reference group, or because you can see that there is a relationship between your own situation and that of the critical reference group:

  > If you've come to help me, you're wasting your time.
  > But if you've come because your liberation is bound up with mine,
  > then let us work together.
  >
  > —Lilla Watson, Aboriginal educator and activist

- A profound respect for those who belong to the critical reference group, and a deep recognition of the legitimacy of their/our viewpoint—feelings, beliefs, ideas, opinions, attitudes and ways of living.

- Such respect is born of direct personal and continuing experience of the critical reference group's situation. Hence such a perspective rests on being in touch with (or knowing how to be in touch with) this experience—knowing how profoundly to see and to feel the lives of critical reference groups and to hear their/our voices.

- A sharply felt dissatisfaction with any conditions impinging on the critical reference group that are identifiably detrimental to the meeting of their/our growth or development (physical, social, emotional, learning, creative, spiritual), needs or interests, or are overtly damaging (unfair, humiliating, hurtful, injurious, abusive, oppressive, unjust or repressive).

- A consequent commitment and determination to work in relation to the critical reference group towards the best way of overcoming these conditions, and corresponding adoption of the appropriate value-driven evaluative research questions.

- The adoption of a collaborative question-raising, problem-solving style involving working in or with the critical reference group. Individual actions stem from, and refer back to, the collectivity.

- The adoption of effective theory and thoughtful practice that focuses also on those groups that benefit (even if unintentionally, and including ourselves) from existing conditions that may hurt critical reference groups, and a preparedness to 'study up', to be sceptical about current dogma, and to have the courage of our convictions to advocate and retain a critical reference group perspective even in the face of any pressures to abandon it.

- the extent of mutual support available to sustain their involvement without loss of their consumer perspective or damage to themselves
- the extent to which providers are able to spend quality time getting to know and understand them and their perspective at deeper and deeper levels.

Just as providers don't 'need' users to participate—but risk getting it wrong—users don't 'need' providers to collaborate with them—but risk inaction through providers' lack of understanding, passive obstruction (even if unintended) or active rejection, thus slowing desired and necessary change.

How does this perspective affect the evaluation?

The use of a critical reference group perspective will effectively shape the evaluation by:
- focusing the evaluation around the values, interests and purposes that should be paramount in applying judgement and reaching final agreement
- ensuring a minimum of extraneous effort, particularly fieldwork
- focusing the selection of options for recommendations and maximising the relevance and applicability of future actions
- ensuring future objectives and standards will be appropriate
- enhancing the chances of appropriate new actions becoming ongoing practice
- ensuring ongoing practice continues to be regularly refined to remain appropriate.

In asking about critical reference groups' evaluations of things—and what they would prefer—we are implicitly asking about their own formulations of both their life needs and deepest values, as well as the images that supply their own standards or criteria. This gives a clue as to why splitting 'needs assessment' off from 'evaluation' is an artificial exercise that can risk severing theory from practice. There are two kinds of needs at issue here. First, there are the guiding values or interests (principles and philosophy) about what is valued, wanted and needed. Second, there are the more specific valued forms in which people are able to concretely imagine their interests being met.

When it is said that 'people don't know what they need' often what is meant is 'I (or somebody else might) have a better specific image than they have of how their needs could be met'. This misses tapping people's wisdom about their own values and interests, and simultaneously risks the 'better' image not being tested with the critical reference group in their own life-world. Conventional evaluation often does not pursue clarification of critical reference groups' views by supplying, or otherwise ensuring that the existence of, a range of specific options for them to consider. This is usually due to a misconception that this would 'bias' or 'contaminate' the results. Deliberative inquiry is, however, a new action research or developmental evaluation approach with the potential to enable a more iterative design and better-informed group of participants.

What of the place of the external evaluator?

Before we leave this matter of the 'parties to the evaluation', it is worth assessing the possible place of 'outsider' evaluators or facilitators of evaluation. While this book has been written on the assumption that people do, and should be able to do, their own 'everyday evaluation on the run', there is great value to be had from the strategic input of certain kinds of 'outsiders'.

Many people have expressed disappointment at the past use of outsiders—particularly of private consultants who might tender for an evaluation, come in, quickly interview a range of people, rush off, write up a report and exit without ever fully understanding the situation. On the other hand, many consider people's own self-evaluations to be always 'suspect', while outsiders are inherently more 'objective'. Let's look at what criticisms have been expressed from both sides about the pros and cons of external and internal evaluation as shown in Guide 3.

GUIDE 3
PROS AND CONS OF EXTERNAL AND INTERNAL EVALUATION

Insiders
Pros
Insiders may have:
- long-held deep understandings of the complex systemic worlds they are in
- deep tacit knowledge of what works and what doesn't and why
- accrued considerable 'practice widsom' based on sometimes documented but often extensive undocumented 'evidence'
- already been practising more or less successful evaluation of their work over many years without ever formalising it as such.

Cons
Outsiders may have been brought in because it was feared insiders were:
- too biased to recognise the truth of matters
- too stuck to see ways of getting out of ruts
- too invested to give up favoured ways of seeing and doing things
- so caught in busy daily practice as to be unable to get reflective distance, see discrepancies, or examine the contexts generating them
- without time to take a step back and look at the bigger picture, including other people's experiences or relevant ideas.

Outsiders
Some outsiders may have been able to:
- ask questions that hadn't been asked before
- notice things and 'hear' things in the fieldwork phase that insiders hadn't noticed, observed or heard as clearly
- come up with new ways of explaining things, or shown things in a new light
- break new ground with solutions
- act as a catalyst for change, for example, inspire with a new vision, or loosen established patterns.

Some outsiders may be reported as having:
- asked questions that were considered wide of the mark
- reported on things that insiders had long known, or that were not central to the practical task or critical question at hand
- explained things in ways that annoyed insiders or made them feel misunderstood, under-represented or wronged
- recommended precisely what insiders had been unsuccessfully suggesting for ages (or missed recommending what insiders had been unsuccessfully suggesting for ages)
- not been listened to either!

Yet the fundamental situation in human and community services is that outsiders can come and go, but insiders are the ones who are there to stay. So ultimately, an outsider can only effect useful change *through* and *with* insiders. Thus it is perhaps regrettable that insiders' detailed knowledge and everyday practice wisdom have often in the past systematically been undermined by the rhetoric of 'independent expert objectivity'. This has often led to a false credibility for outsiders that is not based on their real value as a source of different or specialised ways of seeing things (the value of which can be judged by reference to a critical reference group perspective). This situation has changed a lot over the last fifteen years or so, during which self-evaluation has come to be seen to play a vital part in ensuring continuous feedback to a system, with a specialist external evaluation conducted only when needed.

Indeed, where an outsider is used because no staff have the time to spend on a particular evaluation exercise, it may well be cost-effective in the long run to pay to release the insider and get a locum to carry out that person's job, then pay an experienced consultant for a few hours back-up and assistance to the on-site insider, rather than handing the crucial evaluation task over entirely to someone from outside.

The basic strength of *insiders* is their store of 'local knowledge'—and therefore, the major counter-measure they need to take is, to be sceptical of their current assumptions, beliefs and understandings, and creative about new ideas.

The basic strength of *outsiders* is their fresh perception—and therefore, the major counter-measure they need to take is to 'get grounded'.

Requirements for outsiders and insiders

Useful *outsiders* (in relation to insiders) need:
- strong respect for insiders' knowledge, combined with a capacity to critically question (to be a 'critical friend'—raise a critique, not give criticism!)
- a strong critical reference group perspective (see Guide 2), and the ability to retain it
- their own access to a range of past and current experiences, some of which are in similar areas, and some of which are in completely different areas
- experience in doing other evaluations and knowledge of the logic of evaluative inquiry as well as of methods
- skills in facilitating group discussions, dialogue sessions between differing views, to help clarify complex issues; and in promoting a climate of self-illumination and development
- flexible abilities to theorise and conceptualise (for example, good use of analogy and metaphor).

Insiders need (in relation to outsiders):
- an appreciation of a different perspective and body of experience
- the preparedness to suspend existing wisdom to consider the value of new ideas (including being keen to examine long-held beliefs about how to do things)
- the capacity to bring their own experience to bear on different theoretical ideas
- the ability to exchange old practices for potentially more fruitful new ones, while retaining a strong handle on their deepest values, philosophical principles or guiding missions (derived from a strong critical reference group perspective).

The best spots for *outsider* input are often:
- right at the beginning—to help insiders clarify their purposes and questions
- at the point where a list of questions to be explored in the fieldwork is drawn up
- to assist fieldwork discussions where a facilitator might be helpful
- when material is being analysed and conclusions are being drawn out and recommendations for future action are being considered
- to read a draft report.

For more detail on use of experienced researchers see Chapter 6 in *Do It Yourself Social Research*.

Outsiders can, of course, be asked to actually do some of the work; however, every time this happens it substitutes them for insiders and reduces insiders' chances of contributing, evaluating and learning by doing themselves. If the effort is so big as to require someone else to do it or parts of it, and no insiders can be released, then we must anticipate it migrating out of the bounds of everyday practice and risking being separated from that everyday practice. It also may delay or thwart users, practitioners and group members getting feedback on what they are doing.

Insiders as outsiders—and vice versa

The outsider and insider positions are not intrinsic to people but rather are a function of the context in which one is placed. Under certain conditions, insiders could act as outsiders, or outsiders could 'come on board'. For example, an insider can acquire the perspective of an outsider by using a simple mechanism such as working from home one day a week to get a bit of distance and have a think about things in a way not possible on the job with phones ringing constantly and everything happening. A whole group of insiders are trying to be their own outsiders when they go away for a residential planning weekend. The Australian Taxation Commissioner became a temporary insider in his own organisation when he became 'Trevor the Trainee' on an inquiry counter, answering public inquiries. Indeed, the whole new wave of managerialism devoted to getting down on to the shop floor and making direct contact with customers is in this vein.

There are other ways of outsiders being more of insiders by dint of where they place themselves and for how long. The best traditions of critical anthropology saw, for example, anthropologists carefully 'going native' in order to mitigate the mistakes of previous anthropologists who were only able to offer white, male, colonial or European interpretations of what they were seeing.

For everyday evaluators who have already usefully 'gone native', there are a range of different concrete and practical ways of both becoming outsider-insiders and also of drawing on outsiders to act more like insiders. Each of the methods listed below tries to overcome the drawbacks of outsiders' lack of familiarity and lack of 'connectedness' with insiders' worlds, while utilising their sceptical distance and reflective, question-posing capacities. For example:

- People belonging to similar groups or working in similar services might form peer group networks and meet and assist each other, or ask each other to visit them on site.
- Large service organisations or groups of services or clusters of community groups may be able to designate one full-time or part-time person as having research and evaluative facilitation responsibilities (that is, not to *do* the research and evaluation, but to work with other organisational members to assist *them*). Alternatively, they might engage an evaluation consultant to facilitate evaluative thinking at various times over a number of years.
- Central funding or administering bodies might have (or fund) units dedicated to building in this kind of support to particular groups or organisations. This kind of ongoing support, provided over a long period of time, would be able to build up (and build on) already-acquired knowledge.

Returning to the evaluation question

Thus, the answer you would give to our original question—'How are we going?', or 'How is this service going?' or 'Is it working?'—should now be examined in the light of whose perspective it is from which the questions are asked. Are you a service-user, one of the critical reference group? Or are you a staff person—in which case, do you think your answer would be shared by the critical reference group? Now think about your hunches concerning the reason why you answered these questions as you did.

All the parties to an evaluation will eventually need to be asked these same questions that are asked by the people initially proposing an evaluation of themselves—that is, whatever discrepancies have triggered the initial decision to evaluate need to be checked against the other parties' perceptions, in particular those of the critical reference group.

Most people can give an immediate answer to the question 'How are you going?' This answer—somewhere between 'Great' and 'Terrible'—can then be further drawn out or explicated. Great or terrible for whom? How great or how terrible? Great or terrible compared with what? In what ways? How did we know? Now, as we tentatively offer an explanation for our beginning answer to this tantalising question (why 'great' or why 'dreadful'?), we find ourselves describing the way the service or situation is now, but in relation to the way it isn't. Here we find ourselves saying things like:

'We are all doing . . . instead of . . .'

'It has come to be more like . . . but we were meant to . . .'

'I've noticed they . . . when I expected them to . . .'

'We say we are . . . but we are really . . .'

'Well it is a bit . . . and I think it should be more . . .'

'I thought it would be . . . but was surprised it was actually . . .'

'It was very, very . . . and I'd hoped it would be more . . .'

'It was kind of OK, but . . .'

No evaluation can proceed without these kinds of comparative statements (and if you find you only have one of the parts, then use this to generate the other part). You will need both an 'It is like this', and also a 'but it could or should have been like that'. They embed two essential things: first, a description of the world as observed; and second, a description of a world that had either been planned or expected (or not), or a world that has subsequently been realised to be ideal, desired or hoped for (or not). This latter set of positively or negatively 'valorised descriptions of the world' comprises the beginnings of our 'evaluation criteria'—the standards for critique, or the templates and benchmarks against which we compare the 'is' to the 'expected'.

If we lay on the table at this initial planning stage everything we already think and know, then we can examine our conclusions to date (from previous cycles of everyday 'research'). Do we really know enough? Have we asked all the people who might know the answers (or enough of them to feel quite confident)? Can we refer to any records we might have? Where else could we go for more insight and understanding? We might then go on to generate a further question: 'Why is it so?' Again, people can generally at least have a shot at an answer (often several interrelated answers) to this, and this leads to a hunch or hunches or 'working theories'. These theories begin to give a context for the evaluative comments.

When hunches are turned into sceptical questions, they can become the research questions to be answered. (A hypothesis is a glorified hunch. But it's important that you can imagine what evidence would look like to both confirm and negate your hunches.)

Now our hunches will generally be based on a lot of indirect evidence or 'gut' feelings, which may well turn out to be convincing. However, in the absence of any records to which we can point, we will almost certainly need to touch base with our sources and various stakeholder or reference groups to check more directly whether they see things as we think they do. Remember that the value of something is not intrinsic to it, but is determined by those who define the 'something' and say what it is for. This leads into the essential task of the fieldwork.

FIELDWORK AND INTERPRETATION

Essentially, the fieldwork task involves answering two fundamental questions:

1   *A retrospective question: What are (or have been) our experiences of 'what is' (currently) and what is their value?*

This involves being able to get a descriptive and observational picture of each element of what is being evaluated (who, does what, to whom, when, where, why and how), and getting a sense of why these elements have come to be as they are (history, context, governing logic, rationale, purposes).

At the same time, it involves being able to get a picture of what everyone thinks or feels about each of these elements (the value of who does what, to whom, when, where, why and how and with what effects—intended or unintended, desired or undesired), making sure that the views of the critical reference group are fully recorded, as well as those of all others with an interest in the evaluation or that which is being evaluated. This involves getting people to identify and describe the discrepancies they experience between the 'existing' and what they 'wanted' (or expected) to the extent needed to satisfy the audience.

2   *A prospective question: What do we value (or what are valued experiences) and how can we experience them in future?*

This involves getting a set of ideas, images and descriptions of what people prefer or would have preferred—and why. That is, it involves ways of working out how to get from the actual 'here' to the desired 'there' that are practicable, realistic and about which people are enthusiastic.

The planning of the fieldwork involves choosing ways of getting this two-part picture ('What is the value of current practice?' and 'What future practice would be valuable?'), and hence deciding what would count as answers; who is to meet and speak to whom, about what and in what ways; what reading or observing of what will be required, and with what questions in mind, and so on.

The fieldwork task is to get as accurate as possible a picture of what people themselves think or how things appear to them.

Think of the ways in which you normally inform your own everyday judgement and perceptions. How did you know whether you enjoyed last night's Committee meeting? How would you know whether others enjoyed it? How would you judge its value, worth, merit or significance? On what do you base your ideas? Chances are you not only didn't use Multi Attribute Utility Measurement, but that you didn't even resort to a question-naire! Chances are:

- You *observed* things—you listened, watched, heard and maybe read some things. You watched people's faces and 'body language'; you listened to what was being said, the tone in people's voices; you noticed how many had come and whether they stayed for the whole meeting.
- You *talked* to people—you listened to their comments and then their responses to what you said; maybe you then asked some questions and got further insights.
- You *interpreted* what you saw and heard in the light of past experience until it was mean-ingful. Maybe you went home and thought about it all. Perhaps you talked to a few people about it—maybe an outsider such as a partner at home, as well as some who were there and some who were not.
- You *compared* all these 'descriptions of the world' with what you had expected or wanted (whether consciously or unconsciously) and drew some conclusions. You may also have changed both your criteria and your observations.
- You may have drawn on all these conclusions to *envision* what would be better and to *decide* whether to go to the meeting next month or not!

What you 'expected or wanted' was to get some of your life needs met—perhaps to make a contribution, or for information or convivial company, or in the longer term to ensure you get access to a service in the shape and form you want. You carried a lot of images of how these needs might be met. You were observing and talking to people in order to get them to supply you with signs of whether or not your life needs—as meaningful 'eval-uation criteria'—were being met. For example, there may have been a lot of people there so it looked convivial, but none of your friends was there so it wasn't actually experienced by you as such. Or a lot of reports might have been handed out, but they didn't mean much to you, so you went home feeling there were still things you don't know about. If we were to take 'numbers of people' at the meeting, and 'numbers of reports' handed out as signs or indicators of the meeting having been successful, we may not know why community members like you stop coming to meetings.

A 'grounded' or 'naturalistic' approach

Therefore, we set about finding out about the meanings that are real to people in the same way we do in ordinary life—by getting to know people well enough to understand how they see the world. We 'engage' with life, becoming immersed in it on an 'up close and personal' basis, more like an empathetic anthropologist than a laboratory scientist looking down a microscope. We get out and about among people, with people, where people are, where they live their lives in their own natural settings. When we are self-evaluating, we ask ourselves grounded (not abstract hypothetical) questions, like: 'Why am I doing this particular activity?', 'What does that mean?', 'What use was made of that?', and we ask others grounded questions: 'What made you choose to do that?', 'What made you laugh just now?' and 'What do you think of your experience of such and such?' We ask the same grounded questions of written materials or documents as we would of the people who wrote them. We read the material ourselves—we try to get as close to the original experience in them as we can. We immerse ourselves in the life-worlds of the people or situation we are seeking to understand. 'Do they like this?', 'Are they getting anything out of that program?', 'Does this service provide anything of value?'—and 'How can I tell?', 'What signs am I seeing or "reading"?', 'What are *their* signs and indicators?'

We listen intently, then check carefully for what we are hearing—not assuming too quickly that we understand. We probe a bit more, being sceptical of our assumptions and conclusions. Is there another way of understanding what I'm hearing? Do people have a different explanation? What do people who disagree with us think? *Why* do they think like this? Has it anything to tell us?

And we may make (or draw on) written records—records we hope to make (or hope we made!) systematically, carefully, rigorously and as fully as is warranted by the situation. As Lynton Brown has said in the *Group Self Evaluation Reader*,

> What turns the flow of life into data is the fact that it is recorded. Special attention needs to be given to keeping effective records on topics of concern.'
>
> (Brown, 1990)

Lynton has also suggested that people's wealth of experience might be thought of as 'data on the hoof'! At some point in time, these 'live' recollections may need to be turned into written records in order both to convince yourself that something is indeed happening (or isn't) and perhaps to convince others as well. There might, however, be a tension between those for whom minimal and informal records will suffice (because they are carrying their own wealth of 'hoof data' as background), and those who want masses of formal documentation, often because they have too little personal knowledge of the situation.

Some community health centre staff were asked what they would take to be the signs of success in meeting an objective of 'participation'. There was some baulking at having to come up with the kind of numerical indicator expected by their funding body (such as a mathematical equation of number of subscriber-members of the centre multiplied by 1000 and divided by the total local population). Finally, one said he would take to be a sign 'How many people have keys to our community minibus'. Others volunteered, 'If they come into a meeting room and arrange the chairs or close the blinds'. These are more organically *grounded* signs of 'ownership' of and responsibility for the centre. If many signs like these are pooled, better understandings may be developed. Some signs may be recurrent and could be used for standard comparative purposes between services. But for everyday purposes, idiosyncratic but maximally valid signs will be more important for local purposes than standardised but possibly less meaningful signs that central bodies may want to collect.

Spoof indicators of success suggested by another community health centre were the number of cabbages grown by the community garden group, and number of stitches sewn by the Turkish women's group! But these may speak more loudly for the tendency to choose possibly less meaningful things-that-can-easily-be-counted rather than possibly more meaningful things that can't! (For example, it might be pretty silly to require all community health centres to try to systematically quantify how many people rearrange how many chairs at how many meetings, or how many people have keys to community buses.) It may be that, for managerial and accountability purposes, it would be more useful to know that local people have generated banks of their own meaningful but idiosyncratic indicators, or recounted qualitative or narrative material that serves this purpose, rather than centrally seek the Holy Grail of standardised indicators that are meant to mean the same thing to many different services across the board—apart from a few minimal but sensible and rather abstracted signs of service provision. In Chapter 3, there are some brief suggestions on other ways in which central agencies might satisfy their 'need to know' about local services or activities without having either to distort the data or impose too heavily on people's precious time.

Where users can go elsewhere for the services they need, then providers will be furnished with a strong indicator for their success. But where providers have a monopoly, and users have no other choices, then indicators may range from passive compliance, disinterest and non-attendance through to resistance, conflict and what professionals might call 'behavioural issues'. Where users have no choice, indicators of positive valuing will be more complex. Neither more attendance nor verbal gratefulness necessarily will be signs of value to critical reference groups. All such signs require careful interrogation.

There is a chronic problem in evaluation that is known as the 'yea factor', where people reply in the overwhelming affirmative when asked to evaluate services, particularly by more formal techniques such as interviews and customer satisfaction questionnaires. Most people find it difficult to volunteer dissatisfaction (particularly if they will have to use the service again), even if confidentiality is promised. It may still feel like 'making trouble', or 'being ungrateful', and it may even feel unsafe and threatening to do so given that so many react to defend their hard-won practice. The task is to establish conditions for trust and communication where the subtleties of views can safely and effectively be expressed and heard—exactly as in everyday life when you ask someone's opinion and they say what they think will make you feel good! Often it works better to say you would like to make changes and then ask, 'How can I improve it?' This may give people more 'permission' and leaves the negative judgement implicit rather than explicit.

All techniques used should attempt in this way to get as close to people's own realities as possible. Observations should be checked for context, questions should be easily 'askable' and 'answerable', and answers should be explored to fully grasp their meaning. Remain sceptical for as long as possible—both about your own understandings of people's meanings (keep asking: 'What do you mean by that?' or 'Can I just check I have understood what you mean?') and also about your own conclusions (run them past others, including sceptical others). Accrue much more evidence than you would ordinarily—you need to both convince and challenge yourself, and maybe others too.

In this way, your evaluation fieldwork efforts follow all the ordinary rules of social research, and you can use any or as many of the ordinary techniques of social research as seem fruitful. Guide 4 provides a list of techniques and sources—some more naturalistic and amenable to everyday evaluation use than others.

GUIDE 4
USEFUL WAYS OF FINDING OUT

INTRODUCTORY COMMENTS
Different techniques allow us to capture different kinds of records that exist of the discrepancy between how things are and how we wanted or expected them to be (or not)—whether we are conducting an open inquiry or an audit review-type evaluation.

For example, collecting a file of all your old 'Tasks to Do Today' sheets or of logs of incoming and outgoing phone calls can allow you to examine on a daily basis whether you are getting through what you wanted or expected to, and also results in records that allow you to look back over a longer timespan to see whether all your daily activities are adding up to a balance of work that truly expresses your broader intentions or goals. Or a brainstorming session might provide a way of tabling a range of 'how things could be' in order to evaluate these options for the future. Or the use of a whiteboard in a kitchen or staffroom might give instant feedback on a particular issue; if items are then written down and kept in a file, they might give an interesting overview for later examination from another perspective (such as whether people are able to participate in decision-making about the service or organisation).

Records may be routine and deeply built in—such as case records or project records—or they may be new records that are slightly more built on—such as records of what people thought of an activity or event, which are appended to a routine project file. Or they may be new records that are one-offs—such as a survey or a time-series 'snapshot' set of data (where, say, for three months everyone is asked to describe or give their views about something). Or it may be a single taped and transcribed meeting to enable some more detailed reflection on a vexed issue, or brainstorming what is going really well.

The important thing is that records are collected for consideration. As far as possible, try to meet the following guidelines:

- They should be fairly natural, non-intrusive, enjoyable and immediately useful both to those making the records and to those contributing the information (such as both service providers and users)
- They should not distort unnecessarily the ordinary interactions between people or waste people's time
- They can serve as many different purposes as you can imagine. For example, use the same form to both enrol or register the attendance of someone for something *and* ask for some information—for example, about why they want to come. Or use a form to ask what people thought about something *and* also to inform or give them a chance to make further contact for future stages of the research or for networking. A renewal of subscription form could also be used to seek feedback. Use information already collected to analyse, for example, gender or geographic residence—rather than ask about these again in a questionnaire. Or use an annual report-writing process as a chance for group narrative self-evaluation.
- They need to be systematic, comprehensive and rigorous (for example, if you are going to keep some records of something, keep them properly—don't skip or miss some examples or forget to keep them). If they're too tedious or intrusive or unenjoyable or not useful, then you should consider either not doing it, or doing it for only a sample of time rather than forever, or reducing the volume of items or questions, or asking other questions.
- Written records are not always necessary. If you habitually verbally ask questions and store the feedback in your memory, then your brain is working as your computer and 'management information system' (and the most powerful yet known!). However, if you are losing track because of information overload, or need to remember over longish periods of time, or if your word is not enough for 'others' and they want tangible evidence, then you will need to collect written and accessible records.

WAYS OF FINDING OUT

With all methods, you can ask both open inquiry and audit review-style questions (see Chapter 3).

Group discussions and meetings

These might be routine group discussions and meetings (such as committee or staff meetings), or special-purpose ones (sometimes called 'group interviews' if there is a set of questions, or 'focus groups' if there is a single topic and unstructured discussion). They may be formal or very informal (such as wherever people naturally gather). They might be conducted to collect descriptions of what has happened, or views about these events, or to decide on future actions and the reasons for these (planning or goal setting).

Examples: Search conferences,* group memory work, fishbowls,* stories (narratives and chronologies), brainstorming,* nominal group technique (see *Do It Yourself Social Research* 2011),* teleconferences, public meetings, committee or staff monthly meetings, self-help group meetings, think days, group consultation, kitchen table and coffee break meetings, group self-evaluation,* judicial evaluation model,* and so on.

One-to-one discussions

Again, one-to-one discussions might be routine encounters or special ones such as interviews (where one person is the questioner and the other answers, or where both discuss a shared list of topics or questions, or even conceptually where you question yourself!). They might be face to face or over the phone, formal or informal.

Examples: Conversation, kitchen table/office desk/back fence discussions, phone surveys, phone-ins, anecdotes, reflection, recollections, narrative and storytelling, point of delivery customer/consumer feedback, 'key person' interviews ('influentials'), consultations.

Written questions and answers

While written questions and answers are often the first way that people think of getting information, they probably should be the last! They can be unpredictably difficult, often artificial, and frequently result in an exchange of misunderstood meanings (unless you can clarify things over a sequence of written exchanges from tentative to more formal). They should be as grounded as possible (naturalistic, well-'trialled', etc.). Sometimes called 'questionnaires' or 'one-pagers', they differ from the sheets of questions that might be used for individual or group discussions or interviews (more often called the 'interview schedule'), mainly because you are generally unable to enable clarification or exploration of things. 'Open' questions are useful for trying to get more of the meaning and context (e.g. 'Can you say a bit about why you liked it?') unless you already pretty much know what people will say and only want to know how many think what, in which case 'closed' questions might be adequate ('Did you like it because it was: Familiar, Understandable, Multifaceted, Short, or Other . . .?' Tick where applicable).

Examples: Questionnaires, one-pagers, satisfaction surveys, suggestion boxes, 'ideas' noticeboards, graffiti boards, checklists, cut-off feedback slips, sentence-completion ('I liked it because . . .'), return postcards technique, correspondence, voting, Delphi technique.

---

* *Asterisked items are described in detail in* Chapter 5.
(See the index at the beginning of Chapter 5.*)*

Participant observation

All observation is in a sense 'participant observation', as it is not technically possible to remove the observer from the field of the observed (where would we go?—into another field of observer-observed!). However, at first the observer may not be speaking to others about what they are observing or to clarify meaning (although will soon need to do so to avoid drawing incorrect conclusions). But direct observation 'in the field' of what is being evaluated is possibly one of the most valuable (albeit these days least valued) techniques for collecting information, despite us all pretty much always having our senses 'turned on' most of the time. Thus observation can take place virtually anywhere and at any time—in offices, shops, on the streets, in schools, kindergartens, workplaces, kitchens, refuges, on trains, trams, and buses, at shopping centres, in hospitals, at home, at the movies, in cafes, at reception desks, in waiting rooms, churches, railway stations, pubs and lifts, and out windows! Watch, look, listen get a 'feel' and a 'taste' for what you are observing. Look at people's faces; look at what they do, how and when and where they do it; look at who is doing what and under what circumstances. Look at body language, hear the tones in voices, sense the issues, listen to noise levels and silences. Examine rooms—how the chairs are placed, what are the signs of care or of activity, or of wear and tear, or of creativity? Intuit and then examine what you are sensing. Develop your sixth sense! Observation can be active or passive; the observer can be a participant or the participant can be an observer. Careful notes or records, or video or photographs, and so on may need to be made, as you will need such records in order to talk about what you are observing and reflect on what it means. Remember, meaning is not self-evident—it is constructed by you, by those you are observing and by any others who you might ask.

Examples: 'Hanging around', on-site study, field visits, exchange visits, sociometric or actor network charts, photo essays, videos, interpretive drawing, tape recordings, ethnographies, community studies, case studies, physical traces (e.g. contents of rubbish bins), headcounts, 'walking about' technique.

Existing recorded documents

Sometimes called 'historical analysis' or 'documentary evidence', existing recorded documents are examined by 'interrogating' them with the same questions just as if they were 'live'! What do they 'say' about what are their *implicit* values, purposes, and so on? What insight do they provide into your current situation? How would you want to do things differently or the same in the light of them? What do they 'tell' you about contexts and conditions that cast more light on things? Besides these open questions, you can test your hunches too. Some examples of existing recorded documents to 'interview' follow:

• Files	• Case records	• Archives/histories
• Pamphlets	• Rulebooks	• Minutes/agenda
• Memos	• Posters	• Circulars
• Diaries	• Statistics	• Notes of lectures/talks
• Phone logs	• Newspapers	• Journals, articles
• Books	• Articles/papers	• Constitutions
• Reports	• Annual reports	• Timetables
• Rosters	• Glossy brochures	• Correspondence

- Photos
- Maps
- Television
- Radio
- Films
- Noticeboards
- Meeting times
- Room bookings
- Referrals
- Newsletters
- Field notes
- Research reports
- Demographics
- Budgets/costings
- Magazines
- Bibliographies
- Schedules
- Cartoons
- Mileage records
- Appointment books
- Records of requests
- Oral histories
- Legislation, regulations
- Computerised databases
- Work portfolios
- Daily contact sheets
- Letters of support/complaint
- Longitudinal or time series data
- Resource allocations
- Attendance records
- Visitors books
- Appointments diaries
- Lists of filing cabinet contents

New records

You may wish to purposefully commence new record-keeping. Any of the above techniques could be used—either to 'capture' current practice or describe purposes and intentions. To provide a full evaluation you will again need both—and in relation to each other so you can compare. Thus if you begin to keep a diary, you will need to say what happened plus your reflection on its value relative to your philosophical purposes or your objectives. Or if you log your daily activities, you will need a commentary that judges the value of these relative to either your general purposes or specific objectives. Or if you produce a poster or pamphlet about your service or activity, you will need to reflect on its value relative to your overall purposes (or specific objectives).

Examples: All or any of the above.

The importance of context

From much of the foregoing discussion, it will have become clear that answers to questions about 'value' can only fully be comprehended by reference to their *context*—how people live their lives; who or what else is part of those lives; what else they have done in the past, or hope to do in the future; who or what impinges on, shapes and affects them. We need to go on asking 'Why', 'Why', 'Why' until these contextual meanings are revealed. For example, a new mother from a rural ethnic background is asked about the hospital service and, despite surgically ruptured membranes, a still-unhealed episiotomy, doors left open so all passers could view her labour, no interpreter and post-partum haemorrhage, ticks 'good' on the satisfaction survey—but why? Well, because she came out alive and with a live baby—and she was a refugee from a war-torn country. But will we conclude it was a good service she received? So many questions regarding what is of value (or merit, worth or significance) invoke the response 'it all depends'.

Or the elderly woman with Alzheimer's disease who keeps insisting she wants to go 'up the yard', but is 'evaluated' as having 'behavioural difficulties' by the young nurse who is meant to be giving her a wash but finds she then wets her bed. If the nurse could have inquired into the context of the woman's words, she may have found that the toilet was always 'up the yard' for a woman who has mainly known an era of houses with non-sewered outside toilets. Or the man with Alzheimer's disease who, referring to his new beard, said 'I'm drawing one on', and who was correctly interpreted by a staff member who was aware of his former career as an illustrator.

Contexts for all responses should be sought. Not only should we seek the contexts of users' views and suggestions, but also of providers' actions and the rationales and histories of activities, services and programs. In turn, these sit in still-broader cultural, economic and societal contexts, all of which are constantly changing or otherwise reproducing themselves systemically. The current phase of your inquiry is coming after numerous past cycles of action and research and action. Knowing where things have come from (and how they got there) provides powerful theoretical handles to enable you to shift things to where you want them to go.

Because you went into your evaluation with clear value-driven purpose (referenced to the values of the critical reference group), this now helps you and them to assess where to go next.

FEEDBACK, ANALYSIS, REFLECTION, SYNTHESIS AND DRAWING CONCLUSIONS

You are now in a position to begin to draw conclusions about answers to your two fundamental field questions.

Assessing past and current actions

What are our experiences and what is their value?

You should now have a picture of each element of what is being evaluated (who, does what, to whom, when, where, why and how) and have a sense of why these elements have come to be as they are (history, context, objectives, logic or rationale, purposes).

You and those involved in the evaluation also have a picture of what everyone (and especially the critical reference group) thinks or feels about each of these elements (the value of who does what, to whom, when, where, why and how and with what effects—intended or unintended, desired or undesired).

Thinking about new actions

What are valued experiences and how can we act to experience them in future?

Because the descriptions or images of the world to which a value has been attached were elicited as an important part of the fieldwork, these now supply you or your group with a range of implications and options for future action. The fieldwork also involved getting a range of ideas, images and descriptions of what people thought would be *better* and why, and these were worked through in a dialogue with critical reference groups and other stake-holders.

This supplies a kind of second-stage evaluative task: 'What is the best way to proceed?', 'Should we try doing this?' or 'Should we give that a go?' If the fieldwork has been done thoroughly enough, it will also be clear now how to value the different options in the light of what people have said, and in contexts that are now better understood. The findings and material from the fieldwork must, however, be fully shared for agreement like this to be reached so that things are clear. No further step should be taken until this is the case. If the fieldwork has been fully participatory, then this should be a more or less simple task. There should be few surprises by this stage.

Because people's evaluative comments involve them in comparing the world-in-front-of-them with an imagined world-in-their-mind's-eye, it is often very easy to ask about these visions at the same time—that is, when you are deeply immersed in the original fieldwork. A fatal mistake is to get a whole lot of evaluations of 'how things are now' and return 'home', and then have to imagine what on earth would be better to try next without any field data on the topic.

> Action research is not research followed by hoped-for action! It is action that is researched and changed and re-researched. That is, action research or action evaluation is an active set of *consecutive cycles* of action, observation, reflection, consideration of better ways of proceeding, followed by putting them into action, followed by further observation and reflection, and so on.

Thus, when you asked 'What did you think of *x*?', you should ask also, 'What might you have preferred instead?' or 'What could be done to improve it?' (If the first round of questions did make the mistake of only exploring people's evaluations of current situations, there is now a need for another round of fieldwork to ask what possible ways could be imagined for a desired future.)

Given this sort of understanding, the presentation of an 'options paper' may be more a sign of still unresolved bewilderment or conflict about perceptions, or a too-early stage of ending the initial fieldwork. It should be possible to have had a stage of the fieldwork in which there could have been argument for or against each of the options, drawing on evidence and thinking through implications and showing which of the options looked like the best shot.

This phase involving evaluating possible future practice—assessing the options—also calls for vision, creativity and imagination. Here we are trying to break old moulds of thinking, unfreeze old ways of doing and come up with paths forward that are different from current or past ways. We are trying to shift from one cycle into a new 'gear' to start the next cycle (that's if we are not choosing to continue the existing situation or repeating the existing patterns of action and practice).

But how can we imagine viable ways of doing things we've never done before? How can we imagine the as yet unimagined? Sometimes it's very easy. We know what we should do next, even as we've barely asked the question of ourselves. Sometimes, however, despite our best attempts at self-scepticism, we cannot come up with any better alternatives. In this case, we can do no better than keep trying—perhaps having another internal brainstorm or an external scout-around for ideas. There is no magical way available to us here. In trying to imagine the unimagined or even the unimaginable, all we can do is draw on the best possible sources of ideas available. These may include the following:

- *Ourselves and our critical reference groups.* We usually have among us a tremendous resource of fresh ideas, particularly if we talk or brainstorm in a group. Doing this kind of work in groups seems to work better than relying only on seeking separate individual ideas. People trigger each other's creative thinking. As well, there are always some people in every group who have especially good imaginations, or who can think laterally, or who have seen relevant or interesting things happening else-where, or who have had experiences we haven't had, or who can put two old ideas together into a new arrangement. Other methods that can be of use here are the verbalising or writing of 'future visions', 'scenarios', the use of Delphi-type surveys and forcefield analysis.

- *Metaphors.* These are sometimes shortcuts to associating known things with as yet unknown things—enabling a rich source of implications, illumination and new insight. For example, describing our service for the elderly as a bit like a kindergarten may suddenly help us conceptualise the loss of dignity involved and enable us to suggest alternative, more desirable images. Or we could try asking people to describe their service as a breed of dog, or as a family, and to allocate roles! Or, as Michael Patton has done, take the contents of a kitchen drawer and get people to select an implement and describe how their service is like it!

- *Other people and their experiences.* Inspiration and comparative analysis can come from other groups, or other services, or other areas of comparable practice—whether these are directly observed, or heard about, or read about, or discussions are held directly with them. 'The literature' falls into this category.

But imagination alone can only generate possibilities. A further act of evaluation, or prospective valuation, is required to discriminate among them—and to identify and be critical of the grounds for doing this.

As noted, group discussions are often the best way to both pool options for future action and weigh their pros and cons. As well, when action decisions are made, the last part of the cycle can then be put in place by the same people who have worked on the ideas chosen, effectively making them 'full-cycle' experimental evaluative researchers.

PLANNING AND PUTTING IT INTO PRACTICE

Recommendations for change or improvement can at last be framed effectively—and the current cycle of evaluative research 'ends' with their 'experimental' enactment. Because the evaluation process has involved all those who are to carry out the actions and those who are to benefit, there should be confidence and fewer problems at this stage. Agreement will have been reached and mutual commitment secured. Conventionally, evaluations are presented in written report form, but the more effective the evaluation has been in its internal process of involving all relevant people—no matter how simple or elaborate the evaluation—the less need there will be for a lengthy, formal written report. A written report may serve as a report to those not involved, or as a written record of the process and understandings reached, but the primary forms of (mutual) presentation will already have taken place, along with mutual learning and lesson-drawing.

There should be a more or less imperceptible movement from the evaluation process to the evaluation outcomes—that is, from the process in which people discuss their ideas and reach agreement about the value of past and proposed actions to the outcomes of people

then adopting those new understandings and taking the new actions.
Thus this end of one cycle is simultaneously the start of the next! (Just
as the start of this cycle was the end
of a previous one.)

The new actions or enacted
recommendations are then checked
to see whether they were put into
practice (the audit or monitoring
task—see Chapter 3). They are then
evaluated further to see whether they
'hold up' in terms of still being the
most resonant with deeper values
(the open inquiry task). If they work
well, everyone can return to their
taken-for-granted life! But if things
are still not quite right, or contexts or purposes have changed, and if further unease
or discrepancy is apparent, or there are new ideas for something better, you will need
to start the process again!

Is it science?

There are some important conclusions to be drawn from seeing evaluation in the ways
described above.

Firstly, all the tenets of 'good science' *do* apply to evaluation:

- It must be a well-designed effort that effectively inquires into and draws valid conclu-
sions about the value of things for those who the things are for.
- It must be rigorous, systematic and comprehensive in its scope.
- It must be (and must show it has been) self-sceptical about its conclusions.
- And it must put to the hard test of comparative well-observed actual (although field-
based) 'experimental' practice, the new valued course of action.

Secondly, it turns our view of values round, from seeing them as 'contaminating biases'
to viewing them as the essential driving force of any inquiry. That is, far from evaluative
research being value-laden (much less value-free) it is, in practice, *value-driven*. Indeed, just as
there are no 'value-free facts', there are also no 'fact-free values'. 'Values' are the conclusions
of previous cycles of research that, in turn, shape and drive the next cycle by providing the
comparative frame of reference.

It is not 'values' *per se* we have to be careful of in evaluation, since we must have them
in order to proceed in the first place. What we *do* have to be careful about is whether or not
our observations, hunches and conclusions are 'right' and true for our purposes. That is, did

our previous cycle of research get its conclusions right? No one is well-served by making up or fiddling the findings, or by findings that are unconvincing, incomplete, or that do not address alternative or competing hunches or theories.

They may *look* convincing, *seem* complete and *appear* to address all possible criticism, yet they may *still* be wrong. Nothing can ever be proven—all propositions must always remain open to the possibility of refutation so we can access new and alternative ways of seeing and thinking about things. It is this openness and scepticism about existing certainties that is everyday evaluation's best guarantee of validity, as our cycles of both small and large scale social science continuously correct or modify our understandings in the light of new circumstances. As Einstein has said:

The whole of science is nothing more than the refinement of everyday thinking.

However, while the comparative method remains fundamental to both big science and everyday evaluation, a particular comparative technique—the controlled experiment—may have limitations on the grounds of validity and ethics when applied in the area of people. Attempts to replicate laboratory settings may actually distort the more complex fields of interaction being studied. Naturalistic grounded inquiry in real-life settings may not only be more ethical, but also more methodologically appropriate—even if it is more complex and its measurement may not be able (or need) to be of excessive precision.

As Einstein also observed:

Where there is truth, there is no certainty.
Where there is certainty, no truth.

SIGNS OF GOOD EVALUATION

This chapter's discussion yields some guidelines for accomplishing effective everyday evaluation. When you think about the best piece of evaluation you have known, or when you think of your own best evaluation of a situation, you may find that the following factors were present.

It did not get out of touch with the situation

Evaluation can become overly rationalistic-systematic and sophisticated (or just plain complicated!) Some of

the currently popular logic models have been taken to such extremes and 'fallen over' in their practicability. Not everyone is into these kind of intellectual gymnastics, but pretty much everyone can make straightforward evaluative judgements at a workable scale and have some idea of why they have reached them. If plenty of simple evaluations are done regularly, then services will grow and develop in healthy directions. Most change is incremental—even the best of revolutions are relatively bloodless because almost everyone has already come to see their value. Regular and effective touching base with critical reference groups ensures that things do not get out of hand in the first place.

It did justice to everyone's views and ideas

Everyone who needed to had a say, and everyone's say was listened to. To do this, people need to feel their contribution will be respected, and trust that they will be understood. This doesn't mean that everyone agrees with everything others think or think should happen, or approves of everything that is being described—but that viewpoints are asked for, respected, listened to and understood. Even the person or group we think is most doing The Wrong Thing has a story to tell. And all these stories must be heard and understood if we are to understand why and how their situation came to be as it is. If any person's practices need to change (if critical reference groups are to be better assisted), then it is mandatory that eventually that person's story be told and heard. Not only this, but that person must also be able to participate in reflecting on how alternative practices might be better, and in identifying how he, she or they might be able to move to such new practices. The direct telling by critical reference groups of their stories can sometimes assist this process by presenting the legitimate demands of the group without mediation by secondary groups. Where critical reference groups' needs are already captured in statements of purpose or objectives, then these need to be used to raise questions about how practices reflect them (or not). And where the practices are in place, follow-up observation is needed to check that these objectives are still being met.

This kind of participatory or interpretive research isn't advocated just because it is a nice democratic idea, but because it makes for good science. People's perceptions or 'stories' (where their particular perceptions or ideas are explicated in their social and historical context) are the stuff of our understanding about what is going on in a service or a situation we are evaluating. People generally do the best they can think of under the circumstances in which they find themselves. However, it is good to remember that, even when people are acting from choice, they do not always do so under conditions of their *own* choosing. Finally, people's different biographies mean they may take a wide range of actions for similar reasons, or similar actions for different reasons.

In evaluation, we are trying to illuminate all these circumstances, conditions, contexts, purposes and actions so we can see where we are all coming from. Later we can reach decisions—guided by the values, interests and experiences of the critical reference group—

about what are the best or better ways of doing things. But at the first stage of evaluation we must really grasp well the full nature of the current way of doing things. There is a range of techniques for ensuring everyone freely gets to have a say. These include:

- A modified Delphi technique where everyone writes down their own views and they are then pooled
- or groups where everyone agrees to let each person speak uninterrupted
- or each person has a supply of matchsticks and uses one each time they speak and when the matchsticks are all used up, everyone will have had the same number of chances to speak
- or people are individually interviewed and then the material is aggregated and fed back for a group discussion
- or small homogeneous sub-groups are used where everyone feels more free to speak up, prior to reconvening in heterogeneous full groups for dialogue.

A confounding element to this is if one or more people or a group of people (and particularly those who are not members of the critical reference group) want to short-circuit the effort by getting their way regardless of the views of others. This is the all too familiar territory of power relations. Some people have lower capacities to tolerate other people's points of view and to sit with a process of dialogue or consensus-building (and not run ahead of it), and they may also have greater capacity to intimidate and exert authority, influence or control. Either way, the disempowered (most often the critical reference group) lose out, and so ultimately the services do too. Evaluation facilitators need to work carefully with the currents of power relations and associated emotions to avoid continued protection of poor-quality or even hurtful practices, at the same time as ensuring justice and a voice for all participants.

We learned things from it—it broke new ground

Good evaluation does more than tell us what we already know. It also shouldn't miss the mark or misrepresent us or suggest the impossible. It may have validated some of our private thoughts and conclusions and left us feeling less alone, or it may have given us a stronger sense of what everyone else thought. We may now feel a greater sense of shared purpose—or we may simply have a clearer idea of where we differ in our ideas from others; or we may have come away with some 'aha' feelings, as in: 'Aha—that's why we've been doing such and such!' or 'That's fixed my uneasy feelings about whether such and such would be the right way to go!'

The generation of Good Ideas that come out of Good Understandings is a sign that the evaluation has generated Good Practical Theory. We often feel uncomfortable with the idea of theory. This may largely be because the main source is an often esoteric and sometimes impenetrable academic literature we usually don't read because it doesn't seem like work at work, but it seems too much like work when we're at home! Yet the stronger our theory, the more focused will be our activities, because we will be understanding more deeply why we are doing or valuing (or not valuing) this rather than that, and what the effect has been.

The best way to develop theory and understanding is to follow the open inquiry mode (asking 'Why or what is going on here?', then 'Why that or what is going on behind that?', then 'Why that? again and again'), leading to wider and wider contexts of history, social, community, economic and political elements being admitted for examination and consideration. Where did the service or situation come from? Who first was involved? What were they trying to achieve? What was in their interests, and what wasn't? Even asking 'Why evaluate?' often gets us thinking about the hunches or observations we've been building up—possibly over many years—or it can reveal important matters about the political context in which we are working.

What it came up with was useful

The best evaluation not only develops good illuminating theory, but also gives us leads on where to go next, whether it's to do something we had intended to but had 'forgotten', or to keep doing what we are already doing, or to do something we've only just worked out looks like a more valued solution to a problem. Initially, we will have been satisfied with evaluation if its conclusions merely *look* useful! But the evaluation that really does a good job will be that which led to new ways of doing things that really work *in practice*. Of course, this implies that we turn these into plans or objectives—and someone else will look back over their shoulder in the future to *see whether they worked!*

'Useful' is primarily determined in relation to some identifiable ways by which the needs of the critical reference group are being met. In all successful evaluations, the closer the evaluation gets to the worlds of critical reference groups, the greater the chances are of being able to get this right—and to judge when it has been got right.

'Usefulness' also implies it wasn't actually useless or, worse, hurtful. Evaluation should never hurt the critical reference group or the secondary reference groups who identify with the primary reference group, but should always be illuminative. It should not damage other groups either, although some may be discomforted or feel damaged by loss of power over a situation that was held at the expense of others, or by changes in routines that may have become very comfortable and familiar. If evaluation material reflects badly on some groups whose practices have turned out to be hurtful of critical reference groups, then these too should be discussed with some grace—for example, explaining the context or story that surrounds the practices, and treating the individual people with respect and understanding. There is no doubt that there are powerful class and gender and other differences (like able-bodiedness) that result in conflicts of interests and values between critical reference groups and those who might otherwise want to assist them. Nevertheless, change is best served not only by some faith in there always being at least some shared interests, but also by a wise sense of purpose that justice should prevail and a more extended process of inquiry engaged in to achieve this. This sometimes may involve the simple insistence that critical reference groups' interests will be looked after, even when more powerful groups can't see their way to doing this.

It took time to go 'full cycle'

Another thing that characterises good evaluation is that, it not only draws on a history of previous practices and events and activities and intentions, and takes time to listen to every-one's point of view, and spends time reflecting, explaining and theorising about what to do next; it also then follows the ideas into action and later re-evaluates to see whether the new practices did indeed work. It does not take ten minutes or even three weeks; it takes all the time over which a service or situation develops and exists!

'Oh no!' you say. 'But we've only got three weeks to do it!!' Don't panic. You can do some kind of an evaluation in three weeks, or even in ten minutes or ten seconds. But it will be a smaller-scale cycle. It will still need to have some or all of the above elements for it to be worthwhile, but will be correspondingly modest. In three weeks you might hope to evaluate something like a relatively unproblematic application form used by about 50 people a year. In ten minutes, you might be able to evaluate an hour-long inter-view you just had, or sit in your waiting room and think about its effects on clients (reading matter, colour, smells, voices overheard, languages spoken). But even these apparent 'bits' of evaluation rest on histories backwards and future actions forwards. Large 'quickie' add-on evaluations, even in experienced hands, generally fail to fulfil their promise, apart from keeping up appearances.

The developmental approach to evaluation rests on the reiteration of the familiar action research cycle of action–research–action–research (or, in this case, action–evaluation–action–evaluation, etc.). It involves starting with simple open questions ('What do you think of this?' 'How is it going?', 'Is it working well or not?'), then analysing the responses and returning to ask about particular themes that arose, and so on, until new theory (or a new 'story') has developed to a point where clearer and more effective future actions are able to emerge, and in turn be retrospectively evaluated, and so on.

TWO APPROACHES TO EVALUATION

chapter 3

OPEN INQUIRY AND AUDIT REVIEW

LOCAL AND CENTRAL AUDIENCES FOR EVALUATION

We all know the litany recited to encourage us to do evaluation! It is to help us meet our aims and objectives efficiently and effectively, assist us with planning and accountability, identify both what we've achieved and what we haven't, improve our activities, or support our next funding application!

However, some of the worst confusion that arises in evaluation stems from this common conflation of the needs of two different audiences. One of these audiences typically may be the 'local' audience of on-the-ground providers and users of a service or activity. This audience needs to know the value of what they are doing in order to know how to improve or maintain it in their daily practices. The other of these two audiences typically may be the 'central' audience of those who are responsible for receiving and spending public monies on services and activities that are deemed appropriate and necessary by the elected or appointed representatives of the public interest.* This audience needs to know what is being done primarily in order to monitor for publicly approved appropriateness and value. The local audience is made up of the direct doers or participants. The central audience is primarily comprised of the auditors and transmitters and processors of information about the 'doing' further up the hierarchy and also of policy directions that come down the

---

* These comments also apply to those who spend private monies such as philanthropic trusts or community foundations. In their case, the forms of accountability are more discretionary and there is no system of public accountability via elected representatives.

hierarchy from the elected representatives' assessment of public needs and wishes for new 'doing'.

How you go about handling the requirements of central audiences (such as funders, administrators and any other authorities) may be different from how you respond to the needs of local audiences (such as local service-users or providers). For example:

- There may be differences in the scope and detail—more about detailed areas needing change and improvement for locals; more about 'reporting in' in a more summarised or abstracted way for central people (perhaps on things you are now taking for granted).

- Another difference may be the kind of study called for—open and change oriented for local people; ticking off against a checklist of objectives in a service agreement or standards manual for central people.

Sometimes, however, these requirements can be reversed. Central authorities may assist local services to be change oriented or responsive to users. In Australia, the Victorian Education Department's School Improvement Plan, the State Land Care Plan, the Department of Victorian Communities' capacity-building and the Australian Taxation Office's restructuring called 'People Action' are good examples. Private Trusts or Community Foundations' Deeds of Trust may commit them to community welfare, education or justice activities over longer periods of time. This can mean they have a greater commitment to local efforts to use evaluation for improvement.

On the other hand, local service-users and providers will sometimes merely want to monitor their own performance against their intended program logic using some standard criteria or broad statistics. Examples of this would be when Committees of Management use the Community Health Accreditation and Standards Program manual (formerly CHASP now QUIPs) or the micro-computer Community Health Information and Research System (pcCHIRS) to circulate quarterly statistics reports or write up an Annual Report for their members.

There has nevertheless been an overall trend for evaluation to be used more as an 'audit' or 'review' mechanism by centralised administering authorities (as well as some local service managers) who primarily want to be assured that funds are being used for the purposes for which they were provided, and to check that services are doing what they said they would do. However, local users' and providers' interest in using evaluation as *an improvement method* to check how or why something 'worked' or (didn't work), and to learn from it to see how to do it better, is increasingly being 'built in' to central funding authorities' work. In some areas, these two activities are at last being recognised as two halves of a cyclic action evaluation process where better attention to quality improvement processes decreases overly heavy reliance on after the event quality assurance measurement.

Indeed, some evaluation theorists would go so far as to say that audit, review or assurance activities are not evaluation at all, as they aren't evaluating whether the services are actually of value, but only whether they are being done as promised, according to frameworks of pre-agreed logics and indicators of what *was* of value at that time. For example, the intended actions may have been taken, but change has rendered them less valuable

'HEARING THE VOICE OF THE CRITICAL REFERENCE GROUP'

(a false positive). Or they are *not* being taken, but that turns out to be not such a bad thing (a false negative). However, because such frameworks are *intended* to operate as implicitly valued objectives (which relate back to meeting service-users' needs), formal 'top-down' evaluation-against-objectives techniques are examined in this chapter along with the more developmental 'bottom-up' everyday kinds of approaches that identify what is of value in the first place. The strength of the value of objectives-based logical frameworks (logframes) will rest, therefore, on the strength of the previous cycles of research that led to them. Where this previous research was weak or badly theorised, or inadequately grounded in critical reference groups' perspectives, then the objectives-based logical frameworks will also be flawed. Sometimes the higher purposes or more abstract philosophical principles are better carriers of accrued wisdom about value than the increasingly more highly specified aims and targets that are so popular but often offer a false appearance of certainty about what will be of value.

It can now be seen that these two approaches represent two different perspectives on the same evaluative research cycle (described in the previous chapter)—one looking 'back' at previously recommended and enacted practices to check whether they happened; the other looking 'forward' to a problem-posing and problem-solving effort and as yet unexplored and potentially valuable future practices. The bulk of this chapter examines these two different approaches to evaluation—recognising that *both* might be required by *either* local *or* central audiences, and ideally should be integrated into one evaluation design so each might draw on the other. The new challenge becomes one of retaining local and central parties in a partnership *working together* around the cycles of 'up close and personal' inductive observation to abductive reflection and 'bigger picture' contextualised theory-building about what would

be of more value (and why), to deductive field-based 'experimentation' on implementing the new valued actions and bedding them down and monitoring them as a culture of quality practice, without splitting off into a 'division of labour' and risking Chinese whispers or becoming a Tower of Babel as each speaks the language of only one of these discourses, and loses the whole.

EVALUATION FOR REPORTING AND ACCOUNTABILITY

Before moving on to consider the two approaches in more detail, it is worth pausing for a moment to consider further the risks of separating evaluation used as a reporting and accountability mechanism, from evaluation processes and findings at the local level for quality improvement—especially when those who are central (or otherwise elsewhere) do not know directly what is going on 'on the ground', and those who are local do not know what is being planned or introduced 'from on high'.

A key practical issue from the perspective of the local level is, 'How can central or other audiences best know what is being done down here without us spending a disproportionate amount of time documenting, recording and reporting?'

A key practical issue from the central level is, 'How can we best know that local users and providers are getting and giving the most effective services or activities possible (a) given the available total pot of money, and (b) given the total range of needs and demands?'

A key political issue resulting from separating out evaluation for accountability from evaluation for improvement is that the former generates an inevitable pressure to demonstrate achievement and to show progress towards defined goals, playing down areas where there are problems and showing things in their best light by narrowly orienting to set achievement indicators—usually abstracted as snapshot quantification. Evaluation for improvement, on the other hand, assumes there is room for learning, change and improvement, or the possibility of better achievement indicators, and thus concentrates on where there are still discrepancies between intentions and practice. People need to feel free to share their fears, worries and vulnerabilities, identify problems, come up with what might be done instead, work out solutions and carry out 'in-flight correction' (Lynton Brown's term) through several time point iterations, and then report on 'whole stories' of moving through such processes. These recursive developmental processes can be suppressed by too-regular surveillance or overly close adherence to pre-set logics of achievement objectives. Interestingly, when service agreements were introduced, they worked well as a genuine technique of evaluation for their first year or two when they were seen most clearly as experimental and provisional. Once pinned down, they largely become techniques for promising not just more of the same, but also for lowering sights to the achievable rather than the desirable.

While local audiences may always be more preoccupied with dynamic 'case studies' of local quality, and central audiences may be more preoccupied with counting and comparing services, there are nevertheless several possible strategies of mutual benefit to both local and central levels, to try to integrate these perspectives and methods.

Direct contact

Direct contact is where the central audiences make direct site visits. For all its drawbacks, the old 'inspector' system (for example, in schools and infant welfare centres) had the irreplaceable value of giving direct observational data, and a potential chance to open up questioning and exploration with local practitioners. The best of the old inspectors would have been 'critical friends', using a quasi-anthropological but collaborative approach to gaining understanding, although the 'friendship' would always have been limited by powers to cut funds, affect promotion, and so on. Yet, in turn, these powers are limited by the need to ensure needs are met. Government ministers' field visits with their executive officers to services are another example of direct contact. On-site presentations of local reports in relation to service agreements for a Victorian government funding scheme is another example, as are the networks of regional pre-school child development or health promotion or other kinds of adviser positions. With a more decentralised self-organising approach, we might even call this role one of facilitation—and, like adult education, the learnings are mutual.

Vertical slice

Vertical slice is a variation of direct contact that involves a group of officers from all levels from 'top' to 'bottom' meeting in small groups to collaborate on evaluation for policy development, reflecting on monitoring and reviewing, or service problem-solving or vision-development. This has some shared features of focus groups, although some vertical slice groups may be ongoing collaborative inquiring groups. This approach exposes each to the other's perspective—those both furthest from and closest to ministerial policy and funding levels and management, as well as to critical reference groups such as consumers or communities 'on the ground'.

Network or tree

A network or tree is often a feature of more conventional management structures—whether corporate or hierarchical bureaucratic—and involves those at the 'top' or periphery being part of an intelligence network that means that there is an assured chain of links from them to the centre. For example, there could be regional officers who do direct site visits and have good local knowledge, and central officers who have direct contact with these regional officers, and central managers with direct access to these central officers, and so on. Certainty and reassurance lie in the knowledge that others know the detail (rather than trying to collect and deposit it all centrally). A major drawback is 'editing' that might take place going up the line (as in the famous pass-the-message-along-the-line Chinese whispers group dynamic exercise), and inappropriate or poorly informed direction going back 'down the line'.

Records/written documents

The most unsatisfactory tendency is for central agencies to collect volumes of statistics that are stored in the name of 'risk management'—in the past in endless filing cabinets and now on endless computer drives—but rarely consulted unless a query arises. Sometimes services and community groups experience this as being a little like having to take aspirin every day in case their funder gets a headache! Such reporting should be minimised in the interests of service efficiency (see above for a more 'distributed intelligence system').

This would mean illuminative insights into what is done from natural records—such as those the service or activity would generate as a matter of course, like annual reports, etc.—could be read for meaning more easily. This may be enhanced by the provision of some consultancy to resource deeper reflection. Narrative forms of 'storytelling' reporting, even in the form of the well-chosen anecdote, may also be more illuminative ('We noticed such and such, so we did this and found that, and then decided then to try; and that led to . . .', etc.) than resorting only to surveys with their many possible misinterpretations. Visual presentations, videos, photos, and so on may also have more of a place than was once recognised.

To provide comparative planning data, central agencies should consider what is the minimum they need to know in order to divide up funds between regions or local areas, and leave it to smaller scale units to know more accurately whether a policy is being met. Thus local- or region-relevant data should be sought. Within a locality or region, staff should consider what is the minimum *they* need to know in order to divide up funds or know whether policy is being met. This would condition and limit the kind of data at this level, and overcome the kinds of problems typified by the Herculean efforts being made by central agencies to collect standardised case information continuously about every single individual encounter between a service provider and service-user, in all services within a program, across whole states or nations!

Contractual assurances

Contractual assurances typically have involved central agencies putting in place funding and service agreements requiring a set of requirements and commitments that are subject to regular change and revision in the light of changing purposes or long-term goals. Short-term operational objectives are always means to these changing ends, and should not be treated only as ends in themselves. They need not be overly detailed, but should provide a framework for looking at a year or two or three years of activity with a view to making a little more conscious and explicit where the local people are coming from and heading to, and why. Practice has demonstrated that such written agreements work best if they are in a context of direct contact between central and local audiences (including direct contact with consumers), and focus more on what is needing to change, leaving the remainder as more or less 'tried and true' (so far). One contractual assurance might be to expect (and require) sensible reporting on putting in place more organically developed, grounded and change-oriented local inquiry-type evaluation.

WHAT IF YOU ALREADY KNOW THE VALUE OF WHAT YOU ARE DOING?

Like all research, no useful evaluation can be carried out in the absence of a genuine unanswered question. What is essential is that you work out whether you have a question or issue without a known answer, or whether you already know the answer. If you have a genuinely unresolved problem, you will then be setting out on an exciting voyage of discovery—an inquiry into the unknown. If you already know the answers (or can find them out pretty easily), then you will be in the less-exciting but sometimes just as satisfying business of marshalling existing data or understandings—and carrying out a careful exercise in validation. We face a kind of fork in our path which Diagram 1 (see page 64) sets out.

So work out the answer to the question 'Why do we want to evaluate?' Keep going through the process in Diagram 1 (or use this as a map if you get lost) until you have satisfied yourself that you either need to do a problem-posing evaluation, or more of a validation and documentation evaluation (or a mixture of both, but be clear about which bits are which kind).

In terms of the evaluative research process cycle (see the wall chart on the Allen & Unwin website), the difference is between embarking on a new cycle of self-conscious evaluation and reporting on a cycle of evaluation already carried out (perhaps not so consciously).

Either way, you will find that the question with which we started—'What do I think of my service (or whatever)? How is it going?'—gets asked, but this time you will be clear about what has *preceded* the question and whether or not you have an answer.

EMBARKING ON NEW EVALUATION: OPEN INQUIRY AND/OR AUDIT REVIEW

If, on the other hand, you cannot yet say that you do know the value of what you are considering, we return to consider in more detail the two approaches to evaluation: change and improvement-oriented 'open inquiry', or a check on whether or not we have done what we said we'd do (e.g. by auditing or reviewing against a logframe of goals and objectives and their expected outcomes).

Recalling that evaluation proceeds initially from a sensed discrepancy between the way things are and an image or description of what was expected, we can see that 'what was expected' might be either:

- something that was explicitly and consciously expected—something we realised we valued, wanted and knew we were looking for (maybe even that we had already written down and planned to do), or

- something that was implicitly but not consciously expected—something we only realise in retrospect was what we must have valued, wanted, desired or hoped for (or *not* valued, desired or wanted, etc.)—that is, something we register mentally as a welcome or unwelcome surprise.

Reviewing on the basis of previous conclusions

When we are comparing current practice with what we consciously *planned or expected*, then what we are doing is systematically looking back over our shoulder at the conclusions of a previous cycle of research that were turned into recommendations and explicit objectives. For each of these, we can identify the precedents in our past experience: 'We did such and such in order to achieve *xyz*, and then discovered it had resulted in *abc* . . . We then realised such and such had happened, and concluded such and such . . . and then recommended that we try . . .' We have thus provisionally already decided the value of doing whatever it is, and now are checking to see if we are accomplishing or have accomplished what we set out to.

We are checking current practice off against previously articulated hopes or expectations ('objectives' or 'standards'). For example, we may have decided (as a result of previous practice) that we should have objectives *a*, *b* and *c*, according to principles *x*, *y* and *z*. Now when we look at our current practice (descriptions of the world), we can ask, 'Are we doing "*a*" according to *x*, *y* and *z*. Are we doing

"*b*" according to *x*, *y* and *z*? And are we doing "*c*" according to *x*, *y* and *z*?' See Diagram 2 on p. 66 for a typical set of service objectives and philosophical principles, and the kind of rational grid of evaluation questions it allows us to generate. This is all pretty logical stuff that lets us return to all those previously identified conclusions and use them systematically as our current evaluation criteria.

I am calling all these kinds of retrospective evaluation *'audit' or 'review'-type evaluation*.

It is important to reiterate that this can be done at any time or point in the life of an activity or service. It does not have to be left until the end, and it doesn't necessarily equate with 'summative' evaluation. For example, when you are about to do something new, you can run it through your mind against the goals and objectives already chosen: 'Will this action accomplish these goals and objectives with these outcomes?', or 'How will this accomplish these goals, objectives and outcomes?' This would ensure evaluation was built in from the outset and whatever actions are taken would be consistent with initial intentions, purposes and logical ways that have been calculated to get you there.

DIAGRAM 1
NEW EVALUATION OR WRITING UP OF OLD EVALUATION

Reflection

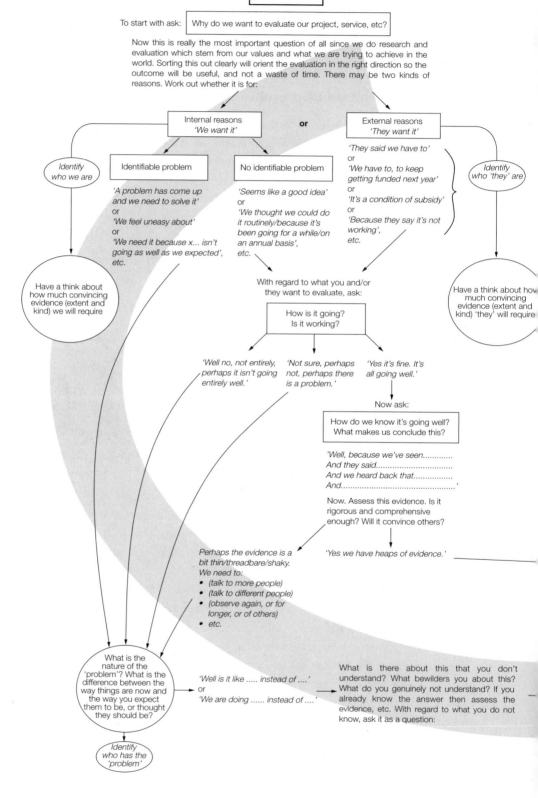

To start with ask: | Why do we want to evaluate our project, service, etc?

Now this is really the most important question of all since we do research and evaluation which stem from our values and what we are trying to achieve in the world. Sorting this out clearly will orient the evaluation in the right direction so the outcome will be useful, and not a waste of time. There may be two kinds of reasons. Work out whether it is for:

Internal reasons
'We want it'

or

External reasons
'They want it'

Identify
who we are

Identifiable problem

No identifiable problem

'They said we have to'
or
'We have to, to keep getting funded next year'
or
'It's a condition of subsidy'
or
'Because they say it's not working',
etc.

Identify
who 'they' are

'A problem has come up and we need to solve it'
or
'We feel uneasy about'
or
'We need it because x... isn't going as well as we expected',
etc.

'Seems like a good idea'
or
'We thought we could do it routinely/because it's been going for a while/on an annual basis',
etc.

Have a think about how much convincing evidence (extent and kind) we will require

With regard to what you and/or they want to evaluate, ask:

How is it going?
Is it working?

Have a think about how much convincing evidence (extent and kind) 'they' will require

'Well no, not entirely, perhaps it isn't going entirely well.'

'Not sure, perhaps not, perhaps there is a problem.'

'Yes it's fine. It's all going well.'

Now ask:

How do we know it's going well?
What makes us conclude this?

'Well, because we've seen.............
And they said................................
And we heard back that.................
And..'

Now. Assess this evidence. Is it rigorous and comprehensive enough? Will it convince others?

Perhaps the evidence is a bit thin/threadbare/shaky.
We need to:
• (talk to more people)
• (talk to different people)
• (observe again, or for longer, or of others)
• etc.

'Yes we have heaps of evidence.'

What is the nature of the 'problem'? What is the difference between the way things are now and the way you expect them to be, or thought they should be?

'Well is it like ..... instead of ....'
or
'We are doing ...... instead of ....'

What is there about this that you don't understand? What bewilders you about this? What do you genuinely not understand? If you already know the answer then assess the evidence, etc. With regard to what you do not know, ask it as a question:

Identify
who has the 'problem'

Where does it all lead? What new actions should we take? What changes are needed? What can we now recommend?

What can we conclude?

Now step back and ask 'why?' What else is going on (especially that people might not be aware of)? What pressures are being brought from outside? What are the effects of the broader social contexts? What is the 'bigger picture'? Check these ideas out too. Talk some more. Collect some more information.

Describe what you decided to do next (and progress regarding this, if it has already been commenced)

What is going on?

The key task here is to work out what you are hearing and seeing. What are people saying? What kinds or answers are you getting?

Outline the various themes that emerged — showing why you came to your conclusions

Analysis, conclusions and planning new actions

Describe any other information collected and circulated (and the sources).

Consider the whole range of other sources and techniques, (e.g. observation, things you can read, etc. — see list in Guide 4)

Say what questions were asked.

How else can you really get to know about the situation being studied?

Say who you had talked to, and how many, where and how they participated.

'We'll need to ask ourselves ..... and .....'
(Try to keep to around 3–10 questions)

Describe in detail how your experiences confirmed and/or refuted your hunches.

Say what your hunches were
'We thought that if we ....
then .... would happen, etc. '

What questions will be useful?

How many? Where and how will you talk with them? Why these? Are there others who would be relevant?

'We set out to work out why x.........
was happening instead of y............,
which we had expected or planned, etc.'

'We'll need to talk with ....
and .... and ....'

Say what was the nature of the original problem.

Identify the 'researched'

O.K. Write it up

O.K. To check out these hunches, what would you need to do? Now you need some more fieldwork.

'There is this ..... and that ......
and ...... and ......and ...... (If
they don't believe this, they
won't believe anything. We've
done the best we can)'

Designing a process of 'finding out'

'Well we reckon it's because ....
and also .... and ....

Why is it so?
or
Why is it happening?
or
What is wrong with ......?
or
Why do they ......?
or
How can we ......?

Why do you think it is so?
Why do you think it is happening?

Pick the main question. That is your main research question, that you now need answers for (in order to know what to do next in your project, service, etc.).

Next, you need some 'leads' to know who to go out and ask what. Start with your hunches (remember they've come from previous 'research'). In answer to your main research question ask:

Identify who is asking the question (you!).
Is that different from who has the 'problem'?

DIAGRAM 2
FRAMEWORK OF PRINCIPLES AND ACTIVITY OUTCOME OBJECTIVES

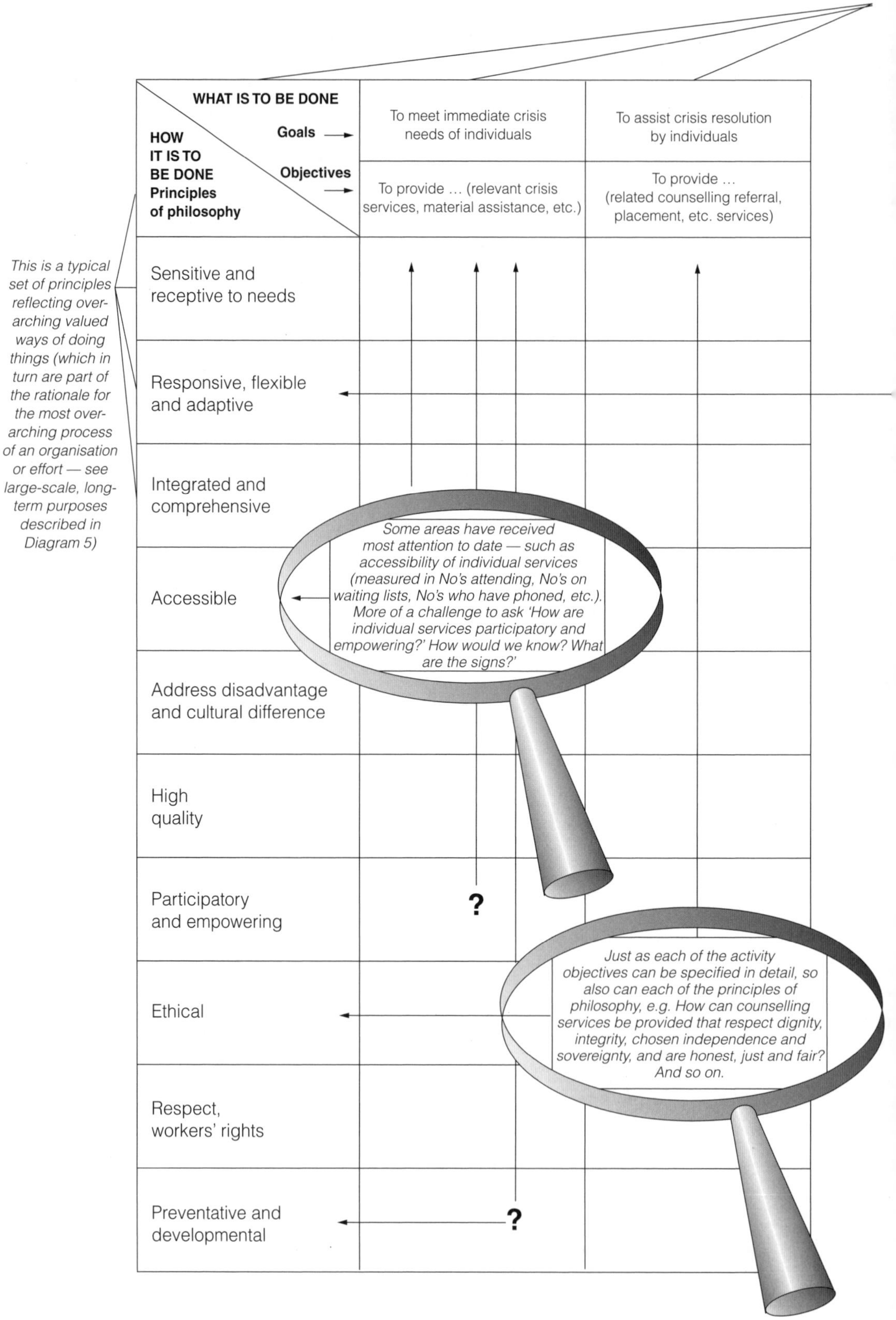

WHAT IS TO BE DONE HOW IT IS TO BE DONE Principles of philosophy Goals → Objectives →	To meet immediate crisis needs of individuals	To assist crisis resolution by individuals
	To provide … (relevant crisis services, material assistance, etc.)	To provide … (related counselling referral, placement, etc. services)
Sensitive and receptive to needs		
Responsive, flexible and adaptive		
Integrated and comprehensive		
Accessible		
Address disadvantage and cultural difference		
High quality		
Participatory and empowering	?	
Ethical		
Respect, workers' rights		
Preventative and developmental	?	

This is a typical set of principles reflecting over-arching valued ways of doing things (which in turn are part of the rationale for the most over-arching process of an organisation or effort — see large-scale, long-term purposes described in Diagram 5)

Some areas have received most attention to date — such as accessibility of individual services (measured in No's attending, No's on waiting lists, No's who have phoned, etc.). More of a challenge to ask 'How are individual services participatory and empowering?' How would we know? What are the signs?'

Just as each of the activity objectives can be specified in detail, so also can each of the principles of philosophy, e.g. How can counselling services be provided that respect dignity, integrity, chosen independence and sovereignty, and are honest, just and fair? And so on.

This is a typical set of activity goals and objectives which classifies the range of valued things to do (sometimes called 'performance areas'). The grid can be used to 'cross' principles of philosophy with objectives to produce operational aims, relevant indicators and targets for outcomes to be achieved

To prevent recurrence or further development of problems	To strengthen conditions for well-being	To promote these conditions elsewhere
To provide … (information, advocacy, screening/ early detection, etc. services.)	To develop … (self-help, group work, community support, community development, etc.)	To initiate … (community action, changes in structures, campaigns of education, etc.)

These can be specified in detail (who will do what, when, where, how often, what outcomes do we expect or hope to see, etc.)

For each 'box' we can ask 'How do we do this in this way?' e.g. How do we ensure group work is able to respond to changing conditions? How would we know? What are the outcomes we expect to see? Are we seeing them?

This kind of matrix, and variations of it, show how questions can be generated about whether we are achieving our objectives and outcomes according to the kinds of principles of practice we value, i.e. whether we are doing what we want to, in the ways we want to do them. The material generated by matrices or 'grids' like this provide the stuff of:

- *Standards manuals and performance indicators (when framed prospectively as expectations or signs)*
- *Service agreements and performance targets (when framed as objectives and targets for agreed outcomes)*
- *Operational manuals (when framed as objectives)*
- *Statutory Regulations and Industrial Awards (when framed as shoulds)*
- *Audit reviews (when framed as 'Are we doing x ...?' or 'Did we do x ...?' questions)*
- *Open inquiries (when framed as 'What is the value of ...?' or 'How can we ...?' or 'Why haven't we...?' questions)*

It can be seen that the matrix can potentially generate enormous volumes of items to be identified and attended to, if all elements of a service are subjected to scrutiny. Often in practice the above kinds of 'tools' attend to those elements that fall into the realm of 'achievable, but not yet taken for granted'.

Moving forward to new conclusions

If instead we are asking about the value of current practice in terms of our observations and 'descriptions of a world', which we have not yet made very conscious but about which we may have strongly sensed or intuitive feelings, then evaluation begins to take us into an open search for new and possibly more valued ways of doing things. This calls for a process of thinking that is often only rational in hindsight, and that challenges us initially to describe the images that come to mind, name our feelings, articulate our hunches and explore ideas as we set off on a journey of discovery.

The aim of this kind of evaluation is to find out prospectively what is of value (merit, worth or significance) and *not* to be constrained by *existing* conclusions and theories about what is already thought to be of value, or established goals, objectives and targets, but to ask unasked questions, observe the previously unnoticed, and consider the value and relevance of ideas and societal developments that may at first not appear to be of any direct relevance. In the course of exploring what people *do* value and think about things, we will work out what are our guiding images, intentions, purposes and vision. These in turn can then be made available for further discussion, dialogue and checking against those of critical reference groups (or checking back with them/us), and finally constituted into more conscious frameworks for future planned and implemented actions.

I am calling these kinds of developmental or prospective evaluation *'open inquiry'-type evaluation*.

In Chapter 4, various evaluative efforts are identified—ranging from the daily and small-scale, right through to the five-yearly or once-a-decade program 'stocktake'—for which *both* the approaches to evaluation discussed in this chapter can be used, at whatever level of elaboration or scale and whether over the short term or long term.

The map and the compass

To describe this metaphorically, if the first ('audit review') approach is to count the boats in the harbour to check they all followed the map to the already known, valued and desired destination, the second ('open inquiry') approach is for a boat to set sail for unknown and uncharted (but seeking more valued or desirable) waters with only feelings as a rudder, the critical reference group's values for a compass, the urgency of its interests for an engine and its observations with which to keep adjusting direction!* When the boat arrives, there is a new map and we can count others when they follow suit—until someone else takes off to new, unmapped but hopefully better territory again!

Now, when we take off into uncharted waters, we may bring along for reference the map of the old harbour to see whether the new coastline resembles it—but if we only

---

*   Interestingly the systems concept of cybernetics (or self-management)—which is about recursively aligning purposes to destination using feedback to chart one's course—is derived from the Greek *kubernetes*, meaning 'steersman'.

allow ourselves to stop in places that resemble precisely the old harbour, we may not be open to finding something better.

As well, the map of the old harbour may be a quite useful and reassuring resource *as long as nothing changes*; however, if there is change in the situation or its context, then it will cease being the best guide for the future, and open inquiry evaluation will again become necessary to re-chart from what is more valued.

There is now much talk about 'building in evaluation', but this is what it means: a perpetual process of learning from our experience in the light of our guiding (and changing) values, purposes or philosophy (the 'why'), in conjunction with a check against a memory or reminder of what we thought we were doing, or had hoped or intended to do (the 'what').

Let's compare the two approaches side by side. Diagram 3 on p. 71 sets out a picture of the characteristics of each of the two approaches.

Putting it together

You may find you want to do an evaluation that combines both of these approaches. That's terrific! You stand a chance of both reassuring yourself that your service is doing what you thought it was doing (and finding the gaps if it's not) and also of breaking new ground that might suggest even better ways of doing it.

Some of us have been experimenting explicitly with how to do both kinds of evaluation within a single design process and have found that if we *start* with auditing against the 'old-cycle conclusions' (i.e. evaluation against objectives), it often has an effect of closing down our minds to thinking only about the value in terms of what we have set out to do. This is still critically important, but it is often very hard then to try to open our minds up again to thinking *what else* may be going on (but which isn't covered by the program logic objectives). Nor do we get to discrepancy-identification about unintended consequences (both good and bad) or creative thinking of ideas for improvement. That is, people often seem to slip into the well-ploughed furrows of looking at familiar objectives and intended actions, and forget to notice or remember the other little observations, insights or nagging uneasy feelings that offer to break out of these furrows and plough valued new ground.

Think about when your questionnaire only asks a lot of audit-style questions such as 'Did you experience x' or 'Did you receive y', and then asks at the end for 'any other comments?' and you can't think of anything else.

To more effectively do both within the one evaluation exercise, it seems to work best to start with even just a few open questions like 'How has it been going?' or 'What have you been doing/receiving and is it going well or not?' or 'What has been of most (and least) value?', especially these questions are asked of the critical reference group, which may have a fresh 'take' compared with practitioners who are focusing on seeing particular things. This sets aside, for the time being, all the previous answers that might have been given to the question, including by carefully prepared service agreements that prescribe and proscribe service practice. Instead, it relies on people's personal and local knowledge and what is at the forefront of their own inquiring minds, including the ideas already accrued through their various belief and value systems.

It turns out we do actually already know a great deal—particularly about what and why we are doing things and their value. It's just that it is all stored on various 'mental computer files' and the existing neural programs don't always retrieve them!

DIAGRAM 3
TWO APPROACHES TO EVALUATION

To Seek formative ↗

OPEN INQUIRY EVALUATION

- Inquiry—'to seek'
- Starts with the questions: *How are we going? How is this service or activity, etc. going? What is happening? Is it working or not? In what ways? What do we think of this service? What is its value? What is of most value, merit, worth, or significance about It?*
- Asks the comparative questions: *What are we doing?* and *Is that good or bad? What are the signs of this?*
- Then asks problem-posing and problem-solving questions: *How could we improve things? How could we do more of what we are doing right? How can we move from the things we don't want to be doing to the things we appreciate more?*
- Implies asking: *What are the needs or deeper valued purposes?*
- The questions are 'opening up' questions implying the need to build new evaluative theory inductively from diverse sources. There isn't necessarily a concrete picture of what the answer would look like at the outset. The process will involve repeatedly asking the question *why are we doing this?*—to retrace the implicit program logic until the fullest and most satisfying set of explanations is achieved. And then asking *'under the circumstances, what would be of more value (merit, worth or significance) and why?'*
- Starts with immediate or obvious 'problematisation' (either of good features or of bad features)—leaves the non-problematic as taken for granted.
- Examines practice in order to be able to extract assumptions and intentions.

Can then develop new and improved evaluative criteria:
- Thus can ask about possible new goals, objectives, aims and activities that might differ from current ones.
- Is developmental, iterative or emergent (or feedback or 'cybernetic' systemic).
- Is improvement and change-oriented.
- Requires drawing on questioning, intuition, observant (interpretive), inquisitive, imaginative, speculative and creative aspects of mind.
  - Use of logic of discovery.
  - Feels more like an art.
  - Aiming at excellence of achievement.
  - Looks for 'meaningfuls'.
- Relies on who is/are the inquirer/s (for example, inclusion of all relevant stakeowners and stakeholders).

AUDIT REVIEW EVALUATION

To check summative compare with Morrison Ross Kerry

- Audit—'to check'
- Starts with the questions: *Have we done what we set out to do? Is this service, activity, etc. meeting its objectives according to the logic of the program theory and assumed outcomes?*
- Asks the comparative questions: *What did we set out to achieve?* and *What are the signs we have done this?*
- Then asks the gap-filling and 'irrelevance'-eliminating questions: *What are we not doing* (that we intended to do)? *What are we doing that we shouldn't be* (that we didn't intend to)?
- Implies already assuming what the needs are or deeper valued purposes.

- The questions are 'closed' questions; implying testing of logic based on theory from pre-existing inquiry cycle sources. (The correct answers are already known and are merely being checked for their existence and implementation). The process will involve repeatedly asking the questions, *are we doing this? Did we achieve that?*—until the full set of possible valued and aimed-for activities have been checked against outcomes.
- Sets out systematically to problematise all possible activities—leaves 'nothing' as taken for granted (except matters not covered by goals, objectives and aims and their logically derived indicators and outcomes).
- Examines practice in the light of objectives (applies known evaluative criteria):

  – Thus starts and ends with existing goals, objectives and aims and their logically-derived indicators, activities and outcomes.
  – Is a closed and causally linear system.
  – Is status-quo (or frozen snapshot) reporting-oriented.
- Requires drawing on systematic, orderly, observant (monitoring), fastidious, highly organised, analytical aspects of mind.
  – Use of logic of accounting.
  – Feels more like a craft.
  – Aiming at competence of performance.
  – Looks for 'measurables'.
- Relies on the quality of previously agreed-upon goals, objectives, aims, indicators and outcomes (and on the level of consensus previously reached).

Then the systematic 'ticking off' exercise can be conducted—showing where intended things are or are not being achieved.

You may find that the open inquiry may have already covered some of this same territory, but now the most significant matters will be to the forefront. In this way, you will have retained the 'gold' once the rest of the 'gravel' of current practice and objectives is sieved through. For example, a large residential agency for people with disabilities commenced the rewriting of its service agreement with a lengthy discussion of what single sentence it thought best represented what it was on about. When it was finished and the agency compared it with its existing mission statement, it found it had made an important conceptual leap from seeing itself as a provider of sheltered care to being a provider of home-like accommodation. The agency may not have got to this if it had instead begun by only checking that its existing mission statement was being addressed.

In another example, the volunteer staff of a community information service explored open questions about their work—and the issue of gender arose (almost all the volunteers were women, the coordinators were male, the service-users were women, etc.), yet when they turned to see whether they were meeting their formal organisational objectives, there was no mention of the gender issue.

Diagram 4 on p. 74 shows a couple of very simple one-page evaluation sheets that have used the two approaches consecutively. Other examples in Chapter 4 show this too. A good example of integrating the two approaches, taken from the area of education, would be the difference between a teacher evaluating a student's creative work of exploring a new idea (using an open-inquiry approach) by reading an essay written by the student, and evaluating whether knowledge assumed to be of value has been acquired by marking a multiple-choice examination (audit review).

If you are conducting a largish effort, it can sometimes work if there is a division of labour around the two tasks. Those whose minds work more happily in an audit review mode could together assess a service against a set of objectives, extracted either from previously written, formal statements of intention or from 'reading off' the objectives from the kinds of services or activities components provided. Another group of more inquisitive souls with a nose for 'problematisation' (both negative and positive) could ferret around for the issues (the word 'issues' is itself almost always a euphemism for 'problems'!) and start applying a 'why, why, why' inquiry mode of questioning to understand better the elements that need to be improved.

When the two groups eventually come back together, they might find overlap, but it will be the areas that don't overlap that will point in the direction of positive change, and the areas that do overlap may confirm the validity of the original evaluative research on which the service was based.

The two approaches in historical context

formative vs summative [handwritten annotation]

'Audit review'-type evaluation after the event continues to be tremendously popular, and is only just beginning to find a better balance with 'front-end' open inquiry approaches. In order for the latter to take their full place within a more comprehensive 'full-cycle' action evaluation framework, it may be helpful to examine the historical context of the rise of each.

The popularity of audit review-style evaluation may stem from the historical combination of introducing new forms of human services in the 1970s, quickly followed by a desire to constrain their growth due to political economic pressures on public spending.

The new forms of service emerged from the 1960s and 1970s when there was a particularly active phase of 'open inquiry', and consequent change in our views about how human services should be carried out. This was in many cases a change from a kind of industrial mode where modern professionals 'knew best', and intervened—often dramatically—in the lives of their patients, clients and other subject peoples with the authority of centralised, highly regimented and hierarchical institutions.

Ironically, these characteristics were associated with a way of providing human services based on the goals and objectives of an earlier era bent on creating a modern society in which 'social problems' were dealt with in a scientific, hygienic, efficient and utilitarian manner, in contrast to an even earlier nineteenth century industrial era when 'problems' were rife and people were left to fend for themselves with only the vestiges of feudal charity for comfort.

DIAGRAM 4
SIMPLE QUESTIONNAIRES USING THE TWO APPROACHES

Questions 1, 2 and 4 are 'open inquiry' - type questions.

Question 3 is an 'audit review' - type question

All the questions on the other 'Feedback Sheet' are 'open inquiry' - type questions (although questions 7 and 9 may be related to objectives — and thus be 'audit review' - type questions).

THE LINKING WORKSHOP' - EVALUATION SHEET

The organisers of the workshop are interested in receiving your opinions about the workshop to assist in evaluating the day and in planning future workshops. Your co-operation in completing this form would be greatly appreciated and please return it to Donna Tonetto, 555 Collins St. Melbourne 3000.
Residential Services, 555 Collins St. Melbourne 3000.

1. WHAT DID YOU FIND USEFUL ABOUT THE WORKSHOP ?

_____

2. WHAT COULD HAVE BEEN BETTER OR CHANGED ?

_____

3. THE FOLLOWING WERE THE OBJECTIVES FOR THE DAY
HOW WELL DID YOU MEET THESE OBJECTIVES ? (Please circle the number that most appropriately describes your view.)

a) OIDS/MOHC Information exchange and to meet each other

1	2	3	4	5
Not at all	In a small way	Reasonably	Quite well	Very well

b) To develop a co-ordinating structure.

1	2	3	4	5
Not at all	In a small way	Reasonably	Quite well	Very well

c) To identify common issues that need to be addressed.

1	2	3	4	5
Not at all	In a small way	Reasonably	Quite well	Very well

4. ANY OTHER COMMENTS

_____

Feedback Sheet

Please let us know what you thought of the Consumers' Fair Go! Kit.

1 Which booklets did you find most useful?

☐ "Need help at home?"
☐ "What to do if you think there's a problem"
☐ "How to improve your community service - get involved!"
☐ "Finding your way around HACC"
☐ "What consumers can expect : putting rights into practice"
☐ "Finding out what consumers really think"
☐ "A complaints system that works : The essentials"

2. Which the least useful? _____

3. In what way did you (or your organisation) use them? _____

4. If doing a second edition is there anything we should add, concentrate more on, leave out or change? _____

5. If we were adding more booklets to the Kit what should they cover? _____

And for what audience(s)? _____

6. Would the booklets or Kit be more useful if in a different format? _____

7. Are you a
☐ consumer representative or advocate   ☐ service provider organisation
☐ management committee member   ☐ government officer
☐ consumer   ☐ other _____

8. (optional) Name _____
              Address _____
              Phone no. _____

9. Who did you get the Kit or booklets from? ☐ direct from us   ☐ through _____

CONSUMERS' FAIR GO! FEEDBACK
Combined Pensioners' Association of NSW
Level 5, 405 Sussex Street
Haymarket NSW 2000

Please return to: HACC

In the post-World War II period, 'evaluation' (rarely formalised or funded as such) by client populations and their sympathetic young professional advocates began to reject this well-meaning but often damaging approach. There was a shift towards understanding the social, political and economic conditions that created and shaped disadvantage (rather than seeing it purely as a matter of personal misfortune or individual wilfulness). Responsibility for people's individual situations had become a social matter—starting with the introduction of government public health, education, welfare and social security schemes, and coming to rest in a set of understandings about how services should be provided to protect and promote people's dignity, self-determination and empowerment.

In the 1980s and 1990s, these became the set of human services program principles, goals and objectives with which we have become so familiar (see Diagram 2 for an example).

Coinciding with this development came the end of the comfortable economic conditions that had underpinned it. More money during the economic boom of the 1960s and early 1970s had seen the expansion of secondary and tertiary education, the growth of a well-paid, credentialled workforce, an intolerance of the 'residue' of poverty and disadvantage, and a determination to deinstitutionalise and resource a range of groups of people, who had literally been locked away from mainstream social and economic life, including people with physical, intellectual and psychiatric disabilities.

However, the economic recession, and subsequent restructuring of industry and consequent demands for government resourcing of business recovery and debt, led to financial stringency, with the 'luxury' of social justice largely being postponed to await further presumed growth in a competitive economy. In 1980 in a Melbourne public lecture at Ormond College Martin Rein described the shift from 'the vision of the social workers' to 'the vision of the economist' at the height of the boom in the late 1960s and early 1970s, when a guaranteed minimum income seemed both desirable and possible, and finally to 'the vision of the auditors'. This latter 'vision' accompanied an era of 'managerialism', 'performativity' and 'leadershipism', as the private sector moved ruthlessly to maximise output and minimise production costs, and the public sector moved to copy this by controlling spending growth and containing the demands of a populace who had come to expect that their human needs might actually be met.

Thus the two groups—those who wished to ensure services were now targeting needs and abiding by more humane principles, and those who wished to ensure that no new services were funded and indeed that some real decreases in funding levels could be attained (we should perhaps see the word 'ration' every time we are told an approach is 'rational'!)—united to introduce techniques such as Management by Objectives and Management for Results, program budgeting, performance indicators and targets. This approach has been in some ways cemented over the most recent decade by the move to tightly prescribing program logics, outputs, outcomes and evidence for these—leaving a silence about how the values underpinning the logics are created in the first place (when once this would have been achieved by needs studies).

This might explain some of the ambivalence with which audit review evaluation is still often greeted by local service providers or users. On the one hand, it seems terribly sensible and indeed helpful to check that one is doing the (good) things we set out to do, or getting the (good) services we were led to expect. But on the other hand, the 'rationality' of such a closed system approach may take critique and further change and development off the agenda. Yet not only growth, but also improvement and development that are within current budgetary restraints, may be impeded if our current logics, practice objectives and outcomes are insufficient or inadequate or inappropriate.

Interestingly, some of the most recent developments in managerialism (beginning with Management for Excellence and extending through quality improvement, to the contemporary strengths-based and appreciative approaches) have been away from reliance on tightly centrally controlled, technical rationalism (which had everyone constantly accounting in advance for everything they were going to do, and being held rigidly to doing every one of those promised things, and unable to do anything 'outside the rules' or unanticipated). The shift at least partially seems to be away from overwhelming reliance on 'top-down' carrot-and-stick motivation and command-and-control management with appearances of 'performance', towards including more 'bottom-up' autonomous and participatory self-management, inspirational leadership and an emphasis on achievement within a broader organisational philosophy.

In important ways, this involves a shift from the excesses of an audit review approach towards integrating some of the characteristics of open inquiry, such as qualitative observation, critical reflective insight and generation of new and better program theory, particularly through sensitively retouching base with the 'customer' or consumers.

Drawbacks of only evaluating against objectives, targets and outcomes

While some of our services' higher principles, deepest values and long-term purposes are the result of decades of painstaking research, theory, policy and practice, we only need to consider how it was that many objectives, indicators and targets were settled on to realise that some change might still be desirable!

Would you say that:

- current practice is the result of planning which *only* came after in-depth, grounded practice, field-based research in which all relevant parties participated?
- this initial front-end developmental evaluation resulted in a high level of consensus and commitment by consumers and practitioners?
- everybody really understood what they were doing and why?
- things proved to be easy to put into practice, as it was obvious what to do?
- you could then tell whether they had or had not been met?
- they were not overly ambitious or, alternatively, too superficial?
- the needs they address haven't changed since they were written?

Yes, Yes, Yes! Fantastic! No need to change yet. On the other hand, if you have been chuckling out loud, then you might be remembering how the new committee put together this year's strategic plan based on the previous one; or a consultant came in to do the consultation that would give the rationale for what had already been decided; or your service manager met with the funding body, and after 'constructive debate and discussion', you 'got up' a few good objectives and you let 'them' get up some of theirs for the sake of peace and to get the funding application or service agreement in before the closing date; or that the objectives were made so vague and general no one could disagree, and things wouldn't be too unachievable; or the pressures of everyday work have meant there hasn't been a chance to really stop and reflect on deeper matters or see what the community thinks.

Yet, in terms of the ongoing evaluation research cycle (see the wall chart on the Allen & Unwin website), the program theory and resulting goals and objectives are theoretical predictions (if we do x, y, z, then needs will be met) until practice provides further evidence that we've actually got things right, or of how we need to adapt further. Until then, they are only as reliable and relevant as the research that led to them (and also depend on no change taking place to those original conditions).

As the saying goes, 'The future is made, not predicted'—so we must retain a capacity to reform, change, develop and improve, or else risk the same ossification that the community workers of the 1970s were suffering from with services designed for the 1940s and 1950s. This means treating service policies, goals, objectives, targets and logical outcomes as valuable expressions of intention and purpose but as always *provisional* and not fixed for all time. For as long as this wisdom can be held, then services remain 'alive'. In this way, they can move constantly between an old consensus and a new one—with evaluative research repeatedly bridging between the two.

So the drawback of audit review evaluation that can result in a preoccupation with measuring the discrepancy between formal objectives and practice (which can result in services adjusting their aims and activities to being more and more modest or achievable to seem to be 'performing') can be overcome by an open inquiry evaluation to continuously re-chart from deeper client-centred values, and free up reflective thinking to develop better service responses.

While it is often an enjoyable, reassuring and valuable exercise (see Diagram 2), a drawback of audit review-type evaluation is that it can eventually therefore feel somewhat mechanistic and tedious about detail to the point of losing meaning. It is actually quite hard—even while worthwhile—to have to consider every little element of a service, especially all the bits that are going well enough and would otherwise be taken for granted. (It would be a bit like being stopped to evaluate your reading speed and comprehension levels every time you turned the page or asked yourself whether you were enjoying reading a novel.)

Sometimes this kind of evaluation—such as that implicit in a service agreement— also becomes repetitive or confusing, as each part of a service is considered under several different headings in regard to its contributions to several different objectives that are connected. It is rare that one service or even a part of a service is only meeting one objective, particularly if an integrated approach is highly valued (possibly as an objective!). This might make audit review-type evaluations rather complex, but the complexity may actually be the price to pay in exchange for greater meaning. To be accomplished strictly within its own driving logic, it calls for a mind a little like a computer. Minds not quite so logically programmed can sometimes mix up objectives with principles of philosophy, or indicators with aims, and so on—but find it easier to tell a coherent story that narratively brings things together more meaningfully. This underpins the recent popularity of narrative evaluation which, while not a complete substitute for audit reviews, can help them make more sense.

So, despite all the detail and attention to systematically and logically evaluating 'all' elements of a service, the more glaring issue with evaluating a service against its objectives is that almost all the really interesting, colourful, 'thick', rich and juicy fabric of a service may actually lie outside the written-down objectives.

To give an example: if you were to evaluate this book, *Everyday Evaluation on the Run*, there are an enormous number of things that could come to mind:

- how it makes you feel, what it touches off in you, where it connects, where it doesn't, what you thought of it, what you could learn from it
- the appearance of the book, the colours, the typeface
- observations about the cartoons
- the language, terminology or grammar
- the style of writing, the examples used
- whether you knew any of the people in the acknowledgements, or what you think of the women to whom it is dedicated
- comparisons you make between it and *Do It Yourself Social Research*
- reflections on other evaluation literature you might have read . . . and you would barely have touched the surface of the colossal array of domains of potential 'data' and 'evidence' on which you might quite unconsciously be drawing to evaluate it.

If you took longer (or I interviewed you!), you might expand into considering:

- its use in your own workplace or when evaluating services you have used or situations in which you have found yourself
- some other people who could use it, or who might find it difficult
- If you had already talked to others who had read it you might recall their comments and compare them with your own thoughts. They might have mentioned its size and thickness, or cost, or value to students, or things it hadn't even occurred to you to think of

and so on and on.

From this wide range of potential aspects, you might volunteer some you had particularly noticed that relate to your needs and interests. This would give strong clues about what is of most value or not of value. This approach, by inquiring about only those elements of interest, could then focus the evaluation on the elements needing change or replication. On the other hand, if you wanted to do a really thorough open inquiry evaluation, you could ask, 'What do you think' of all or many of the widest possible range of aspects.

Both these exercises ('What did you think of the book?' *and* 'What did you think of *this* aspect of the book, and *that* aspect of the book, and this, and this . . .') would give you a more grounded evaluation from the reader's own perspective.

If, however, you started with *your* purposes and intentions and only checked for these ('We set out to do x and y and z: did you experience x, did you achieve y, and was z understood?') you may well have missed out on valuable insights about values, needs and interests you had not realised were there but that were (or were not) catered for.

Sometimes our objectives are relatively cryptic—particularly those for more distant audiences such as funding bodies. For this book, there were four simple operational objectives (or targets):

1   to write a book with the title *Everyday Evaluation on the Run*
2   to have it in camera-ready form for the printer by a specified date
3   to print 5000 copies, and
4   to have it purchased (including by critical reference groups).

The answers to a basic evaluation of the success of these objectives are, more or less, 'Yes', 'Three months late', 'Yes, plus a further 5000 copies in the second reprint' and 'Yes'. Evaluation of this kind strikes many as not quite getting at the full meaning of their work! It is perhaps a little like describing Beethoven's Fifth Symphony as 22 minutes and nineteen seconds long! Now if you're a central program manager who has to ensure that a performance of five pieces of music will fit into the program time, this may be the only evaluation that is required. But if you're asking about the general value of the piece to an audience, then something of the 'colour' and meaning may have been lost! Indeed we don't actually know from this exercise what the *value* of these things is—except by reference to the framework of principles and goals based on the existing (previously generated) theory (If we do this . . ., then that . . . will follow).

The flaw in assuming that one's operationalisation of objectives will necessarily bring about one's higher purposes or intentions might also be illustrated by the example of this book. It turned out that writing a popular and accessible book on evaluation was more difficult and time-consuming than originally thought. Ideally, it should have been left to develop to a further stage; however, the funding service agreement set tight limits around it and constrained its capacity to meet its overall purposes and guiding goal.

Alternatively, you might have proceeded to set objectives (indicators, and measurable targets to result in specific outcomes) for every one of the large range of possible aspects (listed in point form above). Yet would one necessarily want to record formally all this mass of details as part of a rational and extensive standards or objectives-based evaluation framework at all, much less in advance? Or would this be a bit like counting all the leaves to know whether it is autumn?! Perhaps too much rationality of this kind locks us too tightly into a new iron cage.

Often a service will generate an activity that will suddenly take off and head in a really brilliant direction. When evaluated against its formal objectives, such a development may be merely recorded as relevant to objective 'A', or it may even go unrecorded for want of a relevant category. But if the tight restriction of pre-existing audit review evaluation could be released, and a lot of attention devoted to that single successful instance, enormous ground might be covered that might have relevant repercussions for other areas of the service and may even lead to new or reframed objectives.

For example, a service may contribute a stall to a local community festival. If evaluated against its formal intentions, it may appear to have a rather weak 'community education' outcome. On the other hand, if it is examined for what effects it might have had *per se*, those who sat on the stall all day might have returned with insightful stories drawn from the half-dozen remarkable encounters with several members of the public who might never otherwise have approached the service with their stories. These stories may have yielded tip-offs regarding the parlous state of a local private nursing home for the aged, or the germ of an idea about addressing the possible volume of hoarded, unused and dangerous prescribed drugs in people's medicine cabinets at home, or an exciting new idea about how to connect with young people who are carers using the internet.

Rather than the stall educating the community, the community had used the stall to educate the service! This insight might lead to the next stall being explicitly run as a 'person in the street' study, or an even more effective way of tapping community views. As well, another consequence may have been to have the stall appear in the background of a photo in the local paper the following week—reminding a single member of the public to want to join up. Again, when measured against a numerical 'performance indicator', it may not look very valuable. A manager may even move to abandon it in future. But say this single new recruit goes on to lead a successful campaign against the dumping of toxic chemicals in the local creek. And what if, with that new-found confidence, she stands for local government? It might then be interesting to explore what it was about the stall that encouraged residents to talk; what characteristics of the workers allowed them to listen and hear, and so on.

It is this kind of locally contextualised, meaningful and more complex information that may allow a more valid evaluation to be done of that service's activities, yet one can see why such grounded material is both so important and also so elusive:

- Effects may be long term.
- Effects may only be known about by 'chance' or by having excellent local contacts to hear 'up close and personal' or be intuited or deduced.
- Effects may only be connected to the original activity by a fine thread or a complex network of interdependent effects rather than follow a straight line of simple cause and effect.
- Effects may be too costly to trace, but only anticipated 'in theory' (relying on having already been established in painstaking observed developmental practice). That is, it is too time-consuming and expensive to follow up, or only possible to do this very intermittently.

There is the now-famous example of the American War on Poverty's pre-school children's Operation Headstart (followed by Operation Homestart)—which was evaluated as ineffective and subsequently abandoned using an experimental design within only a few years of implementation. Twenty to 30 years later, the evidence came in that children who went through those programs had in fact done significantly better in terms of education and job success. We don't require every teacher to check on their students twenty years down the track (interesting though it may be to be invited to their pupils' school reunions!), yet we can be more or less confident of the value of teaching in the here and now because we have already established strong theory from previous cycles of evaluative feedback research pitched at the appropriate level and the appropriate relationships between practices and later community and workplace settings.

The Australian example of community health centres being evaluated several years after inception and shown not to have made an impact also underlines this point. There is an additional point that can be made here, which is not so much that such services are unevaluable (until they have operated for twenty years)—although this may also be true—but that there are varying indicators of success, and that these indicators match differing levels of intention and action. As a book author, I check today's output against an intention to produce so many pages about such and such a topic—not against whether I have managed to demystify modern Western science to a statistically significant extent! If a community group is funded to produce a newsletter for Heart Week, we don't usefully evaluate it by checking the blood pressure of the population before and after its production. We may more usefully chart a sequence or logical pathway of effects and outcomes, and trace the more proximal of these connections in the first instance.

These kinds of observations underlie the current popularity of 'logic models' that spell out a hierarchy of purposes and practices to achieve them.

Drawbacks of open inquiry evaluation

The fundamental drawback of open inquiry evaluation lies in its capacity to overlook matters that are not obvious to the inquirer. Audit review evaluation will ask about 'all' elements (at least, those that are covered by existing intentions), and if those existing objectives are comprehensive, then the evaluation will also be comprehensive. However, open inquiry evaluation is generally 'only' able to be discrepancy based (whether appreciative or critical) or problem or improvement-focused. This makes it terribly important to ask, 'Whose discrepancies or problems?' and 'Are the problems important?' or 'Significant to whom?', and 'Improvement in what terms, and who will benefit?' If the problems are those of staff, then do they reflect what is problematic to critical reference groups? Or if the 'significant changes' are less important compared with the 'white horse on the table' that everyone is too polite or too afraid to mention, then the evaluation may be misdirected. Or if the voice of the critical reference group is not being heard at all, then the evaluation might well miss its mark.

This again emphasises the importance of genuinely involving critical reference groups in actively guiding the process and direction of inquiry in collaboration with other relevant perspective-holders. Users can introduce perceptions of situations that might never otherwise occur to staff, and can alert to discrepancies in priorities or presumptions that also might not have been obvious to staff.

Open inquiry approaches to evaluation require tolerance of considerable uncertainty and a realisation that evaluation essentially remains a matter of judgement. We can perhaps see why quantification is so strongly associated with audit review styles of evaluation. When one has firmly decided on clear objectives, and may even have converted the signs of achievement into clear performance indicators and worked out precise standards to be achieved, then one can try to detail with considerable precision the extent of compliance (or discrepancy). Sometimes this precision can be expressed without scaling or ranking, such as where questions call for Yes/No answers. For example, if the standard for a 'participation' objective is the presence of a community committee of management—it either exists or it doesn't. Or it can be expressed in terms of how often or how many (people through the door, projects accomplished, etc.); or performances and actions can be ranked, graded, scaled, or scored.

However, for much everyday evaluation, a simple sense or feeling of discrepancy may be adequate (like the shepherd who knows there's a sheep missing without counting them all, or the service-user who knows she is in pain or is being treated disrespectfully without having a device to measure it). However, whenever the extent, degree or amount of discrepancy between a goal or standard and an actual performance becomes crucial, then human beings prefer the reassurance of apparent certainty. Even when such matters remain matters of dubious contextual judgement, we seem to like to imagine that they aren't! For example, when there's a lot at stake, we like to 'know' that the swimmer really 'won' the electronically measured race at 24.003621 seconds and the swimmer who 'only' got there at 24.003622 seconds was definitely second-rate.

When there are scarce budget funds to be distributed among a lot of starving services, the apportioning-type evaluation that says that this service is a '6.3' and the one that loses half its budget was only a '5.8' gives us a sense of 'the right thing' having been done, even if it hasn't. Usually, but not always, there seems to be safety in numbers (especially if you're a 6.3).* We can see again the sense in Albert Einstein's saying 'Where there is certainty there is no meaning. Where there is meaning, there is no certainty.'

If the managers having to make these budgetary decisions cannot get out and about to observe services at first hand (and acquire direct naturalistic data), or have in place a local

---

* Sometimes the ambivalent term 'measures' is used. But this has several possible meanings including:
- size or quantity
- degree, extent, amount
- unit of capacity
- that by which a thing is computed
- suitable action.

Unless quantification is intended, less ambivalent terms are 'identifiers', 'indicators' or 'signs'.

and regional network of people who can reliably do this and compare their naturalistic data, then they may rely more and more on abstracted numerical data. Objectifying in this way may make it easier for managers to avoid being confronted by the moral and ethically contextualised nature of their judgements. However, the further consequences of this may be twofold:

1   Those services that are longer established and have refined their practices so tightly as to be able to time tasks and cost them to the smallest unit and attach a numerical value related to an assessment of needs may do well—even if the practices are no longer worthwhile or meritorious in relation to new more relevant values relating to current community needs.

2   Those services that are newest and most innovative (and may be addressing vital and creative ways of doing things), but are still charting their paths and working out what counts as success and what doesn't, may be most vulnerable to not being able to evidence why they should be allowed to continue.

In Canada, the first services to be cut in a tight economic climate just happened to be the most recently established: services such as those experimenting with self-determination, empowerment and participation of native Indian and minority groups; and low-income groups. There are similar experiences in Australia, the United Kingdom and the United States. Slowly, it is being realised that today's 'tried and true' only got there by being yesterday's 'innovative and creative'.

Yet even the newest and most creative projects can, with some modest assistance, self-evaluate around the particular signs of success that are meaningful within their own local contexts. Over time, and with dialogue, these may become more reliable and comparable signs.

However, not even the most useful evaluative statistics can necessarily be guaranteed a place in the sun. Even when abstracted numbers *do* bear some meaning, they may be rejected—or even abolished! For some years, the Australian federal government collected national emergency relief statistics. Every agency in the country painstakingly kept records of the age, sex, family status and income source of every applicant. Such data enabled the often-quoted statistic that nine out of every ten applicants had been or were awaiting a Department of Social Security pension or benefit. The collection of these statistics was subsequently defunded and discontinued. No statistics—no problem! :-(

Guides 5 and 6 summarise the previous discussion of the strengths and weaknesses of the two phases of the evaluative research cycle.

GUIDE 5
STRENGTHS AND WEAKNESSES OF THE TWO APPROACHES

Audit review
Strengths

- Will call attention to 'all' matters previously thought to be valued/ required—and submit them for attention and check they have been implemented. Within this framework, it can give a sense of illumination to areas that may have been overlooked or forgotten.
- Validity will be high if the prior research base was strong.

- Can be comprehensive and reassure that much is being done.
- Will identify matters (gaps) not yet attended to within the existing framework

- Can affirm previously reached agreements and consensus; can strengthen collective sense of direction.

- Can feel very comfortable and comforting.

Weaknesses

- Doesn't discriminate between the still-valuable and appropriate matters and the now not-so-valuable and even irrelevant or outdated matters (doesn't identify how to change or improve; may lead to preoccupation with mere appearances of performance).

- Validity will be low if prior research establishing value was ungrounded, thin on evidence, etc.
- Can be tedious and feel wastefully time-consuming.
- Will not identify (without resort to inquiry mode) *why* these matters have not been implemented, or whether they should have been, or still should be; nor identify any gaps outside the framework (e.g. unmet needs).
- Can't assist much if the objectives don't represent consensus or generative agreement, or if they are only superficial, or 'paper over' conflict, or if the certainty is trivial, irrelevant, meaningless or leave out the real issues of critical reference groups.
- Can give a feeling of complacency. May encourage inappropriate conserving of the status quo.

Open inquiry
Strengths

- Will call attention to the more pressing or priority issues at the forefront of consciousness

- Problem-identifying focus increases the chances of problem-solving and better outcomes; change for improvement and in areas identified as important.

Weaknesses

- There may be pressing issues that have been repressed into non-consciousness, that need time to surface, or be 'felt through' and reflected on.
- Problem-focus may overlook important matters that no one has yet identified as a problem or alternatively overshadow the strengths, assets and good things happening.

- Assists innovation and creativity and dynamism in special areas (depth).
- Sense of exhilaration at a journey into the unknown.
- Meaningfully grounded rather than abstract, involving rather than excluding.
- Identifies what is of value, merit, worth or significance.

- May not be systematic and comprehensive for all areas (scope).
- Involves uncertainty, suspension of judgement, lack of clarity, and even a sense of chaos, and possibly seeming 'irrationality', disagreement and conflict.

GUIDE 6
WHAT TO DO TO IMPROVE THE TWO APPROACHES

Audit review

- When auditing against objectives, always ensure there is a method of also collecting records about matters that will either require further inquiry or may be significant on reflection—for example, where there is feedback about faulty logic or outdated objectives, or problematic implementation that might imply difficulties with current objectives and intended outcomes, or matters that are otherwise silent or have no obvious place in the current framework.
- To strengthen chances of validity, put in place a parallel or sequential process for open inquiry.
- To mitigate false certainty, recognise the need to move to some kind of change, and publicly identify the existing framework as provisional and contributory to the next phase of evaluation.
- To overcome tedium and wasteful time consumption, keep a full audit review for only occasional use (for example, annually or two- or even three-yearly), and supplement it with more frequent, smaller scale, ongoing, built-in problem-solving or appreciative inquiry evaluation. Focus annual reviews on the areas for change and improvement that have come out of open inquiry.

Open inquiry

- To identify important matters that no one has yet seen as discrepant, touch base with the critical reference group: work out ways for them to speak in their own undistorted voice and be heard without too many intervening 'sound barriers'; encourage and respect even unconventional and (at first) unsystematic forms of input; don't be too quick to judge what is said as being irrelevant or unrepresentative—even the most solitary consumer voice may turn out to be the canary in the mine; later you can check the extent of the view ('Somebody has suggested that . . . What do you think?') if that is necessary. Seek out comparable situations or groups: have they identified problems you haven't? (Again, check out the value of these to your critical reference groups.) Draw on as many sources of different perceptions as you can: read the literature; think up analogies or metaphors that might be useful to reframe old ways of thinking that aren't working.

- Evaluate against higher-order intentions—for example, you may be able to tick off successfully that you have put an equal opportunity officer in every technical college—but has it really decreased women's inequality?

- To counter lack of thoroughness, make sure that, periodically, a systematic review is done—but possibly less often rather than more. Constant, clarifying, problem-solving dialogue and critical and appreciative evaluation shape an organisation in the desired direction and decrease the chances of it ending up in the wrong place.

- To tolerate uncertainty, recognise the desire to improve, and accept moving to some level of agreement through dialogue, then treat what is possible as provisional but give it a chance to survive further trial and error. For example, a group may be reluctant to say precisely when a project will be completed or what its effects will be, but it can be known that those doing it have a track record for completing projects or good work, or it is known that the activity is addressing a notoriously difficult but vital topic. Remember that the more deeply innovative the effort, the longer it will need to prove itself—possibly even years or decades. Measuring Aboriginal blood pressure before and after a twelve-month project where a community worker is attempting to assist Aboriginal communities identify the conditions for improving health may be not just unhelpful but actively re-damaging. If it took 200 years of disempowering by white societies, it may take 200 years of resourcing to show identifiable outcomes. Generate fuller descriptive narratives, especially where abstracted snapshot statistics do not make enough sense on their own.

Questions that address each of the two approaches in sequence

To return to the point about the need for both approaches, a comprehensive evaluation framework would include two sets of questions with both service-users and service providers/other stakeholders. This section sets out to convey the logic of the two different kinds of questions that flow from the two approaches discussed. Note that these may not be the precise questions you or your group might ask (or might ask of yourselves). These would have to be tailored to your own situation (and they can all be expanded or contracted in detail, depending on your time and purposes).

1. Starting with questions to users or critical reference groups
Open inquiry questions for end-users
These are the kinds of questions that ask, 'What is the value of this service or activity to you?', 'What is not of value to you?' or 'Is the service or activity working for you?' ('What works?' or 'What doesn't work?').

If these kinds of questions are too broad, you could break down the service or activity into aspects or elements—'What is the value of x to you?' or 'What is not of value to you about x (or y or z)?' or 'Is element x working?', 'Is element y working?', 'Is element z working?' and so on.

Then you would pursue context by asking, 'Why is that?', 'Can you talk more about that?', etc.

You should get a picture of *what* is being done (description of activity or service), *how* this is known to be of value (description of the signs) and *why* it is working or not working (explanation for it). You may need to ask (or ask yourselves) 'Why?' several times to get a full explanation.

An example of an exchange that captures all three of these elements would be:

Q.   *'Can you say what the value of the self-help group has been for you (or us)?'*

A.   'Well, the meetings of the self-help group I attend are good.'

Q.   *'Can you say why?'*

A.   'Oh well, I suppose it's helped me recover from the grief quite a lot.'

Q.   *'What are the signs of that for you?'*

A.   'Um well, I feel much brighter the day after the meetings! And it just feels less alone when your thoughts drift back—you just know that others have the same thoughts, and that you can move on from them. Some like me take longer, but there's a woman at the group—she only came once—but she's sort of my personal inspiration. I just remember how she's handled it. It gives me a picture of where I want to get to.'

Q.   *'What about the different aspects of the groups—what about the group leader? What about the time, the venue, the topics, etc.?'*

There may be contextual matters that need to be clarified ('Which self-help group?'; 'How did you come to join it?'; 'What were the signs or effects of the grief?' etc.). Or you might want to get more detail on how often the person comes to the group and so on, but the focus of all contextualising questions is to further illuminate the value of the group *to them*. The answers imply their own goals and objectives as well as deeper purposes, intentions and background needs and desires.

Then draw out what was or would be better and why: 'What would you (or we) have preferred?', or 'What would be preferable in future?', or 'What would you (or we) like to see change?', or 'How could it be improved?' Again, ask about 'Why?'—that is, what effects might be expected, and why these changes might be improvements. These questions further clarify the implicit goals and objectives as well as deeper purposes, intentions and background needs.

If service-focused questions prove too narrow, you may need to move more quickly to 'bigger picture' type questions, either about people's own life situations or about the implications of these for better visions for future action.

Audit review questions for end-users

Remember that these kinds of questions test whether the objectives of those who planned or carried out the service or activity were realised. You might say: 'The service or activity was trying to do x, y, z because ... (logic based in context of what is valued). Can you (or we) say whether you/we think these things are happening or have happened?' Don't miss the opportunity at the same time, of asking open inquiry questions about whether these objectives are still of relevance or value to the person: 'Can you say whether that was still a worthwhile thing to try to achieve?', 'What else would be of importance or more important to you?'

For example:

Q. *The self-help group's organiser is trying to provide a group that achieves a number of purposes. Please comment on the following:*

(a) *Have you found the group friendly and approachable? (How much, in what ways? etc.) Is this important to you?*

(b) *Have you found you have learned more about the condition/situation, etc. (that is common to the group)? Is learning more about it of interest to you?*

(c) *Do you have contact with any of the group members outside meetings? Would contact outside the group be of value to you?*

(d) *Do you feel more in control of your situation as a result of being in the group? Is that important to you?*

Finally, examine any similarities and/or differences between the two kinds of material resulting from audit review and open inquiry questions.

2. Moving to questions for providers and other parties

The format for questions for providers and other parties is the same as for users or critical reference groups above—with the exception that they need to clarify whose valuing is sought.

Open inquiry questions for other stakeholders

As soon as you move to questioning providers or other parties, you are asking about their perceptions of value which may be judged by criteria that relate either to themselves or to users or critical reference groups—or to co-workers, funders, managers or administrators. There are several ways of approaching this, each reflecting different purposes and contexts for asking:

- You can frame all questions in terms of the critical reference groups on the assumption that this is the fundamental purpose of their activity (for example, 'Do you think this service is working well for the critical reference group?' 'How do you know?', 'What have *they* said?').
- You can ask for people's own evaluations ('How do *you* think it's going?') and then ask questions to identify who are the reference groups implied in the answers ('Who are the end-users meant to be benefiting?') You may then need to ask explicitly about the value to critical reference groups ('How would you know what end-users thought of it?').
- You can ask what value they think it has for the critical reference group ('How do you think it's going for the end-user group?'), then ask what value they think the critical reference group would place on it ('How do you think the end-user group thinks it's going?') then ask what they think any other parties would think of it.

You would have to think carefully about whether your choice of questions strengthens the assumption that the effort or work is for critical reference groups, or whether it might strengthen the assumption that other parties can judge what's best for critical reference groups—possibly without reference to or respect for critical reference groups' views.

Audit review/questions for other stakeholders

These questions are the same as for users or critical reference groups (as above), but in the context of identifying:

- what are the purposes and intentions ('What are you or were you trying to do for end-user groups?') or what are the goals, objectives, indicators and targets set by you or your service that you are using or have been using? ('What did you set out to do?/What were you meant to be doing?' 'Why were you doing it in this way, in terms of end-users' expressions of needs or interests?')
- were those intentions put into practice (in whose eyes—yours? The critical reference groups'? Others'?)—and was this valuable? (This now reverts to an open inquiry question.) Break it down into separate components and ask about each one—see Diagram 2 ('Did you do *x*?'; Did you do *y*?'; etc.—and 'Was this valuable, important, worthwhile?' etc.).

Tables 1 and 2 are two matrixes that show the two different kinds of questions with two worked examples. Note the value of asking both sets of questions as a sequence.

Table 1: Open inquiry-style evaluation framework

Describe the area, activity or program	*How is it going?*	*Why? How do you know?*	*What do you think is going on?*	*What are the implications for the future?*
ACT/OBSERVE (What was done? or What are we doing?)	**EVALUATE** (Is it working or not working?)	**OBSERVE- ANALYSE** (Why do you say that/What have you noticed? What signs, indicators, factors or evidence?)	**REFLECT- SYNTHESISE** (What else is going on that is creating this situation? What is *really* going on?)	**BUILD NEW THEORY/PLAN** (What changes would you make? What would you do differently?)
I had this new idea for a lesson plan in the classroom …	Some things about it seemed to go well —but perhaps more did not	The children appeared interested, and two said it was great —but I'm not sure they really 'got' it, I had to talk a lot, they didn't realise what was in the pictures	I think the topic was of interest to them, but maybe we explored aspect x when they might have preferred to explore aspect y	Ask them at the beginning of next class to say what they thought of it and why; have small discussion groups and then show the pictures later.

Table 2: Audit review-style evaluation framework

Describe the overall vision or goal/s of the activity or program	Describe the detailed objectives so they show the program logic	What were your indicators and targets for each of these?	Did you achieve these? Show comparative data/measurements Then recommence open inquiry… by asking why (or why not)?	Continue with open inquiry… By asking What could you try instead?
PLAN	**PLAN/ACT**	**PLAN/ OBSERVE**	**OBSERVE/ REFLECT**	**REFLECT/ PLAN**
We set out to … reduce home-lessness	**By doing …** a) reconnecting young people with their families	**We expect to see …** a) at least one family reunion for 50 young people	**What happened …** a) only eight—the conflicts were too great in the other families	**Try next time** a) research building resilient peer groups
	b) by building their self-regard and confidence	b) improvement as per St Luke's self-assessment scales	b) 72% higher—main factor was we'd ensured they had the power to choose	b) repeat same program
	c) by expanding housing options	c) twelve new community units built within two years	c) only three built	c) bring stake-holders together to sort out issues
	d) by restoring Under-18 living allowance	d) an approach made to the local member to introduce a Bill	d) meeting held; approach rejected	d) write policy and run a public-awareness campaign

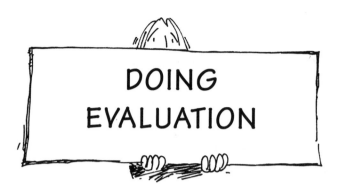

DOING
EVALUATION

chapter 4

DEVELOPING A CULTURE OF EVALUATION

INTRODUCTION

Now you'd like to be doing this more 'everyday evaluation' questioning more regularly, but where to start? Well, it turns out that the best place to start is where you are right now!

In fact, you've already been acquiring all kinds of insights and understandings about your situation or activities or service, right from when you had your very first experience of it. Every day we take *new* actions (new for that day)—whether they are the same as or different from those taken the day before, we are constantly having to make decisions about what is best to do next. As well, most of us daily do some things slightly differently, making regular small adaptations or creative responses to what we do. None of these fruits of our 'everyday small-e type evaluation' should be wasted.

MATTERS OF SCALE

All the time, we're doing or experiencing heaps of things! Some of them seem trivial, small or transient, and some are bigger, deeper and more long-lasting. So the first thing is to have a think about the different levels or scales of activity and their accompanying different degrees of purpose, and decide at what level or scale you are wanting to evaluate.

We have seen how we evaluate small pieces of the world all the time: 'Today is going well'; 'That meeting was a disaster'; 'This newspaper had a lot in it'; 'The computer printout was the wrong one'; 'I liked what that woman just said'.

We evaluate larger pieces of the world less often: 'This year has been a good year'; 'Our group is, unfortunately, starting to drift apart'; 'This shopping centre seems to be changing over recent months and not in a good way'. Similarly, our reasons for evaluating may differ from those for daily problem-solving to those for broader reflect-and-reviews.

Wherever you start, you could reflect for a moment on your starting point's relationship to the whole, and then proceed to evaluate in relation to *its* level of purpose ('We just want to see if this project is on track') consistent with that whole ('The whole—including this project—needs to be focused on resourcing clients' initiatives'). If this balance between level of activity and level of purpose is not achieved, you can find yourself, for example, evaluating this particular piece of a community development process without reference to its ultimate purpose of eliminating unemployment, or evaluating this book only against whether it is close to a certain number of pages long rather than whether it has helped readers improve human services! As mentioned earlier, audit review approaches often confuse levels of scale with different purposes or intentions with the level of activity, such as when a community group's Heart Week Newsletter is evaluated to see whether it brought down the population's blood pressure. However, this is not its immediate purpose—even though the program logic will still need to align it with this big goal in the longer run.

Whether informal and implicit or formal and written down, these issues of scale and the logic connecting them need to be identified so that activities or services are evaluated as successful or not at their appropriate level. At the same time, there can be recourse to higher and lower levels to check for consistency, alignment and effectiveness. For example, at a lower level of 'operationalisation', we might find that people are reporting having happily completed a course of learning about community living for people with disabilities. The material was relevant and the students come away knowing how to live in the community—but did they then move out into their own flats or houses? And if they did, were they able to live happily as ordinary community members? And so on—up to the highest levels of purpose.

Now as noted before, this is *not* to say that a single evaluation needs to accomplish all of this in one study. It may well be a complete fallacy to say that if the students didn't move out into the community, then the course had failed. (This indicates the philosophical problem of thinking that things simply and clearly 'cause' other things in a 'this leads to that' way.) There may have been an unexpected problem with real estate agents' practices. It may

also be wrong to assume that if the students *did* move out, then the course *had* worked. Perhaps they learned how from another source. Evidence needs to be sought for signs that the learning in the course related to the immediate purposes of the course (whether expressed as objectives or not). Diagram 5 illustrates this matter of 'levels' of study and evaluation.

Keeping in mind this matter of levels of purpose (which derive from and express values and interests), it may be helpful to think of these levels as corresponding with levels of practice. For example, we would expect to change our really deep and fundamental purposes only rarely—maybe only a few times in a lifetime. Our big goals may last for a period of many years. Our more immediate objectives may be on a scale of one to three years or so. Our short-term aims may be for a span of months. Our very immediate purposes may be to do things that are this month's, this week's or today's tasks.

CYCLES OF CONTINUOUS MONITORING AND EVALUATION

It is important to practise continual cycles of:
- *observation*—including reaching conclusions about what is going well and what is not, and why
- *reflection* on those observations and clarification of what it is we value and want to sustain or change
- *dialogue* towards reaching agreement about the nature of any changes and improvements in the light of this, and
- *implementation* of the new plans, followed by renewed monitoring and other forms of observation.

These can be practised on *all* our actions, from today's through to this week's, to this month's, this year's, and this decade's, all the way through to this lifetime's. What we reflect on at each of these scales and spans of time is the corresponding level of practice in relation to its place in the hierarchy of immediate and broader purposes, and intended outcomes. This means at one moment keeping an eye out for the big picture—and at the next breaking the big picture down into little bits that are consistent with achieving it.

At present, there is a bewildering range of ways presented for people to carry out evaluation, such as summative, formative, input, process, output or outcome evaluation (see Chapter 5 for these and many others). Many of these kinds of evaluation focus more on a particular *stage* of the process of evaluation, splitting them off as if they were both separate and also, unfortunately, complete. Often this involves talk of doing 'an' evaluation, as if it were always just a step, stage or finite action.

A CALENDAR OF EVALUATION

It may be more useful, in terms of trying to build in evaluation as a more naturalistic element of ordinary activities, to talk of developing a 'culture of evaluation'.

Just as we might talk about an 'ethnic culture', it might be useful to think of evaluation as activities and as a way of thinking that permeates every kind and level of our daily actions and longer-term practices, giving constant rise to particular kinds of questions and observations and, it is hoped, regular spirited exchanges between 'members' of that culture about what is or isn't of value! Current terminology like 'monitoring and evaluation frameworks' is trying to describe how to achieve this as well. The following kinds of opportunities could be seized. If considered 'in toto', these might comprise a comprehensive program of built-in monitoring and evaluation:

- daily informal personal reflection
- weekly reviews
- special-effort evaluations of particular aspects of practice or activities
- monthly collective issue-pooling sessions
- annual what-have-we-achieved and where-are-we-heading-next-year workshops
- comprehensive program 'stocktakes' every three to five years or more.

As noted in the fieldwork section of Chapter 2, for the practical purpose of designing evaluation activities (from a tiny scaled-down version for daily personal reflection, right up to a large scaled-up version for a major program stocktake), we need to ask the following sequence of questions as we traverse the cycle of evaluative inquiry at each of these levels or scales of activity:

Looking back: Retrospective evaluation

Q. What have been our experiences and what was of value?
This involves being able to get a picture of what is being evaluated (who, does what, to whom, when, where and how), and getting a sense of why people think these things have come to be as they are (program logic/theory, history, context, rationale, purposes).

Then it involves being able to get a picture of what everyone thinks of or feels about each of these elements (judgements about the value of who does what, to whom, when, where, why and how and with what effects—intended or unintended, desired or undesired), making sure that the views particularly of the critical reference group are fully heard and

DIAGRAM 5
LEVELS OF EVALUATION RELATED TO PURPOSES

Time Scale	Open inquiry questions	Example	Audit review questions
large-scale long-term	What do we ultimately want to work towards with all of our effort over the lifetime of an organisation or a community of interest?	Action Research Issues Association's purpose: The strengthening of an emancipatory and just culture in which situations identified by critical reference groups (e.g. resulting from discrimination or disability) can be overcome.	Have we worked towards our mission? Have we contributed to strengthening an emancipatory and just culture, etc.? (Remembering that many others are taking different actions to achieve the same ends)
	What do we intend to do to achieve this ultimate state?	To strengthen new paradigm science — viz participatory action (or critical interpretive) research methodology.	
	What will we do to achieve this fundamental purpose?	Develop, support, promote and popularise this methodology.	Have we contributed to our goals?
	What practical actions will we aim to carry out to meet these goals?	Develop models and methods and collect good examples of practice. Publish and circulate accessible written materials about them.	Have we been meeting our aims?
		Set up discussions and networks for the exchange of ideas and experience of them. Assist those with a critical reference group perspective to carry them out — either directly or by providing or referring them to other resources, etc.	
	What can we do to meet these aims?	Establish an association of members who meet. Set up a centre which seeks funding for specific projects in each of these areas (e.g. write a book on self-evaluation, run workshops, have a phone advisory service, establish networks of Friends of Participatory Action Research, Researchers in Community Health, Teachers of Participatory Action Research, contribute sessions to courses and conferences, publish directories, prepare annotated bibliographies, write articles, work with particular groups to assist them to their own participatory action research).	Have we met our objectives? Have we met our targets?
medium-scale medium-term	What do we need to do to realise these objectives?	Call together an initial meeting of interested people ... thereafter the detailed description of all the levels and increasingly tiny actions needed to put into practice all of the above would take up pages and pages rather than the single paragraph available! Nevertheless, every activity objective can be broken down into its constituent bits — ranging right down to the making of phone calls and buying pens to writing the submissions, to paying bills, painting furniture, keeping records and learning new word processing packages, to booking rooms, designing letterhead, getting cost quotes, having meetings, buying stationery, keeping ledgers, paying the rent, writing more funding submissions, doing back-ups, reading reports, correcting drafts, making tea and coffee, recycling paper, fixing the stapler, fixing the printer, talking to groups, making appointments, changing appointments, drawing posters, writing pamphlets, preparing minutes, doing mail outs, talking to visitors, travelling to and fro, writing invoices and receipts, talking over dinner meetings, looking up the dictionary, dialling phone numbers, speaking to audiences, assembling overhead projectors, using the photocopier, fixing the photocopier, writing reports, reading articles, reading books, writing commentaries, getting them typed, arranging chairs for a meeting, questioning people, observing, listening, fixing the photocopier, making diagrams, examining maps, looking at the clocks, looking up the phone book, answering the phone, emptying the rubbish and writing things on the whiteboard, etc.	Are the minutiae of the things we do related to our objectives?
small-scale/ short-term	An alternative 'open inquiry' mode of arriving at purposes is to commence by asking 'Why are we doing this?' And then working up through all the answers, asking 'Why?' then 'Why?' and 'Why?' until the largest scale and longest term purposes are arrived at.		While it is appropriate to check that highly specific actions are still identifiably consistent with the highest level of purposes, it is ineffective and inappropriate to try to test them by seeking direct evidence that fixing the photocopier 'caused' a more emancipatory culture! Instead, by establishing a network of corresponding assumptions, each 'knot' in the net needs only to establish its relationship to the 'knots' closest to it.

recorded, as well as those of all others with an interest in that which is being evaluated. This involves getting people to identify and describe the discrepancies they experience between the 'existing' and what they 'wanted' (or expected).

At the end of this summative phase, it should be possible to tell 'the story so far' about what has been done, what people think about it and why.

Now ask, 'Is anything in need of change? Anything in need of change, improvement or replacement by something better? That is, are there any outstanding discrepancies needing deeper reflection and new thinking to generate more valued actions or practices or other states of being? If there is enough energy for this, set sail to map some new uncharted waters by . . .

Looking forward: Prospective evaluation

Q. What are our deep values or our more valued experiences, and how can we make them part of our future?

This involves getting a new set of ideas, images and descriptions of what would be better and why. That is, it involves ways of working out how to get from the actual 'here' of 'what is' to a desired 'there' of 'what could be' that are practicable, realistic and which people are energetically keen enough to bring into being.

This may seem simple; however, it sometimes needs facilitation and resourcing for a range of conditions to be met for it to be truly 'built in'. This is the subject in much more detail of the third book in this trilogy, *Building in Research and Evaluation: Human Inquiry for Living Systems*. Once new courses of action are created and envisioned, planning and implementation will take them into new experimental formative action (trial and error). Eventually, they may settle as more 'tried and true', although retrospective evaluation may continue and still require some open questions to enable a new cycle of change.

The facilitation of evaluation around these cycles of inductive and deductive action evaluation can take place in each of the following examples from the micro to the macro.

Such a culture of evaluation commences in the 'up close and personal' of daily practice, and is repeated upwards and outwards into the bigger picture of whole projects and larger programs conducted over longer periods of time, and possibly throughout many different sites or locations. In turn, these bigger picture activities return to the groundwork of the micro practices that constitute them.

DAILY INFORMAL PERSONAL REFLECTION

Daily informal personal evaluation is the essential basic building-block of any successful self-evaluating group, service, organisation or institution. Groups, services and organisations don't actually evaluate—the individuals in them do. Yet evaluation—even 'personal' evaluation—is also always social. Every sharp observation we might make, every insight we might generate and every adjustment we might make to our individual practice will always have its roots in the more or less common social soil of language, ideas, skills and practices that are shared (or not) by us with workmates, friends, families and neighbours, past and present.

The better we are at daily informal reflection and the more of us who do it—as part of the groups, teams, communities and services in and with which we live or work—the better we will get at being able to think and feel clearly about the value of what we are doing and wanting to do collectively. In turn, the better this effort is at the micro or local level, the better the depth and quality of information, evidence and understanding on which more macro regional or central levels will be able to build.

We need to make time and space in our busy lives for this sort of reflective and reflexive (self-changing) activity. One form of daily reflective evaluation is to stop whenever we feel uncomfortable or uneasy, or have any other 'problematic' sense—or alternatively, when we feel inexplicably or surprisingly pleased, happy or satisfied. Stop and ask:

'What is happening here? What am I feeling?
What has just happened to make me feel this way?'
'What's making me feel troubled—or elated, and why?'
'Why are things not right (or amazingly right!)?'
'What was the context? What else was going on wider afield that may relate to this?'
'What must I have expected—or wanted? Why didn't what I expected happen?'
'Should it have happened—or was it better that it didn't?'
'Do I want to avoid or change it (the problematic situation)—or do I want to extend it (the desirable) situation next time?'

But how can we see clearly what we are so closely involved in?

Seeing the trees *and* the forests, seeing the remarkable individual instances as well as seeing the unremarkable patterns, trying to be frogs that jump out when the water becomes too hot rather than slowly being boiled alive!—these are the knacks we need to cultivate, and to take time to cultivate to remain fully alive to our situations. Noticing the discrepancies; seeing, hearing, listening, observing. Then thinking and feeling quietly about it. Reflecting. Asking ourselves, 'What is making me feel uneasy here?', or 'Why does this seem such a surprise?' Talking about it among ourselves. Working up hunches. Testing them out. Asking questions. Imagining what we'd prefer. Trying out our ideas. Running them past each other. Modifying them. Watching some more. Observing. Listening. Hearing.

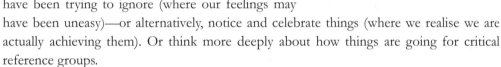

The wise old owl sat on the oak,
The more he sat, the less he spoke.
The less he spoke the more he heard,
We should be like that wise old bird!

Another form of daily reflective evaluation is to routinely try to bring to attention things that we may have been trying to ignore (where our feelings may have been uneasy)—or alternatively, notice and celebrate things (where we realise we are actually achieving them). Or think more deeply about how things are going for critical reference groups.

Think about the times in an ordinary day's activity when it would be good to stop and reflect. Perhaps to write down some of your thoughts and observations, keep a journal or share your thoughts with a friend or colleague. When could you do this? After a meeting? After an interview? After a visit? After a class? Even if only for a minute or two. Stop and ask:

'How did that go? Why?'
'Did it go as I expected or intended? Why?'
'Is there anything I could do differently next time so it would be better?'

Give it a go! Start with the things you can see around you. Some candidates for daily on-the-run reflection might include:

1   filing system that has spread out of the files and is creeping up the walls
2   constantly ringing phone or overflowing email inbox that never lets any real work get done
3   huge pile of daily tasks that never get finished
4   delete key on your phone messages, which is the same as the 'yes' key for your phone banking—thus causing endless confusion.

Observing and noticing

For each of these tiny pots of hot water, first we frogs have to *notice* the discrepancy! We have to actually let it stop us in our tracks, and then plan to do something about it. Articulate it as a question: 'Is this situation not working well?', or 'Is this the best way of doing this?' Second, we have to ask 'what is the value of this?', especially to those whose interests are to be served—how does it assist or impede our critical reference groups getting what they need? What *do* they need?—the information buried two feet in the pile? Do they need to talk on the phone—or do they need us to be doing the 'work' more? What are my deeper priorities and values? And does mixing up the phone pad keys slow you down and make you feel even more stressed than you already are?

Work out which are the best questions:

1   Are there too many files? What are they? What have I been saving and why (describe context, history, etc.)? How do I feel about the situation? What is the value of all these files? Do I need them all? What would be my preferred vision? If I need them, do I need more filing cabinets? If I don't, which should go out and which should stay? (Why? What is my reasoning? Are those reasons still right in terms of my purposes and values?)

2   Am I receiving more phone calls than usual? How many emails can I manage each day? What do they consist of? Why are they coming? How do I feel about them? What is the value of the phone calls and the emails? What can I envisage as a better alternative? What is the comparative value of the work that doesn't get done? If other work is as or more important, can I do it all? Or what could be decreased? How?

3   What does the huge pile of daily tasks consist of? What is the value of each? How do I feel about my workload? What would I prefer? Can I list them in order of priority value? Do they all need to be done? If yes—how? If no—how can I let some of them go?

4   Is this confusion using up my precious energy or slowing me down? Yes! How can I avoid mixing up these two keys on my phone pad?

Do the 'fieldwork'

1   Take time to examine either the whole pile of files or a sample of it. Assess each item. While you're doing that, reflect on how you came to be in this mess! Remember what propelled you to keep adding to the pile (context, history).

2   Record a day's phone calls and emails to see what is coming in and why. Collect information on the time of call, length of call, who called and why. Now examine the emails. Do this in conjunction with evaluation 'project' number (3) below, on your daily task load!

3   Examine the evidence of a day's tasks. How do you know what you have to do in a day? Keep a list for a few days. (Are all the day's tasks listed in one place?) Now have a good look at them. What are they 'telling' you? (What are you thinking in response to them?)

4   Observe closely how it is that you hit the keys by mistake.

Analyse the 'data' of your experiences and draw conclusions

1   You decide some of it is useful but most is worthless. You also conclude you thought some of it might be useful for 'later'—but you didn't know what for, so didn't know where to put it. The existing filing cabinet turned out to be nearly full and you'd never ordered a new one. Or you conclude you could have filed it all, but other things seemed more important at the time.

2   You are surprised to find the 'constant' ringing was only eight calls. But there were 20–30 emails a day. Almost all of them were directly important to your work—indeed they appear to be your most crucial way of operating (information in, information out). Roughly one-third could be deleted immediately, one-third needed responses eventually, and one-third were vital human contact that kept you from feeling like a robotic cyborg. Only four emails and one phone call were super urgent. You realise that the most stress comes from dealing with the emails in the first two hours of the day before you've done your 'real work'. And when in human history did we ever try to respond to 20 or 30 visitors or letters in a few minutes or even a couple of hours?!

3   You ask two other people like you what they make of your day's tasks list. They faint at the thought of accomplishing so much, and then they ask why so many tasks look like they'd take weeks or months rather than a day. You realise why you feel so weighed down.

4   You conclude that if you could somehow mark the 'delete' key—maybe with a sticker—then you might be more alert to the issue.

Make recommendations to yourself for action

1   You decide that only some of the information is critical to your activities. For one week, you will try to throw out things that you now realise are highly unlikely to be useful, and you will set aside two hours on Friday afternoon *for sure* to file it all. You order a new filing cabinet. You also decide to spend one hour every Monday morning *for sure* going through the existing files to throw things out. You write that in your diary too. You do not make appointments at the same times. You will try this for three weeks.

2   You let your group know that you are going to start early and not take phone calls or look at emails until 11.00 a.m. You put that message on the answering machine. You learn not to answer the machine for those first three hours while you concentrate on the most important of your daily tasks.

3   You only put on the daily task list those things you know you can and should get through in one day. You have a longer term list which you revise each month, ticking off what has been achieved.

4   You put half a red spot sticker and half a green sticker on the ambiguous keypad key.

Monitor the action for further discrepancy

1   You find you are getting on top of it—but that it still depends on there not being a crisis or other pressure of work that sends filing down the list of priorities. You resolve

to be more aware of this and, at the end of the year, set aside several days to cull and reorganise the files in the light of changes to the nature of your work.

2   It pretty much works. You are delighted. Problem solved (until a subsequent manager forbids the practice and demands you be constantly on call. This time a 'special-effort' evaluation is needed—see below—to show the impact on work output.

3   You realise you need an even shorter daily list. You pencil in the left-hand margin in order of priority a number against each of today's items. The longer term list goes over several weeks, even to a month. Items from this are assessed and transferred to the daily list. You see the connection with your annual plan and begin assigning a different highlighter colour to each to see the alignments of your monthy and daily task lists.

4   You have never hit the wrong key again!

Now these examples may seem a fraction overdone, but they show the logic of evaluation as it can operate in the micro personal sphere. Much everyday evaluation on the run might be even less formal that this. Some evaluations might take a full 30 seconds from start to finish—or even only a couple of seconds. Try it on more significant matters such as your interaction with group members at meetings, or your choice of reading matter, or your assessment of the uneasy effect a single conversation has just had on you. Try assessing the next new task you are going to carry out—the pamphlet you are about to write, the interview you just conducted, the letter you have just written, the launch for which you are choosing a speaker. From all of this, you will improve your ability to reach your own evidence-based conclusions and develop your own useable store of 'practice wisdom'!

WEEKLY REVIEWS

Using the same process of observing and noticing, and fieldwork-analysis and reflecting, you can extend to something that takes a week. Things that could do with a slightly longer lapse of time might be the kinds of practices that need longer to reveal themselves, or if one were to introduce change it would take about a week to show some effects. Good examples might be someone providing care to an older person with Alzheimer's disease, or a young woman seeking help because she is having trouble looking after her new baby, or a teacher with a rowdy classroom, or a community artist working on a local mural. The same process applies: the noticing and the asking of the evaluative questions, the 'touching base' with criteria for success set by the needs of the relevant critical reference groups, the careful observing and documenting of actions and effects or outcomes, the consideration of context, the drawing of conclusions, and assessment of possible new actions—with slightly longer for each cycle of inquiry.

With these kinds of practice evaluations, diary-type records might be particularly helpful. Some examples follow.

The teacher consultant's diary

See Diagram 6 for an example of a teacher's journal recording her reflections over a period of several weeks. Note that starting with 'plan' would need to be built on prior observation and reflection.

The carer for a person with Alzheimer's disease

Monday *(Initial conclusion and plan action)* The sound of the TV on full blast drives me round the bend. I decide it will have to go, or be strictly limited, or I won't be able to continue. Dear Bill—he doesn't seem to have a clue about what he's watching. He never can tell me who's related to who on those dreadful soaps. I think there really is no value in it.

Tuesday *(Observe-notice)* Last night we were watching *Goodbye Mr Chips* and Bill cried.

Wednesday *(Reflection)* I've been thinking about Bill crying about *Mr Chips* and suddenly wondered whether he is making some sense of all this endless TV he watches after all. Is it possible?

Thursday *(Consult 'the literature'/what is already known)* Decided to ask the Alzheimer self-help group coordinator about what brain function is possible, and she said thinking goes but feeling stays.

Friday *(Inductive fieldwork)* I feel ever so slightly less bothered by the sound of the TV. I've decided to try a little experiment. I asked Bill to point to his favourite videos, and they all had soppy sentimental aspects to them.

Saturday *(Deductive fieldwork)* I brought home *Never Ending Journey* and sure enough, he sat glued to it. I think I'm on to something. He always was such a loving man despite being such an apparent toughie—maybe I haven't lost as much of him as I thought.

Sunday *(Further evaluative research)* I wonder if I could get over feeling embarrassed about talking about emotions with him and get a response from him about his beloved tellie programs? Now I wonder why he seemed to like that documentary last week—the one filmed from the air. Perhaps I should watch part two with him this week and see what interests him most. Maybe it was because it was where he served in the war? Or because it gives him a feeling of freedom? Mustn't make any assumptions this time!

Other weekly efforts

There are other ways to build in evaluation on a weekly basis—for example, if you are involved on a daily basis in your activity, you might consider having a start-of-the-week

DIAGRAM 6
THE TEACHER CONSULTANT'S DIARY

PLAN	ACTION	DATA COLLECTION	REFLECTION	REPLANNING	ACTION
2 months into consultants position. Need to get more organised. Feel like an Octopus. What is my job all about??	• maintain "to do" list • organise an "Action Folder" to best suit ME • attend Unit Review day.	Information from Lee Wooster, at action research ISE 1) copy of Castlemain's Work Journal 2) single sheets of: • Minute sheet • Phone log	Need to spend time with myself to think this process through, what will best suit me/my purpose. How can I visually substantiate how I spend my day	At Traralgon High H.S.C. study camp Brainstorm my 10 areas of work. Think about physical layout of Action folder.	Cut out square pieces of paper. Brainstorm all *the tasks, • activities • functions • events • expectations Organise into logical work areas: 1 Formal meetings 2 Informal meetings 3 Field work 4 Administrative duties 5 Follow up, Questions, backup 6 Attending work related activities 7 Writing 8 Preparation 1 product 2 9 Conducting supporting programs and information nights 10 Professional Development

PLAN	ACTION	DATA COLLECTION	REFLECTION	REPLANNING	ACTION
Define 10 areas of work and write out my definition to each area.	• Write each definition out in full, so people will appreciate what I mean, and clearly clarify my thoughts about my areas of work • ask for MM for feedback		Need to reflect more closely after I have trialled my Work Journal for Term 3 Focus on • areas of work. Are they appropriate? • layout of journal page • layout of "to do" lists	Make up my A4 folder. Ask Vicki about layout (materials Production unit)	• Definition notes to be typed up and placed in my Action Folder • put in Action Folder a page titled "Improvements for my Work Journal" fill this in during term 3 • acknowledge all possible improver points on this page

PLAN	ACTION	DATA COLLECTION	REFLECTION	REPLANNING	ACTION
• To keep an accurate weekly Work Journal during term 3	Fill in Work Journal at end of each day, under the appropriate area of work • Check if I have done everything on my "To Do" list	Each day in term 3 (comprising 11 weeks)	3rd week, need to incorporate time component need an overview of the tasks I need to do in a week. Maybe a weekly coversheet.	Draw an inside line in each column for time component. Draft up a weekly coversheet	Estimating the time spent on tasks in 15 half hour and 1 hour blocks. Don't make it a pain to do so.

PLAN	ACTION	DATA COLLECTION	REFLECTION	REPLANNING	ACTION
To do some professional reading on Group Self Evaluation and Action Research.	Visit G.I.A.E. bookshop and purchase these books.	Professional Reading The Action Research Planner Deakin University 1988.	Formalising the model. I can now see my	Still would like to talk to someone about Action Research.	Talk to Rob Collins about Action Research.

PLAN	ACTION	DATA COLLECTION	REFLECTION	REPLANNING	ACTION
To distribute draft 1 of Work Journal to colleagues in the Educational Program Unit at LVSSC.	Photocopy and leave on their desks.	Their feedback both formally and informally	Need to incorporate travelling time component. Colleagues were proud of my individual effort because it • people outside the	Show other people my Work Journal • husband • Mum • Aunty • people outside the	Maintain my 'improver page' for Work Journal 1. Be really critical about work journal.

PLAN	ACTION	DATA COLLECTION	REFLECTION	REPLANNING	ACTION
To attend Time Management Workshop, August 28th 2011. (All day commitment)	Made a commitment to the group to improve on one main time management problem • present my strategies to group on Sept. 21st 2011	• to keep a 15 minute log in week 9 of term 3. • to keep a phone log.	Reassuring to discover that I did what I had planned to do. Also knowing I was honestly recording my daily tasks happening in Work Journal helped to keep me on task. I feel like I am finding my feet simply by recording what I am doing. I'm task oriented instead of being an 'octopus'		• write up findings from time log and present it to group • to record each phone call as it happens • place phone sheet beside

I found
(even th
points w
ideas in
Term 4.

reflection on where everyone is at and what people are planning to do. Then you might have an end-of-the-week ritual of finishing an hour early and having a drink together to chew over the week's work. Use these times to share observations about incidents or events, successes and disasters, worries and reflections. (Does everyone know about the observe–reflect–plan–act cycle? Might it be helpful to all share that 'mental architecture'?)

Some records or statistics may be cumulative and need attention on a weekly basis. Do they tell you anything on a weekly basis? Are there any other records you could usefully be looking at each week?

Maybe you meet weekly. Most meetings now keep 'action by' records (who'll do what by when, etc.) which provides some nice little audit review opportunities. There should, however, also always be chances to raise new issues (AOB—any other business—is one traditional way). Try seeking this out at the start of the meeting so it doesn't get lost once everyone is preoccupied with the current business.

Try reviewing your calendar planner or diary once a week. How does this week compare with last? What is it telling you about what your priorities have been in practice? What would you have preferred? What would you like to do (or do more of or less of) next week?

A duty lawyer in a legal service decided for one week to phone every client she'd seen over a week, two months earlier, to see how they'd gone. She was so impressed by the value of the feedback that she built the practice into her routine case management.

SPECIAL-EFFORT EVALUATIONS OF PARTICULAR ASPECTS OF PRACTICE OR ACTIVITIES

A 'special-effort' evaluation uses the same process—but scaled up. You might still be able to do it more or less 'on your own', or you may want to involve others. First, you might seek confirmation of your original observation and perhaps unease, and even of your beginning hunches. You might choose another person or several to talk over the matter that you are either troubled by, or feel in the dark about, or wish to 'problematise' (even though it may not appear to be a problem). Identify what it is you want to  evaluate and see whether others share your interest. Say why you wanted to evaluate it. Maybe take it to the whole group or a staff meeting. Alternatively, the group of which you are part may already have 'commissioned' it after a monthly meeting where it was decided to focus on the particular topic.

Start by posing yourselves the following questions: How is it going? Is it working? What do we think of it? Systematically pool all your versions of the issues—what you are experiencing and what you had expected or hoped for or planned.

Assess the evidence. What more do you need to know? What would count as firmer evidence for or against your hunches? What do your critical reference groups think? How do you know? What is the strength of this evidence? How could you collect more? Does it already exist? Should you have been logging it or keeping notes? Can you now do so (say, for a trial period)? Is there a quick way to ask people, such as the ubiquitous 'one-pager' or discussion with them in a group? Or will you need individual input to really do justice to people's differing views, observations and experiences?

Some examples of the kinds of 'pieces' of practice one might want to evaluate at this level are:

- a quick evaluation of a physiotherapist's pre-natal exercise class, or a formative evaluation week by week of a series of workshops held to convey a consumer perspective to professional carers of people with Alzheimer's
- an assessment of the value of a campaign to stop a government funding cut to home and community care services
- consideration of the value of a newsletter to members of a group—and the value of it in hard copy compared with email

Each of these 'special-effort' evaluations is considered below.

Evaluating a group-work class or series of workshops

Group work or workshops might call for slightly more formal processes and slightly more extensive amounts of information. The usual response is to reach for a questionnaire! And that might still be helpful. But let's look first at the wealth of 'data' that already may be available to us. To take the examples above: the class and workshops have actually already been developed in response to all kinds of 'data'—perceptions, observation, feedback—possibly built up over quite a long period of time. As well, you are continuing to get such input every time you hold them. Let's 'unpack' this evidence base. Perhaps write it all down. Keep pushing yourself from the initial question, 'How do I think they are going?' Whatever your response is, ask: 'What makes me think that?' or 'What are the signs of that?'

You might make the following kinds of observations:

'I think they are going well because:

- People keep coming. Lots of people keep coming.
- People not only come on time, many come early for more chat.
- People seem enthusiastic—there's lots of happy conversation; people's faces are animated; there are not many silences.
- People seem to be confident enough to ask questions, they ask relevant questions; most of the discussion is on the topics planned.
- I overheard conversations in which people said how helpful the sessions had been and how comfortable they felt coming there. One said she'd encouraged a friend to attend.
- I met some of the people again at a later date and they gave examples of how they had used what they had learned.'

Now 'interrogate' these signs. Are they all good signs? Could they mean other than what you think they mean? For example, you might not want to be too quick to reject noisy conviviality as disruptive of learning—as it may actually be a necessary condition for it. Nor should you necessarily see silence as a sign of disinterest or lack of comprehension—it may be a sign of intense concentration. On the other hand, you might be wrong! Ask the people in the class what they think. Can *they* think of alternative interpretations? Asking people usually generates fresh ways of seeing—including enabling going more deeply into what they themselves *really* think, especially if they see you are really interested and listening. If you have time, keep records for a while so you can assure yourself (and others) of the strength of your impressions.

You could then be even more systematic and go more deeply into the various aspects and constituent elements of the classes or workshops. What do people seem to think about, or how do they respond to each? Write a list of the program logic elements (who does what, when, where, how and why) of your session in terms of:

- the material conveyed by the convenors
- the topics and exercises
- the rationale behind each element
- the hopes, purposes or intentions of attenders
- the needs and desires of the attenders
- style of presentation
- venue
- size of group
- length of time of sessions
- the times of day.

Here you are starting to generate as full as possible a description of what is done and why. Now ask, for each element, how the critical reference group seems to be responding or what they are getting out of it. Only when you have exhausted this, shift to what *you* were trying to achieve—your intentions, rationale, purposes, 'objectives', standards and hoped-for logical outcomes (as opposed to what people actually seem to get out of it). You will probably find that much of what people did (or didn't) get out of it will relate to your intentions (you'd have done a less effective job of your previous 'research' if that were not the case!).

However, you might—by suspending these expectations in an 'open inquiry' mode—have noticed that people were getting something else out of it that you hadn't planned or realised (or getting more out of some things and valuing other things less than you would have thought). Or that it turns out their situation wasn't exactly as you'd thought or imagined. Or that they'd had previous experiences that shaped them in ways about which you weren't aware. You can then move to adjust or adapt what you are doing (or revise your theory, goals and logic, and perhaps even revisit your deeper purposes of your activities. For example, the physiotherapist may find that, in describing what she thinks the women using her exercise classes are getting out of them (or what she hopes they will get out of them), she finds herself 'forgetting' to mention the exercises! The exercises may have become effective means to all sorts of other related ends, rather than being the most centrally important ends in themselves. Or they may remain a focus or achieving health, but physical health is now seen as part of a much more holistic way of thinking about health.

Moving beyond what you already know (just from searching your memory), you might want to 'touch base' with your end-users in a more systematic and comprehensive way. Here, you will do best to build on the kinds of ways people already use to express their own personal evaluations. You might ask the whole group to discuss the value of the sessions. You will undoubtedly get some good feedback (but it may be the 'yay' factor again). So ask people to suggest improvements, or mention some of your own doubts or hunches, then listen carefully for people's responses. Check also with a sharp eye any who are quiet, or who seem ambivalent or reluctant. Maybe catch them later and say how you were really looking for ways to improve the sessions and you noticed them looking thoughtful so are they sure they can't suggest anything at all? (It often 'loosens up' evaluation if you ask about *how* to change or improve things, rather than just *what* people think of them as they are now. People's valuations are then implicit in their suggestions.) Ask several of the more articulate to judge how they think *others* saw it—again stressing your need for any observations that might help you.

Here, you are trying to supply as much 'permission' to express unmet needs or desires as possible. Do you visit (follow up) any of the attenders? Can you talk to them in their everyday situation—at home or on the job? See whether they can tell you ways in which they have actually *used* what they learned in the classes or workshops. Use any opportunity to research their needs further by observing how they go about whatever it was you were trying to teach them more about. For a pre-birth exercise class, see whether you can attend some of the births (or parts of them, at least). Take notes.

If it is a sensitive, disempowered or otherwise culturally different area (such as foster care, acute psychiatric hospital practice or non-English speaking disability) you may need to employ a member of the relevant group to conduct the discussion and collect people's responses for you. That may need some self-confidence, but the effect will be worth it if people realise how serious you are about hearing from them.

Take time for you or your group to reflect on all these encounters. You might want to be even more rigorous—and, just as an occasional one-off, ask *all* (or a hefty sample) of those attending what they thought. Or follow up later to see whether they can identify ways in which they applied what they learned (remembering that just because some people can't identify their practice with particular messages they have heard, this doesn't necessarily mean that they didn't actually absorb anything). In trying to establish the value of a practice, one of the joys of evaluation can be in trying to establish links between practice and effects. Given the difficulty of this, we should never waste time trying to re-demonstrate effects that others have already painstakingly established in similar situations (while remaining open, as always, to changes or new input).

If you do decide to try to tap everyone's view, you may resort to the apparent ease of a pen-and-paper question sheet. Mostly, these supply useful information, even if they are of the 'Did you enjoy this: yes or no?' or 'Were your expectations met on a scale of 1 to 5?' variety. But people's responses (and situations) are generally far more complex than this. For example, a verbal response might be:

Well, yes, I quite liked the workshop because at morning tea time I met someone who turned out to be a neighbour I didn't know. But I didn't learn anything much that I didn't already know in Session One, although I quite enjoyed it. Session Two I didn't enjoy because it made me feel really uncomfortable about some things I'd been doing without realising their effect; and the afternoon session interested me greatly although it wasn't what I'd come to hear.

Here we can see that hanging an evaluation only on 'enjoyment' or on prior objectives might result in material that turns out to be highly ambivalent. 'Enjoyment' turns out to be a good indicator—but of an unintended factor in one case (the neighbour), and a bad indicator in another (where discomfort was associated with generating a valuable perception of discrepancy). Thus a written tick-the-box response may have rated Session One highly and Session Two lowly, and missed out entirely on knowing about the valuable encounter at the tea break. Nevertheless, we can carefully ask a set of questions that touch on most possibilities, and provided we realise that written responses give only the most abstracted and partial feedback, then even abstract and partial written feedback can be better than none at all.

The other thing to keep in mind is that, just as the use of all other techniques needs to get at both how people see the world in relation to their needs and interests, and also how they see the world in relation to your intentions and objectives (which ultimately are meant to relate back to critical reference groups' needs and interests), so also should question sheets (and their face-to-face versions—interviews) capture *both* open inquiry and audit review elements. Diagram 4 showed a very simple sheet that tried to do this. Diagram 7

DIAGRAM 7
ALZHEIMER'S WORKSHOP FEEDBACK SHEET

Alzheimer Society of Victoria

Title of seminar ....
Workshop held for: .... ; date: ...../...../.....

Evaluating This Workshop

Identifying information (your name or a codeword) ....

In order to help the workshop leaders understand the usefulness of this workshop to participants, we ask you to respond to the following questions.

QUESTION ONE—To be answered before the workshop starts,

1. What are 3 things you would like to get out of today?
   (i)   ....
   (ii)   ....
   (iii)   ....

REMAINING QUESTIONS—To be answered after the workshop,

2. Were there things in the seminar today that helped you understand Alzheimers disease? (Tick one answer)

   Yes: – a lot   ❏
   Yes: – a little   ❏
   No: – not much   ❏

   Can you say how?
   ....
   ....
   ....

   Can you give one or two examples that relate to your own personal experience? (e.g. 'Now I understand why Mrs. so and so did ......')
   ....
   ....
   ....

3. Has the seminar given your any new ideas on how you could handle some things differently?

   Yes: ❏
   Not sure   ❏
   No: – not really   ❏

   If yes can you give an example of how?
   ....
   ....
   ....

4. What stood out as the most interesting thing or things that were said today? (If you can remember something in particular that was said, please write that.)
   ....
   ....
   ....

5. Any particular comments to help us improve the seminars?
   ....
   ....
   ....

Thank you.

Please hand this in at the front registration desk

shows a slightly more detailed version that sets out to check more purposively for what the session-providers were trying to convey.

None of this, however, substitutes for observation and reflexive conversation—what we might call in-depth naturalistic or interpretive 'fieldwork'. An example would be the physiotherapist who checked regularly whether her careful choice of music was contributing to a comfortable and relaxed and ethnically relevant environment (rather than to a leotards-and-fashionable-aerobics-type exercise class). She learned to evaluate whether the music led to people 'sinking into the mat', or 'feeling at home' or 'floating in the air', and so on. These are the kinds of grounded nuances that questionnaires will never be able to explore in such sophisticated depth.

Following are some of the ways in which we might improve how we ask written-down questions so as to get more useful, extensive, rich or meaningful responses:

- Have in mind what people are likely to be thinking about when they pick up your question sheet. Maybe they have just had a session of ideas and information, and are now keen to get off home before peak hour. Don't automatically ask about age, occupation, ethnicity or gender. (If you really need to know how many Greek-born men, aged between 39 and 60 who are factory workers, do or don't think such and such, and your sample size is big enough, then leave those 'characteristics' questions until last.)

- *Do* start with a question that 'leads' the person in to evaluative thinking. This might be the kind of question that would parallel a naturalistic question between two friends emerging from the session who might ask each other, 'Well, what did you think of that?' You might ask, 'Can you say just in a few words what you thought of today's session?' or 'Can you rate today's session on a scale of 1 [least] to 10 [most] in terms of how much you got out of it?' These may not be tremendously valuable questions in themselves.[*] But they do help put the respondent into an evaluative frame of mind.

- Rather than ask 'Did you enjoy or find suitable the venue (or the time or music or discussions)?' ask 'What were some of the best things about the venue (time/music/ discussion)?' and 'What were some of the drawbacks for you about the venue (time/ music/discussion)?' Don't ask the question in the form 'What were the good or bad things about the venue (time/music/discussion)?' unless you are sure there *were* some.

- As mentioned, encourage all possible 'nay-saying'—for example, by saying 'We are keen to improve' or 'We are going to make changes. Tell us how', or include a finish-the-sentence item, 'If only it had been more . . .' or 'Next time it would be good to . . .'

- Specify elements of the session to jog people's memories. Don't just ask 'Was the workshop worthwhile?', ask 'Can you comment on when *a* spoke?, or on the discussion

---

[*]   Although the rating may have some reliability given that most people have gone through an education system that taught us the meanings of 'marks out of ten'! (In addition, this slightly wider scale gives people more room to discriminate than a smaller one of three or five items.) A binary yes/no scale generally means an even more dramatic loss of depth of meaning when asking about extents or matters with contexts that are not self-evident. Most people hate being confined to a simple yes/no question ('Do you enjoy life? Yes or no') unless it is of an easily answerable kind (such as 'Did you attend *x*? Yes or no').

group about aspect *b*?, or on the exercise regarding *c*?'. It's very irritating to be asked for a single global rating of a session or a day that included a great speaker but a badly facilitated group discussion (or vice versa).

- Always have a space for people to volunteer things you haven't asked about ('Any other comments?' or just 'Comments'). Or if that doesn't seem encouraging enough, say 'Is there anything else you can think to tell us?' or 'Any other comment that comes to mind?' This is an important 'open inquiry' element.

- If you can keep it down to one page (or two sides at most), you will be rewarded by more of them being filled in and returned. As a rule of thumb, try to ask only about five to eight questions. And remember that you will have only scratched the surface of everything you *could* have asked in relation to everything you were *trying* to achieve—and that that is inevitable!

Michael Patton (1990) has some quite good and detailed things to say about asking questions (see the Further Useful Reading section at the end of this book), although I think his rule about not asking people 'why' only applies under certain circumstances. I've found that people can often give quite illuminating explanations for why they think things, and that this helps spell out the underlying assumptions of program logic and theory. Alternatively, you can explore this with questions like 'Can you say a bit more about that?' or 'What do you think was going on there?' The sequel to this book, *Building in Research and Evaluation: Human Inquiry for Living Systems*, has a whole chapter (Chapter 3) about a sequence of questions that effectively get you full cycle from 'how things are' to 'how things could be better' and thence into practice.

Evaluating a campaign

To assess the campaign, the coordinator or coordinating group might also start by asking themselves, 'How's it been going?'. Maybe there's an answer in the negative—'Frustrating' or 'Problematic'—or in the positive—'Good' or 'Terrific'. Now is the chance to document what is being done and to explore the reasons, so you might say, 'Well, what have we been doing?', and get down on paper everything that has been done so far (i.e. descriptions of each element of practice) with evaluative comments and reasons beside them. These elements might include:

- working with the local council, including partnering with adjoining local councils to get a joint position on the issue
- getting the community health centre board to do the same with other community health centre boards
- raising awareness among staff
- getting local press coverage.

If documented fully enough, each strand of action can then be assessed. By breaking it down into parts, it may be found that in some cases there was a very satisfactory payoff for effort, but one particular element of the work where there was nothing like the realisation of expectations. This is where the full contextual explanation (gained by asking why, then why, then why again, until the situation is better revealed) can be sought out in order to assess the next possible range of actions. That is, the bigger picture of context and history can illuminate the value of the expectations (or evaluation criteria), and suggests whether a new strategy should be tried. Ideas for this can be sought by touching base with the critical reference group, particularly if informed by an understanding of the factors blocking success. Creativity and imagination are needed, as always, at this point of the evaluation cycle.

Evaluating a newsletter

To assess the newsletter, the group producing it may like to start with a group self-evaluation—doing a 'Round Robin' of everyone and pooling all their own ideas and reasons (for pride or suspicion!) Asking 'What do we think of it, and why?' may yield some good hunches.

A readership survey by use of a questionnaire conveniently included in the next issue may yield some further insights—but first seek out more naturalistic signs that might prove fruitful indicators—for example:

- Have people been known to mention to each other things raised in the newsletter?
- Are there ways of knowing whether people hand their copies on to be read by others?
- Are there signs that readers have, for example, come together as a group to discuss any of the articles in it?
- Have people reported being usefully informed by it?
- Have any of the information sources referred to in the newsletter experienced greater demand? Have those making the demand mentioned the newsletter as their source of information?

Some suggestions of methods follow:

- Can members of the group each undertake to phone or meet with half a dozen people to get some feedback on the last issue? See whether people can recall anything of it. Then go through it page by page asking 'Did you see that?', 'Did you read that?', 'What did you think of this?', 'What did you think of that cartoon?', 'Was that interesting or not?'
- Would it help to collect examples of other newsletters and compare and contrast them?
- Try a simple 'Would you like to keep receiving this newsletter? Please cut off and return slip, in the next issue (although you will still have to interpret the response rate!).
- Pick a small random or purposive cross-sectional (cluster) sample of readers and get them to come in for a group discussion. (Offer light refreshment!) Brainstorm reactions and ideas. Alternatively, pick a selected sample of people who are known always to have opinions and/or bright ideas and/or reliable perceptions of what other people think.

Try to cross-check for opinions and actual usage. For example, people might object to a paternalistic tone but nevertheless find that some of the practical information contained in the newsletter was very useful. You may need just to 'be around' people to learn these kinds of things.

Start with a broad opening-up question like 'Do you like getting the newsletter? Can you say why?' Or, if it requires a choice to get it (for example, to pay a subscription), you could ask 'Why do you keep subscribing?' and 'If you ever stopped subscribing, why might that be?'

Questions like 'Do you read it?' may be less useful. Instead, try to pin down actual contextualised practice. Ask 'Which bits do you specially read or enjoy?', 'When or where do you read it' or 'How much time would you typically spend reading it?', or 'Do you:

- skim read it?'
- skim and read one or two pieces?'
- read most of it?'
- read all of it?'
- other . . .?'

Ask about specific use made of it. For example, 'Can you recall making use of anything from the last issue/last few issues?', 'Have you ever followed its advice/or . . . [whatever's relevant] . . .?' If the newsletter follows a regular format or there have been major themes or articles, list the format or some of the themes or articles and ask people to say whether they read it/them; get them to rate them out of ten, or rank the sections in the format from favourite to least favourite. Ask people 'Why' if that seems a useful thing to do. Sometimes people may reveal needs you had no idea they had (even if it's that the newsletter is exactly the right size for the bottom of the cocky's cage!).

List possible areas for change (illustrations, cartoons, more or less of whatever) and get people to express opinions about them. Later, when these ideas have been pooled, people could rate or rank any options that seem worth considering.

If you're having trouble settling on a few questions (don't ask more than a page or two sides' worth), then go out and talk more to people to try out questions and get a better idea of what is 'askable and answerable'.

Finally, in an open inquiry mode that reconsiders the higher purposes of the newsletter, you might conduct a broader discussion about preferred general style or 'feel'. You may also want to consider other ways (alternative to newsletters) for keeping in touch with members, and assess them in comparison to (or as well as) the newsletter.

MONTHLY COLLECTIVE ISSUE-POOLING SESSIONS
Tabling discrepancies

Sometimes a monthly time devoted to simply asking 'How are we going?' in various areas can mean the tabling and logging of evaluative comments about issues that are preoccupying or puzzling people can be a terrific way of strengthening an overall evaluation program. For example:

- New issues can be raised when people haven't yet reached committed conclusions. Often, the longer that issues can be held and reflected on at this stage the better.

- Issues about which there is clear consensus can be identified for action, and future reporting back (What action? By whom? By when?).

- Issues about which there is divided opinion can be placed (and possibly kept) on the table for people to think about and return to the following month with suggestions. Too-early conclusions or votes should generally be resisted, as they often result in storing up dissatisfaction. Maximum time for reflection and imaginative solution-generation should be given.

- Issues that reappear over and over again without resolution may be referred to a special group evaluation exercise that could then report back to a monthly session.

- Issues that can be left for an annual inquiry or review could be placed on notice for handling at that time.

The discussion about group self-evaluation in Chapter 5 is relevant here. Think about the people-resources in your group with a view to maximising the value of this kind of monthly effort. Think about who are the most interested 'organic' or 'indigenous' researchers in your group:

- *Who's good at observing?*
  'The other day I was sitting watching . . . and I could see that . . .'. Or someone else says 'Have you noticed how when . . ., then what happens is . . .?' Or someone else says 'I've been looking at the stats and I think there might be a pattern emerging . . .'

- *Who's good at developing hunches?*
  'Well I reckon it's because . . .', 'I've been thinking there might be a link between . . . and . . .', 'I've noticed that every time we . . . then . . .'

- *Who's good at asking critical questions?*
  'Why are we doing it like this?', 'What about considering . . .?', 'Has anyone asked our users?'

- *Who's creative and imaginative on reflection?*
  'Perhaps we could try . . .', 'I've had an idea!', 'What about . . .', 'This is a bit unorthodox, but what if we tried . . .'

- *Who's sceptical?*
  'What makes you think that?' 'But it could be because . . .', 'Do we really know that for sure?', 'What if . . .', 'I'm not so sure. It might more be a matter of . . .'

- *Who's good at judging which are good ideas?*
  'I think that idea would work because . . .', 'We could try idea x first, and idea y if x works', 'I can't see that idea working at this stage because . . .'

Everyone can play all these questioning roles in an evaluation inquiry process, but some people are good at identifying these inquiry preferences—either in themselves or in other people. It's a bit of an art. You could try 'electing' people to these roles by a modified 'Delphi' technique if necessary. Or watch how people accomplish these skills when they need to. Later the jobs can be rotated and everyone can get the hang of them for their own evaluations. But the most important thing is for all these different evaluative research capabilities to 'be at the table'—and *stay* at the table *together*—so all can traverse the inquiry cycle 'full circle' and none risks being neglected or superseded.

Reporting on reflexive evaluations

Such monthly sessions could also be used by people to report on personal or small-group self-evaluations, with the fruits of this labour being shared. The emphasis of these should be on telling the story of what had been observed, what had been tried instead, what had been learned and what further improvements had been planned or made as a result. Narrative reports on development like this are illuminating and set a valuable tone for others to try the same kind of 'whole-cycle' exercise:

> Firstly we noticed that ... Then we decided a fruitful direction to pursue would be ... When we tried it we found that ... And that showed us we needed to do more of ... and less of ... So we concluded that doing x in tandem with y followed by z worked best, and we thought that was because of ... Now we're about to give this all another go over at [another location].

You could do this with a different person, project or program component each month.

This kind of evaluation work is very close to what some might call quality improvement or organisational learning, and the essential elements of these two concepts are indeed shared.

'Business as usual' (and all the congealed interests and power relation and familiar ways that that entails!) will threaten to swamp these sessions—exactly like everyday busy-ness threatens individual self-reflection efforts. The same discipline and determination will be required to preserve even the smallest monthly reflective times. Sometimes this needs clear leadership to ensure it continues until it becomes built in to the culture of 'how we do things round here'. If interest flags and few people are presenting, try asking what people are Really Interested in evaluating.

What *are* people really interested in *right now*? Work on that. Try bi-monthly or quarterly if that works better, but do not stop unless you want your service or activity to ossify.

ANNUAL WHAT-HAVE-WE-ACHIEVED-TO-DATE AND WHERE-ARE-WE-HEADING-NEXT-YEAR EFFORTS

Discussion meetings

Annual discussion meetings could be held at the group's ordinary first or last general meeting of the year, or at a special 'day away' or residential workshop of up to two or three days' duration. While they are often called planning days, in fact they cannot do their work without first reviewing past practice, and auditing it against previous goals and intentions and logically expected outcomes, and also scanning the changed context or environment in which things are now being reconsidered. It can help to 'lead in' by commencing with an 'open inquiry'-style session. During this session, people might start by discussing their general reflections, observations and evaluation of the previous year's work, and then be in a good place to start envisioning the future year or beyond.

Inquiry review (retrospective)

First, each person might report very briefly on what they've been doing during the past year and what its value was. This needs to avoid being too much of a familiar descriptive litany, as this may risk not seeing valuable new leads for change and improvement. For example, try telling the story as a narrative of change from the *previous* year, and end with where you think it might need to go next. People could do some reflective preparation for this prior to coming. The writing of an annual report can be a good way of doing this. These retrospective narratives can supply a 'collective memory' as a point of shared reference. Ideas, suggestions and questions could then be posed to the other members of the wider group.

Envisioning the future (prospective)

People could then set aside their current activities or formal objectives and, by orientating themselves to the situation of the critical reference group (members of which should be present as the primary partners in this work) and in relation to their wider contexts, volunteer their visions both for the future of the *general* enterprise and for the *specific* contributions they could make. This could also be placed in the context of a directional narrative from a point in the past towards a point in the future. Here people are rearticulating their deepest and most important values, standards or templates—some of which they may not have put into words before. Brainstorm these ideas. Get them all listed before examining them with a view to practicability for trying out.

As a contribution to this, it can be helpful to step back from the up-close work to ask 'What is going on in the bigger social, geographic, economic and political contexts in which we or/and the critical groups are living?' 'What trends or changes are we seeing that are impacting (or could effect) what we and they are doing or hoping to do?' This is sometimes called an environmental scan.

Identifying what needs to be done

People could then talk about the steps necessary to take forward any of the visions or ideas for the future. As part of this, people might like to brainstorm or volunteer ideas about what they think is either blocking or would enable their achieving the situations they want for the future. This kind of SWOT analysis (Strengths, Weaknesses, Opportunities, Threats) could be assisted by the techniques of group self-evaluation and force-field analysis described in Chapter 5 or the sequence of questions in Chapter 3 of the third volume in this trilogy, *Building in Research and Evaluation: Human Inquiry for Living Systems*.

Deciding on achievable steps

The final consensus may be a mixture of:

* some more of the same
* some changed practices (some completed, some improved, some abandoned)
* some entirely new practices.

It will stem from a revised and rearticulated general vision, informed by ideas that will have developed during the course of the meeting. The fine details can then be settled by revising the previous formulation of the group's purposes and intentions, theory and logic, objectives and targets—such as a funding agreement. Each clause of the agreement can be revised in the light of the inquiry review—adding, subtracting and revising. The group then ends with a *new* articulation of its formal plan for the coming year.

Other annual efforts

There are a number of other kinds of evaluation that can be carried out on an annual cycle, many of which we may not have thought of as such. For example, they can include your annual office clean-up:

- cleaning out your desk and unfinished in-tray before or over the holiday break
- revising your own or the organisation's filing system
- rearranging the furniture
- going through your last year's diary and putting the dates in next year's diary
- updating your teledex or address book.

A *Self-evaluation Kit* (Wilson, 1989) was used by local citizens' advice bureaux—particularly as an annual audit on their progress in implementing their objectives. The cancer support groups' example (see Diagram 8) has been built in to the groups' annual calendar of meetings as a way of providing more 'bottom-up' inquiry information on participants' hopes and purposes, and also feedback on ways to improve and develop the groups.

COMPREHENSIVE PROGRAM STOCKTAKES EVERY THREE TO FIVE YEARS

There is something of an expanding scale from alignment between personal reflection on individual components of activities, to group evaluation of clusters of activities that make up services or campaigns, to participating in organisational evaluation of whole programs comprised of many services. Just as it would be disastrous to leave small, daily problems to build up for years (we've all seen examples of that!), it is equally disastrous to attempt total program reviews regularly, or even annually.

Indeed, if regular daily, weekly, monthly and small-scale special-purpose evaluation is practised, many of the big, total, disruptive program reviews of the past might become unnecessary. Total program reviews may continue to be useful in retrieving programs out of large, deep, routine ruts or, alternatively, to defend programs against sudden, irrational or uninformed external threat (requiring extensive documentation and justification for audiences that are completely isolated from the local practice).

But a current flaw of many major program reviews is that they attempt to carry out *all* elements of evaluation, from the local and micro right up to the central. Program reviews should evaluate only at the scale of what belongs to the whole program—not every tiny element of every service that comprises the program. Program evaluations need to rely on and build on a fabric of more detailed evaluation activity 'at the coalface' that has been going on at smaller scales over the previous three to five years. These take their place in the program evaluation's standing back at a longer distance—something that is not possible or desirable on a very regular basis or without being able to consult longitudinal or time series-type records.

The following is an example of a committee self-evaluation of a funding program, where the committee had experienced three years of operation and funded many projects, giving them a perspective that would otherwise have been difficult to achieve earlier. As the program was of modest size, it was possible to evaluate specific elements, although this material largely confirmed what was already known (from more regular feedback sources) about these. It was the program redesign that was the real breakthrough and, while this had already emerged from daily practice, the main value of the program review was to bring together these insights for sharing, and formalise the process of reaching consensus about the desirability of taking this direction.

An example: A three-year evaluation of a grants program

The Australian Consumers' Health Forum wanted to know whether its research grants program was working. It approached the matter by using several sources of observation and reflection to illuminate the various levels of intention: from the most general and philosophical (how to strengthen the voice of health consumers *per se*), to middle-level purposes (how to develop a health consumer research sector), to more specified levels (how to empower consumer, community and self-help groups to carry out their own value-driven efforts to 'find out'), through to the highly specific (how to assist groups to do their own participatory action research and evaluation).

It assembled a critical reference group-centred view of the elements of the program using a logic or organising framework based around consumers' sequential chronological experience of the program—that is, their first hearing of it, barriers they faced in preparing and submitting their application, experience of the Forum's staff, use of the application form/kit, experience of the assessment procedure, notification of outcomes, any changes made to the groups' budgets, the presentation of cheques ceremony, ethics procedures, administrative matters, alternative sources of funding approached, outcomes of project and unexpected things learned by and from the projects. Within this, both *open-inquiry* questions ('What were your general impressions, specific impressions related to the elements of the program, plus ideas for change?'), and also *audit-review* questions were asked (which checked against the Forum's objectives—for example, 'Was there active consumer control over the project, an emphasis on prevention rather than treatment, action research to inform and achieve change rather than only academic/theoretical knowledge, were there multiplier effects, the addressing of oppression or disadvantage, the giving of voice to consumers, good geographic spread, and the addressing of issues of gender?').

In this way, it not only examined highly specific elements but also enabled a major shift in the program to be recommended (a shift from all the money going to projects proposed from the field to dividing the funds into three buckets—one to respond to proposals from the field, one for strategic projects identified centrally from the Forum's experience of the myriad efforts needed to advance the whole field, and one for a resources network of local consultants and publications and tools to assist groups to prepare better research proposals and carry out more effective research and evaluation themselves).

DIAGRAM 8
CANCER SELF-HELP GROUPS' ANNUAL REVIEW QUESTIONS

ANNUAL REVIEW OF OUR GROUP

Anti-Cancer Council of Victoria
Recognised
Cancer Support Group/Service

It's the start of the year, and we thought it would be good to reflect on what we've got out of being part of our mutual support group, and what worked over the past year, and what hasn't.

Procedure:
We start by each filling in the questions ourselves. Then we will pin them all to the wall. You do not need to put your name on it. We will then read each other's contributions, and then come back into the group to discuss them further and decide on how to do things this year.

This gives us all a chance both to have our say and also to see everyone else's ideas—thus pooling our collective wisdom!

1. Why do we come to the group? What do we hope to get out of it?
   ....
   ....

2. What were the first impressions when we came to our very first meeting?
   ....
   ....

3. What have been the best things about the group?
   ....
   ....

4. What have we found less useful?
   ....
   ....

5. Has being part of the group had an effect on us? (e.g. on what we do, or feel, or think?) *Give actual examples.*
   ....
   ....
   ....

6. If we didn't come to the group, what would be the effects on us?

   The good things that we would miss   The drawbacks of coming that we would not miss
   (the disadvantages of not coming).   (the advantages of not coming).
   ....
   ....

7. Are there ways we can think that the Anti Cancer Council could help us? (e.g. support, ideas about something, courses, leaflets, contact person, feedback about other groups and their activities, etc.)
   ....
   ....

8. What would we like the group to do this year? (e.g. speakers and talks, activities, outings, visiting people with cancer, public speaking, support work). *Give new ideas as well as say what existing things should be continued.*
   ....
   ....

9. Any other comments you'd like to add?
   ....
   ....

Take your time. When finished, pin your sheets up on the wall and then read each
other person's contribution. If the other sheets make you think of new things, bring
these ideas into the group discussion which will follow.

The evaluation drew on the following multiple sources of observation and reflection using a range of methods:

- questionnaires followed by feedback and group discussions, plus participant observation of past and current members of the Grants Committee itself
- individual discussions, questionnaires followed by group discussions, plus participant observation with past and current members of the Grants Committee secretariat
- questionnaires and individual and group discussions with grant recipients from all three years
- questionnaires and individual and group discussions with unsuccessful applicants whose proposals had been worthy of funding
- a previous research study of the needs of the full field of potential applicants (successful and unsuccessful) for research resources, barriers faced in applying, etc., using on-site visits, observation, small group and individual discussions and content analysis of the groups' research studies
- use of file material on decisions made each year, and other written materials generated by the program—including newspaper advertisements, pro formas, various letters sent to applicants and grant recipients at various stages of the process, correspondence with the minister, grants processing procedures, etc.
- a content analysis of three years of sequential files on projects awarded funds, initially to examine progress, but—by using an open inquiry mode—also to become aware of themes and issues emerging from groups' experiences. (Files included initial application, subsequent correspondence, progress and final reports, groups' own evaluation reports, and any output—reports, pamphlets, publications, posters, videos, etc.)
- participant observation attendance at a cheque presentation ceremony, and attendance at a grant recipient's performance of a funded health education play (performed by young people who had been paid out of the grant as peer action researchers).

This national evaluation work was substantial enough to have been a specially funded project in its own right; however, instead of farming out to an external evaluator, the Grants Committee chairperson—herself a consumer representative—conducted the evaluation as a participatory group self-evaluation, including adding her own reflections on the three years' experience. These excellent conditions generated a report that was both well-received by and useful to the rest of the Consumers Health Forum as well as key external audiences (who had either an interest in the program or a sceptical view of it). Nevertheless, this relatively elaborate evaluation probably did not yield a substantially different outcome to that which might have been achieved from a less detailed and more informal exercise. It may, however, have provided more confidence and reduced some uncertainty about reaching these same conclusions—a common function of more costly external evaluation.

CONCLUDING REMARKS

Experienced evaluators heading towards the end of long careers in evaluation often report that they see less and less need for large formal evaluation exercises and more and more need for smaller-scale, more built-in, naturalistic and responsive end-user focused approaches. Some end up calling their work professional development or continuous quality improvement, finding it to be integral to organisational development and even indistinguishable from 'whole-systems' human development *per se*. What remains of most value is the use of 'full-cycle' evaluation (see the wall chart on the Allen & Unwin website) or evaluative inquiry *per se*, which:

* explicitly notices and names the 'discrepancies'—both those that are life depleting *and* those that are life enhancing, assisting us to more consciously formulate questions to examine the former, or seek more of the latter
* ensures the inquiry effort is driven by the values and interests of those whose life or lives are to be enhanced, by benefiting from the evaluation
* expands to include all others who are relevant to partnering to achieve this
* rigorously, thoroughly and comprehensively gathers new observations, evaluative perceptions and context-based understandings
* self-sceptically develops new theory and its associated logic on the basis of this evidence
* re-values actions and formulates new and practical actions consistent with this
* implements and monitors these actions as part of a continuing and ongoing cyclical process of learning from our experience.

It is useful at times to think of evaluation as 'research' and even 'science', because this magnifies the self-conscious and purposive aspects of our efforts (regarding relative truth-finding, careful experimentation in the relevant life-worlds, the importance of evidence and meaningfully theorising that evidence, etc.).

Everyday research and evaluation *not* raised to this level of self-consciousness, but which proceeds through ordinary capabilities of sensing, feeling, intuiting and thinking *may* be equally effective (just as it has for thousands of millennia!). For example, people or groups we recognise as 'naturally' effective or competent—the sustainably living Indigenous community, the gifted teacher, the good nurse, the outstanding community worker, the successful self-help group, the 'professional' community group (when the word 'professional' is not being used in its pejorative sense!), or influential campaign workers—all operate as intuitive scientists and 'communities of science' of their own practices. Those who recognise their value—including peers, service-users or managers—are also fine intuitive evaluators!

However, those of us who can perceive all the as-yet imperfect states of affairs, who see continuing injustice and unnecessary hurt or disadvantage, who see the damage that has been done to natural human inquiry processes by our socio-political culture, and who have not yet identified the most effective ways of taking action against all this life-depleting activity, may be impatient to enhance our chances of 'getting it right' for life.

Resorting to more conscious, theorised and articulated evaluative practice can offer to shortcut some of our otherwise slower processes of individual and social learning. There are no miracles—just fewer pots of water for us to boil to death in! Or pots in which pretty much no one boils to death any more, because we have learned from evaluative feedback how constantly to adjust the heat for it to be life-giving.

THE EVALUATION INDUSTRY'S TOOLBOX

chapter 5

MODELS AND TECHNIQUES

INTRODUCTION

Everyday evaluators will probably rarely need to resort to the professionals' toolbox—built up now over more than 40 years—the contents of which can range from useful to overly sophisticated attempts to capture and codify all nuances of logic and definition possible, right through to rather confusing jargon and even some mystifying 'snake oil'.

Everyday evaluators are as subject to the waves of passing fashions in evaluation as professional evaluators themselves (who think them up!) and evaluation clients and funders. Often 'old fashioned' methods have a lot of wisdom and might later be rediscovered (like CIPP), or new methods might have been overlooked at the time but return later in a new guise that proves popular (like action research or 'positive evaluation', which have been taken up as 'appreciative inquiry'), or are still ahead of their time (like 'ecological evaluation'), or are the next big thing (like 'systemic evaluation').

So this section of the book is a bit of a Cook's tour through a wide range of terminology and evaluation approaches about which you might have reason to wonder. It carries a message that there is no obvious 'one best methodology', although it may help you to 'place' them better in their context. To that end, there is also a list of questions you might usefully ask about the different approaches.

This chapter presents:

- some key *models* of evaluation processes (general design or pattern, or framework of logic and content)
- some associated *methods or techniques* (specific ways of gathering evaluative data, hearing people's experiences or assisting them to engage with differing perspectives for understanding their social contexts)
- some major *methodologies or 'paradigms'* of evaluation (deeper-orienting philosophies of knowledge or 'epistemologies').

Often the different models, methods or paradigms are highlighting one aspect or another of the full evaluation research cycle (see the wall chart on the Allen & Unwin website—for example, the current preoccupation with 'program logic', the 'why' of practice, after so many years focusing on the 'what' of action; an emerging interest in the 'how' of interconnectedness in complex whole systems; or the value-drivers of asking 'for who/for what'.

Terms described in the companion volumes, *Do It Yourself Social Research* or *Building in Research and Evaluation: Human Inquiry for Living Systems*, are not repeated here (with only a couple of exceptions).

The nearly 100 models, techniques and methodologies in this chapter are in alphabetical order for easy reference. Some theorists have attempted to classify these to give some idea of their logical connections or genealogies (lineage or ancestry). At the end of this introductory section to the chapter, several book references are listed for the enthusiast who wishes to delve more deeply into this.

In the hope of giving readers a way to navigate this chapter, frequent references are made to the framework and terminology already used in this *Everyday Evaluation on the Run* book. Cross-references to related models, methods or methodologies *within* this toolbox chapter are **shown in bold type**.

In conclusion, this chapter offers a glimpse of what the academic and intellectual heavies in the field are up to, as well as a small insight into the debates that have raged in the professional evaluation community over four or five decades. It also offers deeper insight into the whole business of evaluation—a little like learning a language by seeing how it is used by many different speakers over time.

However, as this book is for the small-scale everyday evaluator with a need for immediate, accessible, everyday evaluation processes, this section may be a little overwhelming. If this happens at any point, then *immediately stop reading* and return to contemplating either the wall chart on the Allen & Unwin website, or the view out your window!

EVALUATING THE EVALUATION APPROACHES

Attempts have been made to try to classify this bewildering array of models, approaches and techniques into similar or related groupings. However, there is often a lot of overlap, and some models only focus on one particular dimension of evaluation. One would really need a 3D map on which to try to plot a fuller picture (and even then, some of the techniques would have to move back and forth between one category and another). References in which these different classifications are discussed are listed below.

It might be more helpful to pose questions of each approach as a way of identifying where it stands in relation to *your* situation and purposes.

Questions regarding whose values drive the evaluation method

Q. Who is this evaluation method oriented towards assisting?

A. Anyone? Managers? Clients? Stakeholders? Program staff? Critical reference groups? All of these? Only some? Who is left out?

Q. What (and whose) are the purposes of this evaluation method?

Q. Does it get you 'full cycle' from describing the value of how things are now, to identifying how they could be of greater value? Or does it only tell you the value of things as they are?

Q. Why has this evaluation method been decided upon rather than any other?

Q. Has it been developed or chosen by people in my situation—or the people I want to assist?

Q. What can I see in it that might be of use to me?

Questions about the conduct of this evaluation method

Q. Who will be able to carry it out?

Q. How will the evaluation method be used?

Q. Who will be familiar with it—or need to know more?

Q. What are likely to be the outcomes of using this method?

REFERENCES DESCRIBING A RANGE OF DIFFERENT EVALUATION APPROACHES

Armstrong, A. (1986) *Evaluation Models and Strategies*, Evaluation Training & Services Pty Ltd, Melbourne.

House, E.R. (1983) 'Assumptions Underlying Evaluation Models', in George Madaus, Michael Scriven and Daniel L. Stufflebeam (eds), *Evaluation Models: Viewpoints on Educational and Human Services Evaluation,* Kluwer-Nijhof, The Hague.

Owen, J.M. and Alkin, M.C. (2006) *Program Evaluation: Forms and Approaches*, 3rd ed., Allen & Unwin, Sydney.

Patton, M.Q. (2001) *Qualitative Research and Evaluation Methods*, 3rd ed., Sage, Newbury Park, CA.

—— (2008) *Utilization-Focused Evaluation*, 4th ed., Sage, Thousand Oaks, CA.

Stufflebeam, D.L. et al. (2000) *Evaluation Models: Viewpoints on Educational and Human Services Evaluation* (Evaluation in Education and Human Services Volume 49), 2nd ed., Kluwer-Nijhof, Dortrecht. See chapters 2 and 3 on evaluation models.

Stufflebeam, D.L. and Webster, W.J. (1983) 'An Analysis of Alternative Approaches to Evaluation', in G. Madaus, M. Scriven and D.L. Stufflebeam (eds), *Evaluation Models: Viewpoints on Educational and Human Services Evaluation,* Kluwer-Nijhof, The Hague.

Wadsworth, Y. (2010) Chapter 3 Cycles of research, evaluation and inquiry for life, in *Building in Research and Evaluation: Human Inquiry for Living Systems*, Action Research Press, Hawthorn, and Allen & Unwin, Sydney.

INDEX

Accountability

To be accountable means to account for that for which one is responsible, and to those to whom one is responsible. In its most archetypical form, it involves being able to say how funds have been spent on what they were meant to be spent on with the intended outcomes or results. However, to show, account for, demonstrate or report after the event on what has been done (which has a pre-agreed value) is conceptually different from working out what is of value in the first place in order to plan worthwhile and valuable things to be implemented. This latter may better be termed evaluation for improvement. Thus, strictly speaking, to demonstrate accountability is to report retrospectively on audit review results, but to evaluate is to embark prospectively on open inquiry processes to identify the value or worth of something. The increase in talk of 'need for accountability' largely reflects the increasing gaps between those who know what is being done and its value because they are proximal (close) to it, and those who should know or want to know but are more distal (at a distance from it). If those who do not know are the critical reference groups, then this should serve as a sign that something is wrong in the everyday practice of the work. If those who do not know are other stakeholders (e.g. representing broader constituencies or other interested parties), then accountability may be experienced as 'rendering unto Caesar' if it is not clearly 'power for' (critical reference groups). 'Accountability' thus seems often to be an ambivalent term—that is, who is accountable to whom? Services to funders and managers—or funders, managers and services to critical reference groups?

Accreditation

(*See also* **Standards programs**)

As the name indicates, these contain the typical features of *audit review* approaches. Interestingly, they usually begin by being developed 'bottom up' by and from inductive inquiry processes within the field (most often from staff who are part of a movement for client- or community-focused quality services). Then, as they become institutionalised, all new services experience them as top-down audit-style reviews based on a deductive logic (if you do x then y will follow). For example, the Community Health Accreditation and Standards Program (CHASP), which was initiated by the Australian Community Health Association, followed this pattern (and was later even further institutionalised as part of the Australian Hospitals Standards). The peer-organising professional body began by overseeing the formative stage (for example, posing descriptive questions rather than relying entirely on verificationist questions), and this assisted it to achieve relevance and avoid early rigidity. As a result, many of the questions required more holistic and non-quantitative data. A typical selection of questions is illustrated.

Reference

Fry, Denise and King, Lesley (1991) *A Manual of Standards for Community Health*, AGPS, Canberra.

A CHASP Review

AN EXAMPLE OF A STANDARD AND ITS INDICATORS

Standard 4.4 - **Accessibility and** - **Availability** The community health centre/service will be located and operated so that its activities are accessible and available to the community it serves.	**Assessing a Standard** The CHASP Review team assesses the extent to which a community health centre/service has achieved the standard. The review team compiles and summarises its comments for each indicator, in order to assess the overall attainment of each standard.

Indicators
No.

Comments For Each Indicator
No.

4.4.1. Are the centre's premises located in a visible and convenient part of the area it serves?

4.4.1 Centre is in main shopping area and has a prominent sign

4.4.2. Can the centre be easily reached by public or community transport from all parts of its area?

4.4.2. Generally yes, but residents from X Heights have no bus service to X.

4.4.6. Does the telephone system operate efficiently, and is it answered 24 hours a day? (It may require an answering machine)

4.4.6. Insufficient clerical assistance means a recorded message is used in lunch hour. An after hours recorded message gives information on emergency services, and how to contact the community nurse on weekend roster.

4.4.9. Does the centre have easy access to an interpreter service that covers the languages spoken in the area served?

4.4.9. Interpreter service available, but it's sometimes difficult to get a female Arabic interpreter for pre-natal classes.

4.4.15. Does the health centre use other venues in the community from which to conduct its activities (e.g. homes, schools, workplaces)?

4.4.15. Many programs conducted in schools and other community venues. Primary Medical Services provide no home visits.

The CHASP standards have indicators that:
i) **suggest how the standard may be achieved,**
ii) **can be used to assess the level of achievement.**

The CHASP Review Report includes comments on how each standard has been achieved by the centre/service.

(Fry, Denise and Lesley King: 1991)

Action research/action learning, action evaluation

Everyday evaluators might call these kinds of responsive field-based approaches 'trial and error'—a kind of **naturalistic** experimental approach often conducted over longer periods of time (through several iterations of feedback). Seventeen tenets of action research are described in the excerpt from a paper by Robin McTaggart (1989).

Action learning is a small-group, workplace-based process of catalysed learning from peer-presented case studies that shares some fundamental assumptions with action research. Its origins were in the post-war industrial reconstruction collaborative inquiry work of the British researcher Reg Revans (the origins of second-wave action research were in post-war settlement in the work of Kurt Lewin, an American researcher).

Evaluative action research and learning is often thought of as following a cycle or spiral of action, observing that action, reflecting on those observations and the values that guide and help the evaluator judge those actions, questioning further, developing hunches about what is going on and why, drawing conclusions, evaluating alternative options, settling on a new theory or logic, and planning the new valued action, then implementing those new actions, and observing and reflecting again, and so on. The spiral, it is hoped, goes up towards improvement—but it can also go down (if people compound their errors).

So action research or action learning are not merely research or learning that it is hoped will be followed by action! It is action that is intentionally researched and modified, leading to learning what to try in the next stage of action, which is then again intentionally examined for further change and learnings, and so on as part of the research itself. Life itself is a kind of action research project when you think about it in this way!

Much conventional and academic research proceeds as if it starts with hypotheses and ends with conclusions, but this is a formulation of only half of the full inquiry cycle (Wadsworth, 2010) (*See* **Systems Analysis, Systems Theory**). First, it does not take seriously the *source* of the (value-driven and experience-based) theories or hunches—which is critical to getting more *meaningful*, *relevant* and *useful* hypotheses worthy of people's time and effort. Without this, services are even more likely to 'get it wrong' and require excessive amounts of data collection for after-the-event audit review to alert people to this (often incurring a wall of defensive response if things have gone awry). Second, it does not take seriously the matter of putting the conclusions to the *practical* test (with the value of the actions being judged by those whose interests were to be served by the evaluation in the first place), and thus also to getting beyond the defensive reactions to realising when things are not going well, and back to reflecting on the positive values and desired states being sought.

Some theorists believe that evaluation stands separate from research; however, this book has argued that the two elements are part of an integrated action evaluation process, and are bound together by the *purposes* of the exercise (and thus by the critical reference group which has those purposes grounded in its needs, interests or desires and the values that express these). In practice, whenever we try to describe a 'fact', we find we are constructing a description of the world in which there already attaches some kind of a value-interest, whether mild, strong, positive, or negative, conscious or unconscious. Even in just 'choosing'

Principles for Participatory Action Research

A paper presented to the 3er Encuentro Mundial Investigacion Participativa (The Third World Encounter on Participatory Research), Managua, Nicaragua, September 3–9, 1989.

1 Participatory action research is an approach to *improving social practice* by *changing* it and learning from the consequences of change.

2 Participatory action research is contingent on *authentic participation*: it is research through which people work towards the improvement of *their own practices* (and only secondarily the improvement of other people's practices). Through dialogue among participants, regular checks are made to ensure that the agenda of the least powerful become an important focus of the group's work.

3 Participatory action research develops through *the self-reflective spiral: a spiral of cycles of planning, acting,* (implementing plans), *observing* (systematically), *reflecting . . .* and then re-planning, further implementation, observing and reflecting. One good way to begin a participatory action research project is to collect some initial data in an area of general interest (a reconnaissance), then to reflect, and then to make a plan for changed action; another way to begin is to make an exploratory change, collect data of what happens, reflect, and then build more refined plans for action. In both cases, issues and understandings, on the one hand, and the practice themselves, on the other, develop and evolve through the participatory action research process—but only when the Lewinian self-reflective spiral is thoughtfully and systematically followed in processes of group critique.

4 Participatory action research is *collaborative:* it involves those responsible for action in improving it, widening the collaborating group from these most directly involved to as many as possible of those affected by the practices concerned.

5 Participatory action research establishes *self-critical communities* of people participating and collaborating in all phases of the research process: the planning, the action, the observation and the reflection; it aims to build communities of people committed to *enlightening* themselves about the relationship between circumstance, action and consequence in their own situation, and *emancipating* themselves from the institutional and personal constraints which limit their power to live their own legitimate educational and social values.

6 Participatory action research is a *systematic learning process* in which people act deliberately, though remaining open to surprise and responsive to opportunities. It is a process of using 'critical intelligence' to inform action, and developing it so that social action becomes *praxis* (critically informed, committed action) through which people may consistently live their social values.

7 Participatory action research involves people in *theorising* about their practices—being *inquisitive* about circumstances, actions and consequences and coming to *understand* the relationship between circumstance, actions and consequences in their own lives. The theories that participatory action researchers develop may be expressed initially in the form of *rationales* for practices. They may develop these rationales by treating them as if they were no more than rationalisations, even though they may be our best current theories of how and why our social (and educational . . .) work is as it is. They subject these initial rationales to critical scrutiny through the participatory action research process.

8 Participatory action research requires that people put their practice, ideas and assumptions about institutions to the *test* by gathering *compelling evidence* which could convince them that their previous practices, ideas and assumptions were wrong or wrong-headed.

9 Participatory action research is open-minded about what counts as evidence (or data)—it involves not only *keeping records* which describe what is happening as accurately as possible (given the particular questions being investigated and the real-life circumstances of collecting the data) but also *collecting and analysing our own judgements, reactions and impressions* about what is going on.

10 Participatory action research involves participants in *objectification of their own experience*, for example, by keeping a *personal journal* in which participants record their progress and their reflections about the practices they are studying (how the practices—individual and collective—are developing) and their learnings about the process (the practice), of studying them (how the action research project is going).

11 Participatory action research is a *political process* because it involves us in making changes that will affect others—for this reason, it sometimes creates resistance to change, both in the participants themselves and in others.

12 Participatory action research involves people in making *critical analyses* of the situations (projects, programs, systems) in which they work: these situations are *structured* institutionally. The pattern of resistance a participatory action researcher meets in changing his or her own practices is a pattern of conflicts between the new practices and the accepted practices of the institution (accepted practices of communication, decision making and educational work). By making a critical analysis of the institution, the participatory action researcher can understand how resistances are rooted in conflicts between competing kinds of practice, competing views of social (and educational . . .) positions and values, and competing views of social organisation and decision-making. This critical understanding will help the participatory action researcher to act politically towards overcoming resistances (for example, by involving others collaboratively in the research process, inviting others to explore their practices, or by working in the wider institutional context towards more rational understandings, more just processes of decision-making, and more fulfilling forms of social work for all involved).

13 Participatory action research *starts small*, by working through changes which even a single person can try, and works towards extensive changes—even critiques of ideas of institutions which in turn might lead to more general reforms of projects, programs or system-wide policies and practices. Participants should be able to present evidence of how they started to work on *articulating the thematic concern* which would hold their group together, and of how they *established authentically shared agreements* in the group that the thematic concern was a basis for collaborative action.

14 Participatory action research starts with *small cycles* of planning, acting, observing and reflecting which can help to define issues, ideas and assumptions more clearly so that those involved can define more *powerful questions* for themselves as their work progresses.

15 Participatory action research starts with *small groups* of collaborators at the start, but widens the community of participating action researchers so that it gradually includes more and more of those involved and affected by the practices in question.

16 Participatory action research allows and requires participants to build *records* of their improvements: (a) records of their changing *activities and practices*, (b) records the changes in the *languages and discourse* in which they decide, explain and justify their practices, (c) records of the changes in the *social relationships and forms of organisation* which characterise and constrain their practices and (d) records of the development of their expertise in the conduct of *action research*. Participants must be able to demonstrate evidence of a group climate where people expect and give evidence to support each other's claims. They must show respect for the value of rigorously gathered and analysed evidence—and be able to *show and defend* evidence to convince others.

17 Participatory action research allows and requires participants to give a *reasoned justification* of their social (and educational . . .) work to others because they can show how the evidence they have gathered and the critical reflection they have done have helped them to create a *developed, tested and critically examined rationale* for what they are doing. Having developed such a rationale, they may legitimately ask others to justify their own practices in terms of their own theories and the evidence of their own critical self-reflection.

Robin McTaggart, Deakin University, Geelong, Victoria 3217, Australia.

Extract from *Everyday Evaluation on the Run* by Yoland Wadsworth, Allen & Unwin, Sydney: 2011, pp. 133–4.

to see *this* fact rather than that fact, there has been a valuing action taken. So wherever we try to describe a value, we find we are describing value-states or valued-activities. That is, just as there is no such thing as a value-free fact (or value-free research to 'collect' them), there is also no such thing as a fact-free value (in that our values are valued-states we have learned about through previous cycles of everyday action research or action learning).

In a way, social research or social science has as much to learn from the value-explicit nature of its evaluation elements, as evaluation has to learn from the evidence-seeking and hunch-testing nature of its essential research process.

References

Kemmis, Stephen and McTaggart, Robin (1988) *The Action Research Planner*, Deakin University, Geelong, Vic.

Lewin, Kurt (1946) 'Action Research and Minority Problems', *Journal of Social Issues* no. 2, pp. 34–46.

McTaggart, Robin (1989) 'Principles for Participatory Action Research', paper for Participatory Action Research Encounter, Nicaragua.

Revans, Reg (1980) *Action Learning: New Techniques for Management,* Blond & Briggs, London.

Stringer, Ernest (1996) *Action Research*, Sage, Thousand Oaks, CA.

Wadsworth, Yoland (1998) 'What is Participatory Action Research?' *Action Research International*, Paper 2, www.scu.edu.au/schools/gcm/ar/ari/p-ywadsworth98.html>.

Advocacy evaluation

This is a model for internal evaluation within an organisation that is halfway between people doing it themselves and bringing in an external evaluator. It involves designating one person who is part of the organisation to be the evaluator. The role shifts from a traditional one of neutral expert to that of active organisational change agent. Important elements include using an advocacy philosophy; ensuring the evaluator is optimally located in the organisation; and selecting for the role imaginative, iconoclastic people who possess extensive 'operational' experience and are good listeners, communicators and negotiators. Case studies show high rates of implementation of recommendations and a shift from a preoccupation with 'quantity' to one with 'quality'. The approach, emphasising timeliness and relevance, shares much in common with **decision-theoretic** or **client-centred**, and **utilisation-focused** evaluation.

Reference

Sonnichsen, Richard (1988) 'Advocacy Evaluation: A Model for Internal Evaluation Offices', *Evaluation and Program Planning*, no. 11, pp. 141–8.

Appreciative inquiry (AI)/strengths-based evaluation

Appreciative inquiry is an **action research** methodology using a '4D' approach (Discover–Dream–Design–Deliver, i.e. Observe–Reflect–Plan–Act) which is currently popular as a way of focusing on **positive evaluation** criteria rather than on what is going wrong or is *not* of value. This proves to be a fast track out of endlessly going around in closed loop circles of observing and measuring and reporting on what is wrong without ever moving to research what to do about it.

A typical 'discovery' question is to try to start by appreciating or noticing what is the best about 'what is'. Examples might be 'When did you most feel like you were able to be the kind of person, e.g. social worker, nurse, doctor, you wanted to be?' or 'Describe a time when this service was being its best'. A 'dream' question is moving to focus on 'what might be' and envisioning this—for example, 'Make three wishes for this program's future'. The 'design' questions ask how to co-construct a strategy to bring this new ideal into practice, and the 'deliver' (or 'destiny') questions work out how to enact, adapt, improvise, adjust and empower the new practice.

There are alternative groups of four alliterative words being used by various other people to differentiate their AI approach from David Cooperrider and Suresh Srivastva's original 'take' on this methodology (from the Weatherhead School of Management, Case Western University, USA.

Strengths-based evaluation and practice approaches (such as that of St Luke's in Bendigo, Australia) also focus on questions that foreground the strong, the good and the positive—in St Luke's case, in the organisation's work with children, families and communities.

There are now whole professional societies, institutes and websites devoted to these kinds of approaches.

References

Cooperrider, David and Srivastva, Suresh (1987) 'Appreciative Inquiry in Organizational Life', *Research in Organizational Change and Development*, no. 1, pp. 129–69.

Cooperrider, David and Whitney, Diana (n.d.) *Appreciative Inquiry: A Constructive Approach to Organization Development and Social Change*, Corporation for Positive Change, Taos, NM.

McCashen, Wayne (2005) *The Strengths Approach*, St Luke's Innovative Resources, Bendigo, Vic.

Autocratic evaluation

This definition was developed by Barry McDonald in the education field, and can be contrasted with two other kinds of approaches defined by him: **bureaucratic evaluation** and **democratic evaluation**. He saw autocratic evaluation as a 'conditional service' to government agencies with control over the allocation of resources, offering external validation of policy in exchange for compliance with the recommendations. Its values derive from the individual expert evaluator's perceptions of the constitutional and moral obligations of the bureaucracy. The evaluator focuses upon issues of merit, and acts as an 'independent' adviser (often academic). His or her techniques of study are seen as yielding evidence-based proofs that give scientific assurances to compliance. Contractual arrangements are meant to guarantee non-interference by the client and the evaluator retains ownership of the study. The report is delivered to the bureaucracy, but is also published in academic journals. If the recommendations are rejected, policy is not seen as validated. The evaluator's court of appeal is the research community and higher levels in the bureaucracy. The key concepts of the autocratic evaluator are 'principle' and 'objectivity'. Its key justificatory concept is 'the responsibility of office'. The subsequent commercialisation of the public sector along economic liberal lines distorted some aspects of this model (e.g. commercial-in-confidence clauses that preclude publication or even sharing of data among participating stakeholders).

Reference

McDonald, Barry (1976) 'Evaluation and the Control of Education' in D.A. Tawney (ed.), *Curriculum Evaluation Today: Trends and Implications*, Schools Council Research Studies, Macmillan, London.

Baume Report approach

Reflecting trends in the United States and the United Kingdom to economic rationalism, in 1979 an Australian Senate Standing Committee on Social Welfare published an influential report entitled *Through a Glass Darkly: Evaluation in Australian Health and Welfare Services*. Chaired by Senator Peter Baume, the committee's report was a meta-evaluation (an evaluation of evaluation) which, despite some notable efforts to the contrary, came down heavily on the side of a strongly rational-technical approach to evaluation involving:

- **program-based** and **objectives-based evaluation**.
- **zero-base budgeting**
- **quantitative statistics and measurement focus**
- a central **management** and funding body perspective emphasising value for money and accountability.

Coming as it did at the end of the 1970s, with an economic recession triggering panic amongst governments about spending, the Baume approach to evaluation quickly took over from the more needs-based approaches popular in the 1960s and mid-1970s such as conventional surveys and some more **phenomenological** efforts (which mirrored the American **naturalistic** critique of rational **experimental** approaches). These new managerialist approaches to after-the-event' audit review continued to conflict in the field with the need for more qualitative, inductive and formative evaluation to establish and regularly re-establish what might be of value *per se*.

References

Lawrence, John (1980) 'Preface', in Rosemary S. Sarri and John R. Lawrence, *Issues in the Evaluation of Social Welfare Programs: Australian Case Illustrations*, UNSW Press, Sydney, pp. iii–vii.

Senate Standing Committee on Social Welfare (1979) *Through a Glass Darkly: Evaluation in Australian Health and Welfare Services*, Vols 1 and 2, AGPS, Canberra.

Bradshaw's typology of needs

In 1972, Jonathan Bradshaw published a short article in the English *New Society* journal entitled 'The Concept of Social Need'. It subsequently, despite critique, became over-whelmingly popular (and remains so to this day) as a fourfold way of defining 'needs'. While needs-based evaluation is recognised as a distinct school of evaluation, in practice all evalua-tion refers in some way to who or what it is for, even if this is left implicit. There is a debate about whether we should speak of critical reference groups' 'needs', 'values', 'interests' or 'desires'. However, the vast majority of human and community services practice hinged on a language or 'discourse' about 'needs' until the 1990s, when the focus shifted from (seem-ingly unmeetable) service-user needs to (seemingly curtailable) service providers' capacity, with needs having to be cut to match the capacity of providers.

The four ways of identifying 'needs' that Bradshaw described are:

1 *Normative.* What the expert, professional, administrator or social scientist defines as need in terms of a 'desirable' standard.
2 *Felt.* Need defined as want, expressed directly by those who have it.
3 *Expressed.* Need defined as felt need turned into concrete behaviour or action, or demand that is expressed indirectly in some way—for example, by a waiting list or by purchasing behaviour.
4 *Comparative.* If consumers get a service in one area but not in another, it is assumed the unserviced area has an unmet need.

Bradshaw never intended his four categories to be *definitions* of needs, but rather saw them as four *methods* of identifying the needs people have. That is, there aren't four differ-ent *kinds* of need, but four different *ways of finding out* what they are. Three out of his four, however, are other people's ways of judging critical reference groups' needs, with those other people occupying usually very different class, power and cultural backgrounds. Only one of the ways attempts to tap directly critical reference groups' own judgements, yet Bradshaw notes that even this way is 'widely considered' 'unreliable' and an 'inadequate measure of "real" need'. Rather than then moving on to address the requirement for a well-informed populace to avoid forms of colonialism where people are seen as having 'limited perceptions', or otherwise not wanting to 'confess a loss of independence', Bradshaw fails to recognise his own elitism.

For example, one could reshape and expand some of his categories using the approach of this book and add another four ways of identifying need:

5   *Volunteered*: where critical reference group members directly, explicitly and verbally articulate and request their needs (as they experience them) be met.

6   *Signified:* where members of the critical reference group have not been given opportunities to, or are not otherwise confident or able to volunteer explicitly their needs verbally, but freely offer non-verbal or other signs—such as a person with Alzheimer's disease who uses body and facial signs that can be 'read' by someone using a critical reference group perspective.

7   *Sought:* where one group with a critical reference group perspective mobilises the volunteering of information from other critical reference groups to identify relevant ways, that may not otherwise have been explicitly volunteered or signified by that group, but may have been by another group.

8   *Professionally or administratively defined*: where a person trained in a specialist body of knowledge defines need from their own point of view with or without direct reference to the experience of the people to whose needs that body of knowledge is meant to refer.

Some of these debates have been addressed by a relativist perspectival 'stakeholders' approach, or more recently by a systems approach that identifies the critical stakeholder as the critical reference point or 'inquirer' in dialogue with other co-inquirers (with other more or less aligned interests).

References

Bradshaw, Jonathan (1972) 'The Concept of Social Need', *New Society*, no. 496, pp. 640–3.

Fitzgerald, Ross (ed.) (1977) *Human Needs and Political Practice*, Pergamon Press, Sydney.

Brainstorming

This still regularly used technique is intended to increase a group's access to a range of ideas through purposeful free association. It is a seemingly simple although really quite sophisticated technique that can easily be used by everyday evaluators—although it is often difficult to maintain the ground rule that suggestions are made *without any critical comment* in the first place. (Pros and cons are assessed later on the basis of previously collected in-depth observational knowledge of the relevant fields of action.) Brainstorming involves bringing together a small group face to face (fewer than ten people works best). The topic for which ideas are required is presented, and on a board or butcher's paper *all* suggestions are recorded. Apparently irrelevant, impractical or problematic suggestions are encouraged, recorded and discussed later when the group evaluates all the offerings. It is often used to generate creative and imaginative new solutions, although it may not immediately come up with the best solutions. Sometimes it is helpful for people to be able to go away and chew over all the ideas and possibilities in relation to the issue, problem or desired future they address, and then come back to meet again later.

Reference
Rawlinson, Geoffrey (1981) *Creative Thinking and Brainstorming*, Gower, Aldershot, UK.

Bureaucratic evaluation

This, along with **autocratic** and **democratic evaluation**, was a term developed by Barry McDonald in the education field. He described bureaucratic evaluation as an 'unconditional service' to those government agencies that have major control over the allocation of resources. The evaluator accepts the values of those who hold office and hold the resources, and offers information that will help them to accomplish their policy objectives. The evaluator acts as a management consultant, and his or her criterion of success is 'client (management) satisfaction'. The techniques of study must be credible to the policymakers and not lay them open to public criticism. The evaluator has no independence, no control over the use that is made of his or her information and no court of appeal. The report is owned by the bureaucracy and lodged in its files. The key concepts of bureaucratic evaluation are 'service', 'utility' and 'efficiency'. Its key justificatory concept is the reality of 'authorised' power.

Reference
McDonald, Barry (1976), 'Evaluation and the Control of Education', in D.A. Tawney (ed.), *Curriculum Evaluation Today: Trends and Implications*, Macmillan, London.

Client-centred models

(*See also* **Consumer evaluation**)
These models of evaluation take the 'user' or 'commissioning agent' as their driving force. 'Users' may be defined by this approach as managers, government departments, a funding body or a self-help group. That is, the term 'client' is an ambiguous one that may cover any of the conceptual parties/stakeholders in an evaluation (whether *those it is for*—to help, *those it is for*—to inform, convince or influence, etc., *the evaluators, the evaluated* or the *self-evaluating*). In the literature, client-centred models might include some **management** approaches, **responsive evaluation**, **stakeholder evaluation**, **utilisation-focused evaluation** and **consumer evaluation**—that is, those approaches that directly involve in the evaluation the various groups that want the evaluation.

Over time, and with the growing understanding of the importance of end-user or end-beneficiaries not just in 'receiving' services but also in actively participating in their design and implementation, client-focused *services* require different approaches by evaluators than does client-focused *evaluation*. Consumer evaluation has become more common to describe the former (*see also* **empowerment evaluation**).

Reference
Patton, Michael Quinn (2008), *Utilization-Focused Evaluation*, 4th ed., Sage, Beverley Hills, CA.

Collaborative evaluation

This refers to evaluation that proceeds with the **democratic** or **participatory** involvement of **stakeholders**. Some or all of the various parties to evaluation come or are brought together. For example, a collaborative evaluation in a school might—like client-centred models—involve a range of stakeholders:

- those who it is for in the sense of the stake*owner* to be benefited), such as students
- those who it is for in the sense of also deriving value from the critical reference group being benefited by it, such as parents, teachers or employers
- those it is for in the sense of being informed, influenced or convinced, such as regional departmental authorities, central funders or policy-makers.

The collaboration is between people with different interests or values but who have enough common ground to be able to collaborate. While the warm, fuzzy meaning of 'working together in a joint enterprise' is usually intended, the secondary dictionary meaning of 'aiding the enemy occupying forces' may provide a cautionary insight! For example, if professional staff and a self-help group collaborate, or large institution managers and social workers and consumer-employed community workers collaborate, then active provision should be made for addressing imbalances in power relations.

The great value of collaborative evaluation is the involvement of all parties who might be expected to change their practices—and who need to experience, both directly and personally, the inquiry as it yields the evidence for value, merit, worth or significance and be part of the consequent arguments for change. With strong **interpretive** or **phenomenological** underpinnings, such **dialogic** evaluation can effectively enable the mutual illumination of differing parties' beliefs, perceptions, world-views, ideas, visions, contexts and histories. A collaborative evaluation of psychiatric nursing practices—involving both nurses' and patients' perceptions in dialogue—might, for example, more effectively lead to change than either patients' complaints or a media exposé of bad practices, or a staff inventory of quality assurance activities they undertake. It will certainly have a better chance of succeeding than a managerialist evaluation that doesn't draw on the experiences of both the 'troops' and the 'civilians'. Collaborative studies might run aground if one party is unable to listen, or hasn't enough of a desire to understand another party's perceptions in their context, or if any party can't wait any longer for any other party to see their situation, and either leaves in frustration or continues on in frustrated silence.

Reference
Reason, Peter (n.d.) *Collaborative Inquiry*, Newsletter, Centre for the Study of Organizational Change and Development, University of Bath, UK.

Complaints mechanisms

Complaints mechanisms range from feedback systems like the humble suggestion box through to highly formal semi-legalistic bodies like state Ombudspersons, or health services complaints offices. They can provide feedback to the service as well as give consumer redress. Conventionally, they are a last (or later) resort when more everyday avenues have been exhausted. Characteristics associated with greater success include:

- being accessible (the suggestion box should not be under the direct watchful eye of the service provider!)
- allowing for consumers' confidentiality or protection against reprisal if confidentiality cannot be maintained
- allowing the complaint to be received by someone other than the direct provider
- giving the complainant enough support to have confidence to lodge a complaint
- giving the recipient of the complaint power to make changes
- ensuring the complainant receives feedback about the change/s made (or reasons if they do not).

Over time, 'complaints' have come to be seen as more formal, while 'normal complaints' are more often seen as 'feedback' and somewhat more routinely sought out, accepted and acted on than in the past. They are also more often seen as part of a larger quality and satisfaction program (Wadsworth in ongoing association with Epstein 2001; Kilner and Were, 2000).

References

Kilner, David and Were, Keith (2000) 'Complaints: Our Frontline Feedback', Part 3 of *Pursuing Customer Satisfaction in the Human Services*, Social Options Australia, Stepney, SA.

Mohr, Rick and Lunney, Rowan (1989), 'The Essentials: A Complaints System that Works', in *Consumers' Fair Go! Kit*, Combined Pensioners Association of NSW, Sydney.

Wadsworth, Yoland with Epstein, Merinda (2001) *The Essential U&I: A One-volume Presentation of the Findings of a Lengthy Grounded Study of Whole Systems Change Towards Staff-Consumer Collaboration for Enhancing Mental Health Services*, VicHealth, Melbourne, pp. 87–9.

Congruency and compliance models

These terms are used in the evaluation literature to refer to evaluation models that look at whether program operations are consistent with or divergent from **objectives**, **performance indicators** and **outcomes**, such as those found in **funding and service agreements**, and whether funds have been spent as agreed (not just whether they have been spent *per se*). typical congruency and compliance models would be **management by objectives**, **program budgeting**, **service agreements**, and techniques like **critical path analysis** (for example, PERT). The term 'compliance' indicates that these are generally operated as non-collaborative top-down management approaches where successful achievement is considered mandatory (often in high-risk areas such as child protection or public safety), but may be too rigid if there is change, which means discretion, adaptation, creativity or improvement are needed.

Reference
Armstrong, Anona (1986) *Evaluation Models and Strategies*, Evaluation Training and Services, Melbourne.

Connoisseurship model

Elliot Eisner developed this evaluation model from within the American education camp. It uses the metaphor of the arts critic to represent perceptive observation drawing on experience and imaginative criticism (critique or disclosure) deemed sufficiently experienced as to be able to reveal deeper underlying characteristics, truths, values or structures. The fine nuances noticed by someone who has devoted years of attention to refining evaluative judgement in a particular area are given credit and sought out. The chief drawback occurs if the perception, and hence insights, have emerged from a particular life context characterised by different values or interests from those involved in or those who will benefit from the current evaluative field. Judgements may also rest on a large amount of unexplicated intuition or undocumented evidence, making it difficult for others to use the technique themselves or to cross-check the sources or bases of the connoisseur's evaluations.

Reference
Eisner, Elliot (1983) 'Educational Connoisseurship and Criticism: Their Form and Functions in Educational Evaluation', in George F. Madaus, Michael Scriven and Daniel F. Stufflebeam (eds), *Evaluation Models: Viewpoints on Educational and Human Services Evaluation*, Kluwer-Nijhoff, The Hague, pp. 335–8.

Constructivist/constructionist evaluation

Constructivism is an epistemology (methodology for knowing) based on the idea that reality is socially constructed. That is, it holds that 'reality' is not only always apprehended by the 'intervening' **interpretive** individual human mind—itself a store (or perhaps these days, a neural network) of mental models built from such interpretations of sensing or observational experience, acquired over time, and deeply encultured and relational in their multiple and changing meanings—but also that such 'experience' implies such learning takes place through action in the world. The latter action orientation of *constructionism* also stressed the individually embodied nature of this mental enterprise, even while what is individually embodied remains profoundly shaped by the social (both enabled and constrained).

Thus research or evaluative knowledge is not in any simple sense 'gathered', 'collected', 'described' and 'passed on'; rather, through complex communicative interactions (verbal and non-verbal), people come to grasp or approximate (more or less) the mental constructs in the minds of others (and convey what is in their own) in order to build shared-enough understandings of the world to enable social communication, cooperation, collaboration or competition, and individual action within that social context.

As applied to evaluation by its theorists, Egon Guba and Yvonna Lincoln, constructivist, or *'fourth generation'*, evaluation draws on and extends radically some of the old tenets of **interpretive** social research, leaving behind a *'first generation'* of evaluation that was preoccupied with measuring test results; a *'second generation'* of objectives-based and outcome-oriented evaluation; and a *'third generation'* of judgement and decision-oriented evaluation, on the grounds of their various tendencies to disempower legitimate parties to the evaluation, their failure to accommodate other values, and their over-commitment to a narrow old paradigm objectivist science. Instead, it proposes that the central concern of evaluation is negotiation over, and construction of, the meanings of the value of what is being evaluated—involving the evaluators, the evaluated and the evaluated for—in relation to context and with an action orientation. The various stakeholders may, however, differ in their centrality relative to the purposes of that which is being evaluated (and there remains a risk of existing power relations determining outcomes, despite an ethics of 'dignity, integrity and privacy' and hope of enfranchisement of all stakeholders). But certainly Guba and Lincoln make the quantum leap from old paradigm to new paradigm science. The evaluator no longer evaluates, but instead sets in place processes that assist all relevant others to self-evaluate and co-evaluate.

References

Berger, Peter and Luckmann, Thomas (1967) *The Social Construction of Reality*, Anchor Doubleday, New York.

Guba, Egon (1990) *The Paradigm Dialog*, Sage, London.

Guba, Egon and Lincoln, Yvonna (1989) *Fourth Generation Evaluation*, Sage, London.

Consumer evaluation

Some prominent evaluators used to regard 'consumer evaluation' as that where an expert evaluator acted as an 'enlightened surrogate consumer' and judged what was in the interests of consumers by reference to the functional purposes of the evaluand (e.g. a car would need to be driven to assess its driveability). However, the term is now more likely to be understood as consumer-conducted evaluation, as it has become clearer that the actual consumer is the only one with the relevant context in which the (relative) truth of the matter can be determined.

'Consumer studies' conventionally have also involved professional researchers going out and asking consumers for their views of services. But more recently, these studies have been conducted by consumers themselves, or by their organisations or consumer advocacy bodies. Conventional science often considered such work to be 'biased and subjective'; however, the critique of old paradigm science in conjunction with an increasing body of consumer studies, suggests that strong driving value-interests increase the pressure to accomplish relevant and valuable work. When **reflexive** and self-critical, it is also more likely 'to get it right' because consumers literally can't afford to get it wrong—it is they who will directly suffer any mal-effects. 'Bad intelligence', like the covert military operations from which the metaphor is drawn, is not in consumers' interests (even if the findings are 'liked'). Consumer evaluation, or that done by critical reference groups, may involve **self-evaluation** or **group self-evaluation**, or it may 'study up' or be **collaborative**. An assumption of this kind of evaluation is that users, consumers or end-beneficiaries of services are the ultimate arbiters of the value, merit, worth and significance of those services, since the essential indicators of service success must relate to *this group's* needs (there being critical limits to how 'good' a service or intervention can be if consumers do not experience or agree that it is).

References

Mohr, Rich and Lunney, Rowan (1989) 'How to Have Your Say' and 'How to Improve Your Community Service', in *Consumers' Fair Go! Kit*, Combined Pensioners Association of NSW, Sydney.

Wadsworth, Yoland (1998) 'Coming to the Table': Some Conditions for Achieving Consumer-focused Evaluation of Human Services by Service Providers and Service Users', *Evaluation Journal of Australia*, vol. 10, nos 1–2, pp. 11–29.

Context, Input, Process, Product (CIPP)

This is an early **systems** model, developed by Daniel Stufflebeam, which has been popular in education circles. It was developed in the late 1960s in reaction to Tyler's (decontextualised) behavioural objectives-based testing and experimental designs, and is based on the view that the most important purpose of evaluation is 'not to prove but to improve'. It offers four different kinds of evaluation in response to four different kinds of decision-needs:

1 *Context* evaluation: this identifies strengths and weaknesses, assesses needs and judges relationships to objectives.
2 *Input* evaluation: this identifies and assesses system capabilities and alternative plans (procedures, staff, budgets, strategies, etc.).
3 *Process* evaluation: this assesses and guides implementation by identifying defects, refining design and procedure.
4 *Product* evaluation: this identifies and assesses outcomes and relates to objectives, in order to serve 'recycling' decisions (continue, terminate, modify, refocus, etc.).

The model was initially intended as an *open inquiry* approach for guidance in service development and improvement, but it was later to generate *audit review* records for accountability and reporting, and lost some of its value as a 'whole-cycle' model. It is still being used and might benefit from a change in the name of the 'Product' step to 'Product-outcomes', to illuminate its actual definitional usage.

Reference

Stufflebeam, Daniel L. (2000) 'The CIPP Model for Program Evaluation', in D.L. Stufflebeam, George F. Madaus, and T. Kellaghan, *Evaluation Models: Viewpoints on Educational and Human Services Evaluation*, 2nd ed., Kluwer-Nijhof, Dortrecht.

Cost-benefit analysis, cost-effective analysis

These evaluation methods (and associated **program budgeting** and **zero-based budgeting**) are ways of evaluating spending, investment and funding, but by reference to a variety of criteria such as benefit to population served (value for money), efficiency (maximum value for minimum money), and so on.

Originating in the market economy, cost-benefit analysis has been controversial in human services, where the price mechanism is less meaningful—with 'price' being set not in the marketplace, but in a sense by the ballot box (when people, including service-users, vote for a government that employs the human services funders and policy-makers who in turn price-fix their fellow professionals' service provision, and then tax/bill the voters/service-users). Even when there are comparable private sector services, account has to be taken of the way in which public sector services are already partly a result of 'market failure' (that is, already having been deemed to represent 'inefficient' resource allocation by the competitive, profit-driven market).

Cost-effectiveness analysis is an attempt to relate costs to non-monetary internal criteria or to objectives. It has also been called 'performance budgeting', and this is its link with **program budgeting** (PPBS). Thus, the nature of the debate is more about the effects of spending this much rather than that much, or spending this much on this rather than on that.

In practice, it has meant human service managers have been encouraged to cut costs in almost every budget with the 'competitive market' being *between themselves*—with a driving logic of being rewarded for spending less money rather than being rewarded for increasing service. This can be something of a 'perverted market' where ensuring the most service for the least outlay can mean it is 'better' to have an *appearance* of a service (even if it is dangerously thinly spread, and there is no real follow-through). Part of the response to this has been a paradoxical focus on outcomes and program logic models to detect and theoretically correct such situations.

References

Levin, Henry and McEwan, Patrick J. (2000) *Cost Effectiveness Analysis: Methods and Applications*, Sage, Newbury Park, CA.

Thompson, Mark (1980) *Benefit Cost Analysis for Program Evaluation*, Sage, Beverley Hills, CA.

Critical friend

This is a term that is increasingly being used while its origins remain slightly clouded. It almost certainly arose in the 1970s in the context of critical theory and the Frankfurt School's Habermasian thinking about achieving the conditions for 'communicative competence' (Connerton, 1976) in the education domain. A popular way of understanding the concept is to see it as referring to someone who is able to be *both* a trusted person *and* ask challenging questions, draw attention to matters using an alternative perspective or point to different 'facts', information or experiences that might offer a critique of someone's thinking or writing. 'A critical friend takes the time to fully understand the context of the work presented and the outcomes that the person or group is working toward,' while being an 'advocate for the success of that work' (Costa and Kallick, 1993).

References

Connerton, Paul (ed.) (1976) *Critical Sociology*, Penguin, Harmondsworth.

Costa, A. and Kallick, B. (1993) 'Through the Lens of a Critical Friend', *Educational Leadership* vol. 51, no. 2, pp. 49–51.

Critical path analysis

This technique—and versions of it, such as **PERT** and **GANTT** scheduling—is a way to sort out and establish a kind of an evaluative framework for the chronology of implementation tasks for a service, while still at the planning stage. It is a way of setting down a description of an expected set of timed activities so that actual progress can quickly and easily be compared for any discrepancy, and rectifying action taken (or explanation made for diversion). While designed as a decision-making tool for managers, the essence of this approach can easily be applied by everyday evaluators. The technique in its simplest form can be done by pen and paper; in its more complex form (for example, for more than 100 activities), it is done by computer program. The danger of the computer program is that, when calculations turn out to be wrong, everything can be adjusted by a few keystrokes so no apparent discrepancy remains! See **PERT** and **GANTT** for examples of how the technique looks. The critical path is the total expected time path after all calculations have been made. You can calculate worst possible scenarios (longest path) or best (shortest).

References

Education Department of Victoria (1985) 'Critical Path', in *Destination Decisions*, Curriculum Branch, Education Department of Victoria, Melbourne, pp. 43–6.

Hoffer, Joe R. (1977) 'PERT: A Tool for Managers of Human Service Programs', in F. Cox et al. (eds), *Tactics and Techniques of Community Practice*, F.E. Peacock, Itasca, IL, pp. 287–98.

Decision-theoretic approach

This technique is aimed at clarifying the relationships among multiple goals that may represent conflicting values and interests. It can use statistical and quantitative techniques for measuring values and uncertainties regarding outcomes, and the probability of those outcomes. In its broadest sense, it is about evaluating with a view to decision-making. In its simplest sense, it is accessible to everyday evaluators—that is, it encourages us to ask about the value of our decisions and also to assess new ideas with a view to what will be done in practice as a result of them. Later logic models and program theories-of-change have their precursors in this approach.

Reference

Edwards, Ward, Guttentag, Marcia and Snapper, Kurt (1975) 'A Decision-theoretic Approach to Evaluative Research', in Elmer Struening and Marcia Guttentag (eds), *Handbook of Evaluation Research*, Vol. 1, Sage, Beverly Hills, CA, pp. 139–82.

Deliberative Polling®

Deliberative Polling® is a Stanford University-owned franchised method that incorporates some insights from action evaluation (e.g. collaboration between various stakeholders, in an iterative process, to enhance understanding and critical discernment capacity). It also uses elements from market or public opinion research in a new method that is intended to be more democratic. It starts with a random, representative sample of people being polled on their opinions about the targeted issue/s. This comprises a baseline dataset before deliberation. The population 'members' of the sample are then invited to gather at a single place for a weekend in order to discuss the issues. Briefing materials that are intended to be 'balanced' are sent to the participants and are also made publicly available. The participants then engage in dialogue with competing experts and political leaders, based on questions they develop in small-group discussions with trained moderators. Parts of the weekend events may be videotaped and broadcast. After the deliberations, the participants from the original sample are again asked the same questions. The resulting changes in opinion represent the conclusions that it is assumed would be reached by the public if they too had the opportunity to become more informed about the issues.

Reference
Fishkin, James S. (n.d.) 'Deliberative Polling®: Toward a Better-Informed Democracy', Center for Deliberative Democracy, Stanford University, Stanford, CA, accessed 22 February 2010 at <http://cdd.stanford.edu/polls/docs/summary>

Delphi Technique

Like its name (which alludes to a famous oracle of ancient Greece), this technique attempts to get a handle on predicting the future. Originally developed by the Rand Corporation in the 1950s for predicting the value of technology for use in war, it has since been taken up in the education and community services areas. While it reached a peak in popularity in the late 1970s, it is occasionally still used today, particularly by managers, to elicit quickly a range of ideas from, and then also consensus among, a group of people deemed to be experts. The format involves an initial round of open-ended questionnaires seeking the issues people see as important. The results of these are circulated to all those who contributed to the original questionnaires, with a further questionnaire asking people to rank all the possibilities now before them. Convergence tends to ensue as an artefact of the technique, even though it should allow the possibility of revision of individual items. A key drawback can be the loss of complex connectivity between the ideas and the people and the contexts from which they were generated. Another drawback arises if the pool of items (after the first round) represents less than an ideal pool of wisdom. If better options are required and no one can imagine them, then frustration can arise in the second round when people are forced to choose from the pool of less than desirable options. If these less than desirable options are then ranked, a 'numbers game' ensures everyone is then stuck with the result. That is, the 'consensus' isn't reached by discussion, reflection and empowered/informed contributions, but rather by someone crunching the numbers. It may be unfortunate that some of the original defining characteristics of the technique have always been stuck to so rigidly. These include:

- the elimination of face-to-face contact and discussion in order to minimise the 'emotive effects of group dynamics'
- the insistence on reducing the 'inconvenience' of time-consuming travel for decision-makers
- the method's reliance on forced choices, and
- the emphasis on involving only those deemed to be 'experts'.

Its basic iterative format, which attempts to democratise input, supplemented by more 'real group' (community of practice) interaction, could be more helpful to everyday evaluators for getting individual ideas onto the table from their real-life contexts, and for helping the group move towards selecting from among its ideas. It can also be useful for clarification of intentions or purposes. **Search conferences** overcome some of these drawbacks. **Brainstorming** and **nominal group techniques** (see *Do It Yourself Social Research*) also address similar needs.

Reference

Delbecq, A.L., Vandeven, A.H. and Gustafson, D.M. (1975) *Group Techniques for Program Planning: A Guide to Nominal Group and Delphi Processes,* Scott Foresman and Co., Glenview, IL.

Democratic evaluation

This is a third kind of evaluation defined by Barry McDonald, along with **autocratic** and **bureaucratic** evaluation. Democratic evaluation is a kind of 'auto-information service' to the community about the characteristics of a program. It recognises value-pluralism and seeks (indirectly) to represent or (more directly) to involve people with a range of interests in its own formulation of issues. The basic value is an informed and active citizenry, and the evaluator acts more as a facilitator and broker in exchanges of information between differing groups. Techniques of data-gathering and presentation must be accessible to non-specialist audiences. The main activity is the collection of definitions of, and reactions to, the program. The evaluator offers confidentiality to informants and gives them control over the use of information. The report is non-recommendatory, and the evaluator has less chance of information misuse because of the transparent sharing of the work. The evaluator engages in periodic negotiation of his or her relationships with sponsors and program participants. A critically important criterion of success is the range of audiences served. The report aspires to best-seller status. The key concepts of democratic evaluation are individual 'confidentiality', 'negotiation' and collective 'accessibility', and the key justificatory concept is 'the right to know'.

Reference

McDonald, Barry (1976) 'Evaluation and the Control of Education', in D.A. Tawney (ed.), *Curriculum Evaluation Today: Trends and Implications,* Schools Council Research Studies, Macmillan, London.

Development evaluation

Approaches to monitoring and evaluation across different institutions and sectors are passing through a decolonising period in which fieldworkers, development practitioners, academics, donors and policy-makers are realising that the value of their contributions are intimately related to how they are implemented, researched, monitored and evaluated. Participation by recipient countries' peoples—local communities, government and non-government agencies, religious bodies, and so on—has become as compelling as it has in human services for the most excluded and disadvantaged in the West. Watch for keywords like the initial 'P' with M&E—that is, Participatory Monitoring and Evaluation frameworks (PM&E)—or notice when they are missing. Case studies are a critical method of presenting, supplanted by more recent technologies like Rapid Rural Appraisal (which morphed into

Participatory Rural Appraisal) and **most significant change**. The key issues and challenges involve the transfer of power and control over resources from donors who are 'helping' to those being 'helped'. National economic and policy interests, and the cultural clashes between rich countries encountering 'poor' countries, come into play, making it a particularly 'hot button' form of evaluation.

References

Estrella, Marisol et al. (2000) *Learning from Change: Issues and Experiences in Participatory Monitoring and Evaluation*, IDRC, Sussex.

Selener, Daniel, with Purdy, Christopher and Zapata, Gabriela (1996), *Documenting, Evaluating and Learning from Our Development Projects: A Systematization Workbook*, IIRR, New York.

Developmental evaluation

This is a term being used by a number of evaluators and evaluation consultants who have identified the value of working with services or organisations over time in contrast to the fly-in-fly-out, one-off style of evaluation consultancy. Michael Patton, the American evaluator, in particular has contributed a valuable literature around the concept. By building both working relationships and trust between themselves and the organisation or service, and by building a store of experiences and skills for those within the organisation or service to self-reflect and explore questions and gather data over time, evaluation facilitators or consultants can overcome some of the wastage associated with the style of after-the-event consultancy that still predominates. In **organisational development**, it may be called 'process consulting'. It has some things in common with **action evaluation**, **client-centred models**, **participatory** and **reflexive evaluation** and the new dynamic forms of **Systems** thinking.

Reference

Patton, Michael Quinn (1994) 'Developmental Evaluation', *Evaluation Practice*, vol. 15, no. 3, pp. 311– 19.

Patton, Michael Quinn (2010) *Developmental Evaluation: Applying Complexity Concepts to Enhance Innovation and Use*, Guildford Press, New York.

Dialogue/dialogic evaluation

Dialogue developed out of dissatisfaction with the social science tradition of one-way interviewer–interviewee question-asking and answering. In less structured interviews, more depth and understanding was found to be forthcoming from *an exchange* in which matters could be explored, clarified, revised and refined. Beyond the 'qualitative turn' in one-to-one exchanges, however, came the realisation from participatory forms of research (particularly action research) involving multiple stakeholders that even greater discernment was possible in exchanges within and between groups. Some of the now familiar properties of dialogue began to emerge to enhance such exchanges (Bohm et al. 1991)—and in particular what dialogue was *not* (e.g. arguments, posturing, holding forth, defensiveness, bantering, discussion and other forms of adversarial communication where we don't discover anything new or really connect with each other because fixed positions are being held).

Particular use of the approach is called for where people are working with diversity or conflict, community-building, organisational development, deliberative democracy, public participation, dispute-resolution, healing and transformation, education, human services, and so on.

Here are some basic guidelines for dialogue that can be discussed and agreed to by a group and posted around a room to remind participants:

- We talk about what's really important to us—and are keen to hear what is really important to others.
- We avoid monopolising the conversation. We don't talk for too long and we make sure everyone has a chance to speak.
- We really listen to each other. We see how thoroughly we can understand each other's views and experiences.
- We respect our own views and how we got to them, just as we make space in which to respect others' views and are keen to hear their grounds for thinking what they think too. We can be 'right for us' without the other therefore being wrong.
- We try not to get stuck in old thoughts and feelings. We see what we can learn by being curious and exploring things together.

See also **collaborative evaluation** and **constructivist evaluation**.

References

Bohm, David, Factor, D. and Garrett, P. (1991), 'Dialogue: A Proposal', Hawthorn Cottage, Broad Marston Lane, Mickelton, Glos., England, paper accessed online 24 November 2009 at <www.david-bohm.net/dialogue/dialogue_proposal.html>.

Labonte R., Feather, J. and Hills, M. (1999) 'A Story/dialogue Method for Health Promotion Knowledge Development and Evaluation', *Health Education Research*, vol. 14, no. 1, pp. 39–50.

Wadsworth, Y. and Epstein, M. (1998) 'Building In' Dialogue Between Consumers and Staff in Acute Mental Health Services', *Systemic Practice and Action Research*, vol. 11, no. 4, pp. 353–79.

Wadsworth, Y. (ed.), with Epstein, M. (2001) *The Essential U&I—A One Volume Presentation of the Findings of a Lengthy Grounded Study of Whole Systems Change Towards Staff–Consumer Collaboration for Enhancing Mental Health Services,* VicHealth, Melbourne.

Discrepancy Evaluation Model (DEM)

This model, developed by Malcolm Provus in the education area, places heavy emphasis on implementation evaluation and was a reaction to the limitations for field-based practitioners of laboratory-based experimental designs. It seeks to identify the discrepancies between the actual program performance and the ideal program or a standard, having derived the description of ideals from the values of program staff and the client population served. It also argues that evaluation of large-scale—even national—programs must begin at the local level. Decision-makers are assisted to determine how far and in what ways a program deviates from the ideal but can still be said to have been implemented (and be meeting its fundamental criteria). To the extent to which it treats goals as surrogates for needs, and hence the discrepancy is practically between programs and goals/ideals, then it has tended to operate more often as a management audit review tool than as a staff- or consumer-driven inquiry model. See also **standards programs**.

References

Provus, Malcolm (1971) *Discrepancy Evaluation for Educational Program Improvement and Assessment*, McCutchan, Berkeley, CA.

Steinmetz, Andres (1983) 'The Discrepancy Evaluation Model', in George Madaus, Michael Scriven and Daniel F. Stufflebeam (eds), *Evaluation Models: Viewpoints on Educational and Human Services Evaluation*, Kluwer-Nijhoff, The Hague, pp. 79–100.

Ecological evaluation model

This model also emerged out of educational psychology in the 1970s, in reaction to the artificiality of laboratory-based experimental approaches. Like **naturalistic** and **constructivist** models drawing on **hermeneutic** understanding, it sought to orient evaluators' attention to the settings and interactions within and between people's environments, and to understand these not as a set of interacting but separate variables, but more as organically or holistically structuring 'parts' of a combined 'living' context. Ultimately, it fell prey to some of the features of more conventional **positivist** evaluation—such as 'objectivism', where the 'external', deemed non-participatory scientist still peered down a microscope (albeit at a whole duck pond rather than just the duck weed!), and did not engage actively in the process of participation and interaction characteristic of a more **interpretive** or **constructivist** approach and implicit in an ecological model. Nearly four decades later, ecological and systemic thinking models are front and centre in evaluation (and indeed the wider global world) as the implications of acting non-ecologically come home with a vengeance in the current world oil crisis, climate emergency and their myriad socio-political consequences.

References

Bronfenbrenner, Urie (1976) 'The Experimental Ecology of Education', *Educational Researcher*, vol. 5, no. 9, pp. 5–15.

Wadsworth, Yoland (2010) *Building in Research and Evaluation: Human Inquiry for Living Systems*, Action Research Press, Hawthorn, and Allen & Unwin, Sydney.

Empowerment Evaluation

See entry in forthcoming website accompanying Wadsworth 2010 (link on Allen & Unwin website from 2011). The key reference is Fetterman et al (1996) on p. 211.

Evaluand

That which is being evaluated.

Experimental evaluation

Laboratory-based science yielded a model of research that has its enthusiasts in the social sciences. This model proposes that, in order to know whether something has had an intended or expected effect, one should try to control all elements of a situation and only vary the one intended or expected element to see whether the effect is as anticipated. In a simple everyday way, we often use a quasi-experimental approach whenever we use 'trial and error'. However, a full-blown experimental approach tries to control all elements and only vary the 'study elements'. Thus it tries to control for all possible sources of difference by, for example, random sampling of subjects; having control groups (which are intended to be identical to the study group, except for the study element or intervention); standardising the physical environment by attempting to eliminate any differing effects of the experiment or experimenter—for example, conducting the experiment so no one (neither researcher nor researched) knows which group got the varied element (double blinding); separating out the variables for analysis, and so on.

Unfortunately, as can be imagined, this method is pretty difficult to accomplish in complex, constantly changing human life with human populations—particularly if the matter being studied is otherwise a natural social process of any degree of complexity (particularly in terms of self-feedback), such as the development of a community, or household-formation or human service provision, or processes of social and political exclusion and discrimination.

The nature of human beings as aware, self-aware and mutually aware; the complexity and interdependency of 'variables'; the constant natural changeability, including that resulting inevitably from any form of research intervention (even so-called 'unobtrusive' research), and the expectation of human ethics (for example, not withholding treatment from a control group when it is already suspected of having value) largely prevent this form of laboratory-based science from having everyday applicability. When attempted, it often results paradoxically in the reduction of meaning and validity and the giving of a false sense of certainty. Where meaning survives, results often feel like one is 'reading Braille through a doona'*—yielding abstract outlines or glimpses of the multiple and socially constructed

---

*   A YW metaphor that translates as attempting to detect meanings through a thick layer of distance, summarisation and reductionism (as in reading Braille through a feather quilt!)

realities they are meant to be representing. Alternatively, it may result in very predictable outcomes since it primarily offers to verify (or falsify) hypotheses if they are already the result of previous theory-building and inductive research or evaluation. The experimental method is frequently further confounded by adherence to **positivist** and expertist assumptions that deny the value of people's experiential truths and knowledge claims. The experimental method becomes critical if hypotheses are plucked from the air, so to speak, where people have no idea what the effects of something would be (e.g. a novel chemical combination made by humans for the first time in a laboratory test tube), in contrast to a natural pharmaceutical such as aspirin which has been 'nature-made' and tried and tested by humans over hundreds of years, in naturally occurring biological ecosystems.

References

Campbell, D.T. and Stanley, J.C., (1963) 'Experimental and Quasi-Experimental Designs for Research on Teaching', in N.L. Gage (ed.), *Handbook of Research on Teaching*, Rand McNally, Chicago.

Cook, T.D., and Campbell, D.T. (1979) *Quasi-Experimentation—Design and Analysis Issues for Field Settings*, Rand McNally, Chicago.

Hawe, P., Degeling, D. and Hall, J. (1990) *Evaluating Health Promotion: A Health Worker's Guide*, MacLennan and Petty, Sydney.

Explication model

This approach tries to avoid the implication of 'judgement' (such as by an external 'objective' expert) that has often given evaluation a negative connotation. Instead, like **illuminative**, **naturalistic** and **constructivist** approaches, it tries—as the name implies—to understand and illuminate by means of clarification, **interpretation** and explanation. It draws on anthropology as a source of techniques such as on-site participant observation, and its key strength is that it may produce richer and more detailed descriptions of both practices and intentions. Its drawback lies in its fear of being evaluative (judgemental), which may mean being unable to produce at least some kind of value-driven comparative analysis (e.g. relative to critical reference groups' purposes or needs). **Constructivist/ constructionist** evaluation overcomes some of these difficulties by using an explication model, but also by shifting the locus of judgement from an independent 'objective' expert back to the participants in the evaluated phenomena.

References

Koppelman, K.L. (1983) 'The Explication Model: An Anthropological Approach to Program Evaluation', in George Madaus, Michael Scriven and Daniel F. Stufflebeam (eds), *Evaluation Models: Viewpoints on Educational and Human Services Evaluation*, Kluwer-Nijhoff, The Hague, pp. 59–64.

McDermott, Fiona and Pyett, Priscilla (1990) *The Meaning of Treatment: An Evaluation Handbook for Alcohol and Other Drug Treatment Agencies*, University of Melbourne, Melbourne.

Feminist evaluation/research

While feminist evaluation is not as strongly identifiable a stream within evaluation compared for example to empowerment evaluation or realistic evaluation, the impact of the women's movement and subsequent women's studies and even gender studies (where a feminist discourse has often been displaced) has arguably been profound as women insisted on bringing 'the personal' to 'the political', the experiential to assessing 'the facts', an ability to question and listen deeply, a preparedness to share and exchange diverse views and vulnerabilities, and the problematisation of and theorisation about men's greater power. In a way the whole of the emergence of the 'interpretive turn' and qualitative research and evaluation may be seen as owing much to the educational and workplace involvement of women in the 1970s and 80s.

Associated with this have been feminist contributions to **collaborative**, **illuminative**, and **responsive evaluation**, as well as to **theories of change** and decolonisation and empowerment projects as well as most other domains of evaluation.

Reference

Seigart, Denise and Brisolara, Sharon (eds) (2003) *Feminist Evaluation: Explorations and Experiences, New Directions for Evaluation*, no. 96, Jossey-Bass.

Financial Management Improvement Program (FMIP)

The FMIP was an influential Australian Commonwealth government budgetary *audit review* mechanism aimed at improving resource allocation decision-making in the 1980s and early 1990s. It was a highly rationalistic and comprehensive attempt to achieve performance evaluation of all programs, based on identified descriptions of objectives and activities with efficiency and/or effectiveness performance indicators, tied to resource usage. It involved several related mechanisms such as **program budgeting** and **management for results (MFR)**—an extension of **management by objectives** (MBO). One feature was the insertion of the expectation that new initiatives must be at the expense of old ones—thus involving apportioning-type prioritisation decisions. (This relates to the popularity, albeit contested, particularly in the health area, of QUALYS—a tool to assist this kind of evaluation activity.) It also involved the introduction of a 'user pays' principle—including where goods or services are exchanged between and within government departments—as a way of assisting managers to evaluate **costs** in relation to **benefits**. The greatest drawback for services from this kind of top-down audit review activity is that there can be a powerful rigidifying of services around a fixed set of objectives. Such an overwhelmingly rational-contractual effort can make it enormously difficult for change to take place in flexible response to communities. The ponderousness of any change to **program budgeting** categories attests to this, as does the lack of discretionary funding power when all items are 'tied down' for at least one full budget cycle. The greatest value is that, like all audit review evaluation, explicitly aware attention can be focused on the value of even the smallest backwater of activity—even if only in the simple and abstract form characteristic of most audit review approaches.

Reference
Linard, Keith (1988) 'Program Evaluation and Resource Management Improvement in the Commonwealth Public Service', paper presented to the National Evaluation Conference, Canberra.

Fishbowl

Fishbowl is still a very popular observational and feedback technique, and involves the simple idea of staging a 'two-ring circus'—with the inner circle comprising a group discussion watched by an outer circle. At a later point in time, the two groups can either swap places entirely or exchange either some members or their perceptions, or those in the outer circle can report on their observations of what the inner circle did. It is a way of organising active participation and silent observation that might be useful, for example, where new leads are being sought around an issue where some points of view are not otherwise getting a good hearing, or where alterative perspectives are not yet available. It depends a lot on the skills of those staging it and the purposes being served. A later technique, called **world café**, has some things in common with this in terms of a sequence of exchanges to generate alternative viewpoints.

Reference
Education Department of Victoria (1985) 'Fishbowl', in *Destination Decisions*, Curriculum Branch, Education Department of Victoria, Melbourne, p. 83.

Force-field analysis

This technique addresses the old maxim 'We act, but not under conditions of our own choosing'! It involves the written-down description of all the 'forces' or social conditions that are *for* the desired action, practice or change on one side of the page, and then all the 'forces' or barriers or conditions *against* it on the other side of the page. The lists may not be the same length—some 'forces' are stronger than others. (This could be denoted in some way.) **Brainstorming** could be used to produce the lists. Again, some of the 'forces' may not immediately be obvious and the connections might only be made later. This kind of technique is useful at the point in the evaluation research cycle when questions such as, 'Why have our valued worlds not come to replace our actual worlds?'

or 'Why have our actual worlds not metamorphosed into our valued worlds?' have arisen. It is also useful at the point of the cycle where possible future options are being evaluated in order to settle on a recommended new course of action. Once the forces have been described, these descriptions could be researched to understand them in more detail (for example, not just mentioning 'professional power', but designating exactly the elements of professional ideas or practices that might work 'for' or 'against' a desired change), or to check their strength. It can be a drawback if the 'forces' are only superficially explored and 'obvious', but less effective solutions are opted for instead of hard to imagine but more informed solutions.

Reference
Education Department of Victoria (1985) 'Force Field Analysis', in *Destination Decisions*, Curriculum Branch, Education Department of Victoria, Melbourne, pp. 53–62.

Foresight

(*See* **Scenarios**)

Formative evaluation

Michael Scriven's influential conceptualisation of evaluation as **formative** (or **summative**) has now become standard in evaluation. The concepts are often seen as two kinds of evaluation, but in practice they designate two moments and functions (and audiences) of evaluation: formative is for *improvement* or while an evaluand is still developing, while summative is more for decision about the fate of a program at some point of closure or 'afterwards'. Both are essentially performed for decision-makers—but 'formative' is more for local practitioners or managers to know how an evaluand is unfolding or being implemented, while 'summative' is carried out so managers can inform funders or others more distant from operation. Thus Scriven saw evaluation for formative purposes as logically subservient to evaluation for summative purposes— indeed, as 'early-warning summative'—and ideally done by an independent evaluator, although it is common practice for formative evaluation to be done internally and summative externally. Formative evaluation is more likely to be ongoing, or of a monitoring nature, with continuous feedback to amend and improve a service or activity. It may focus on inputs and throughputs, although it would be difficult to do without some attention to effects.

Formative evaluation is not necessarily equivalent to **process evaluation** or to implementation evaluation or progress reporting (nor is summative evaluation necessarily equatable with **outcome** or **output evaluation**). Evaluation for formative purposes *may* study outputs and outcomes *to date*, while evaluation for summative purposes may give an account of process, and be unable to report on outputs or outcomes at that point in time.

In practice, these distinctions may be lost, and formative, developmental and open inquiry evaluation may be seen as similar, and summative and audit review also seen as equatable. In, *Building in Research and Evaluation: Human Inquiry for Living Systems*, all these methodologies are seen as playing their part at different points in time when traversing full cycles of evaluative research from present practice through to development of new actions, and from implementing the new actions to them being refined as effective repeated practice.

Reference
Scriven, Michael (1981) *The Logic of Evaluation*, Edgepress, Inverness, CA.

Fuzzy set theory

This theory was developed in response to the phenomenon of so-called fuzzy goals. Rather than treat program staff's tolerance of intuitive and implicit (and possibly ambivalent, unclear, complex, emergent and divergent) goals as problematic, it sees it as more desirable that there be a variety of interests and perspectives in order for people to be able to get on with things. Unlike techniques such as **Delphi, multi-attribute utility measurement** and **decision-theoretic**, as well as all goals-based approaches, which all require a clear list of specific accurate and measurable goals at the outset, fuzzy set theory is an (albeit highly mathematical-quantitative) approach to understanding 'approximate reasoning'. Fuzzy goals (fuzzy decisions and fuzzy programs) can be accepted by evaluators by a kind of reverse estimation of goals from decision problems. **Goal-free evaluation** attempts to shift evaluation right out of reliance on *a priori* goals clarification.

References
Zadeh, Lofti (1965) 'Fuzzy Sets', *Inform and Control*, no. 8. pp. 338–53.

Zadeh, Lofti, Fu, King-sun, Tanaka, Kokichi and Shimura, Masamichi (eds) (1975) *Fuzzy Sets and Their Applications to Cognitive and Decision Processes*, Academic Press, New York.

GANTT schedules

When you read what this is, you will probably be surprised to find it is a Proper Technique with A Name! This horizontal set of bar charts will be familiar to many everyday planners. It works a little like **PERT** as a mild **critical path**-like framework for evaluating (audit reviewing) progress where several (or many) people are sequentially or correspondingly accomplishing activities between which there are logical or chronological links (e.g. one task needs to be completed before another, or several tasks can be carried out at the same time). Unlike PERT, it does not actually show the links between activities. The typical annual organisational calendar, a staff holiday leave schedule or a volunteers' roster are all examples. A GANTT chart for the Action Research Issues Centre's projects might look as illustrated.

	Jan	Feb	Mar	Apr	May	Jun	Jul	Aug	Sept	Oct	Nov	Dec	M T W T F
Books, articles, brochures (SJSA)													M T W T F
Workshops, courses (SJSB)													M T W T F
Networks (FOPAR, TOPAR etc.)													M T W T F
Assistance, consultancy, referral													M T W T F
Special consumer evaluation projects													M T W T F
Research ideas in community health project (RICH 2)													M T W T F
Consumer research bibliography (PNRDC)													M T W T F
Staff annual leave													

GANTT PLANNING CHART FOR THE ACTION RESEARCH ISSUES CENTRE

Reference
Education Department of Victoria (1985) 'Critical Path', in *Destination Decisions*, Curriculum Branch, Education Department of Victoria, Melbourne, pp. 43–6.

Goal Attainment Scaling (GAS)

This approach, like the **well-formed outcome model**, was originally developed in the mental health area to assist clients and therapists or nurses to rate client achievement of goals on a matrix of 'behaviours'. In this technique, people's actions are classified into levels of outcomes from 'least likely' to 'expected' to 'best possible outcome'. Like all *audit review* approaches, its strength lies in making one's 'best guesses' conscious, and its weakness lies in treating these 'best guesses' as the 'right guesses'. It is helpful as a way of being conscious of what is being done (or not). But new *open inquiry* is needed to ask 'Why?', or 'What would be better goals?'

Reference
Kiresuk, T.J. (1973) 'Goal Attainment Scaling at a County Mental Health Service', *Evaluation*, Special Monograph No. 1, pp. 13–19.

Goal-based (or objective-based) evaluation

This is evaluation that *starts* by asking what were a person's, a service's or an activity's formal explicit, written-down, pre-framed, pre-agreed goals and/or objectives, then asks whether these have been fulfilled by the actions that were logically framed (theorised) to achieve them. Some believe this is not evaluation *per se*, but merely a checking exercise as value, merit, worth or significance cannot be reduced to whether goals were met (as the goals may no longer best express these). Nevertheless, it can form a useful framework for detecting discrepancies in implementation if the goals are known to still be of value. That is, they will be more likely to be useful if the prior phases of the inquiry research cycle were well done and there has been insignificant intervening change. Paradoxically, they will be more rigid and difficult to change as they become more and more refined. See sections in this book on the *audit review* approach to evaluation for further strengths and weaknesses (see also Diagram 3 and Guide 5). Related models and techniques include **management by objectives**, **program budgeting**, **PERT**, the **Discrepancy Evaluation Model**, **accreditation** and **PASSING**.

Reference
Most standard evaluation guides, texts and manuals produced by central agencies.

Goal-free evaluation

The preoccupation with evaluating against goals and objectives led Michael Scriven, among others, to propose a way of trying to avoid the associated difficulties of:
- the narrowness of program objectives' coverage
- missing seeing the unanticipated outcomes, which were often viewed as carrying negative connotations or as mere 'side-effects'—but which might actually represent crucial developments or change in the context (suggesting valuable new priorities)
- to avoid the so called 'contamination', 'tunnel vision' and 'perceptual biases' of the observer if the goals (particularly if laudable) are known and familiar, but unexpectedly channel thinking into unhelpful ruts.

While this approach may easily have lapsed into a naive inductivism (assuming that our perception is guided by no pre-formed ideas, hunches or theories) or that change is now so endemic it is no longer worth having even tentative goals, Scriven was clear that he was, in practice, evaluating 'actual effects' against a 'profile of demonstrated needs'.

However, needs statements are often produced in a form that implies some particular kinds of needs-meeting services, activities or programs (and hence informal 'objectives' and 'goals'), particularly when articulated by professional service providers. Scriven also talked of 'national needs' and a wider 'decision audience' of 'national policy formulators' who define needs, rather than those who actually have the needs. While this may free up the evaluator from local management or program staff's articulations, it does not appear to bring the evaluator closer to the life experiences of those assumed to have the needs. Unlike the approach of this book, which directs attention back to the specific, contextualised and concrete expression of needs by those who have them—the critical reference groups—Scriven appears to direct attention upwards to decision-makers or experts, or to broader abstract categories or principles that in practice are again the evaluator's judgement of these. If local service providers and their service-users were to be included, and encouraged to reflect on the services without immediate reference to formal goals and statements of logical outcomes, and examine effects *per se*, other than those intended, then this would be more like an open inquiry approach. In Scriven's version of the goal-free model, there is also ambivalence over the identity and role of the 'client'. While his approach has been called 'consumerist' rather than managerialist, he does appear to place the evaluation's point of reference outside and above that of actual individual consumers or even of their organisations and their more collective consumer perspective.

Reference
Scriven, Michael (1972) 'Pros and Cons About Goal-Free Evaluation', *Evaluation Comment: The Journal of Educational Evaluation Centre for the Study of Evaluation, UCLA*, vol. 3, no. 4, pp. 1–7.

Group self-evaluation (GSE)

Group self-evaluation incorporates the basic elements of **self-evaluation** but in an organised collective setting. It might be a group that wants to work together on exploring its members' individual self-evaluations (for example, those at a service staff meeting might regularly receive and respond to ideas from each other's self-evaluations), or it may be a team that together is providing a service and that comes together regularly to reflect collectively on joint efforts; or a small group of two to three people that meets, with members playing **critical friends** to each other to help clarify their own assumptions, purposes or the observed outcomes of their actions. While like self-evaluation in that group self-evaluation may be an exercise in looking at internal practices, it will generally also extend to reflection on the context and efforts of the practices of others—not in the sense of taking responsibility for what others are doing and giving them Good Advice, but rather in the sense of helping each other observe, reflect, question and understand the context and effects—both enabling and frustrating (see **force-field analysis**)—of their envisioned better practices. There are some important conditions for GSE to work well that align with Etienne Wenger's ideas about a 'community of practice' (1998):

- People must participate voluntarily. GSE cannot simply be mandated for reporting or audit review functions. If it is, then it will become group self-reporting (generally reporting in terms of objectives with a tendency to gloss over difficulties), and it will not function well for open inquiry evaluation and critical improvement purposes.
- The learning that takes place can be credited to the group, but the group should resist any tendency to 'close ranks' to compel individual members to learn particular things in particular ways. The technique for learning relies entirely on individuals swapping their experiences, and trusting and being trusted to ask sympathetic illuminative, appreciative or critical questions.

'Critical' does not mean criticism. A critical question takes the form of a query about the conditions for knowledge and action—why and how people came to know what they know and do as they do, and whether they experience discrepancies between their knowing and doing and their deeper purposes or values. It is essential that the route to current conviction and practice is retraced backwards, and useful questions asked to generate new conclusions and a different route forwards to new ways of knowing and doing. Secretly, you might be convinced that someone is spending a lot of their time doing some things that are unimportant, irrelevant or downright damaging. You suspend your own pre-formed conclusions in the spirit of sceptical science and go back to the start by asking the person what led them to do what they are doing. The forthcoming explanation can be further pursued by continuing to ask logic-seeking questions such as:

- And what led you to draw that conclusion?
- Where did those ideas come from?
- Did you have a lot of evidence for that?
- Why was that evidence so convincing for you?
- Where or when did you first start noticing that?
- What effects did you notice?
- Did that fully satisfy you?

This style of questioning helps each person to retrace their steps and possibly beat a new path in order to finish up in a place different from the current problematic one. People need to do this for themselves not just so they are truly committed to the new way of seeing, but also so their own life-world is enhanced and extended from 'where it is at' rather than someone else's life-world forming the basis for the conclusions about what to do. In fact, we all may have trouble 'doing as we are told'! This is because these are in effect *answers* at which others have arrived from the vantage point of *their* life-worlds. But we *may* benefit from others' *questions* if these can help us to think through our own inquiry processes. As the old Chinese proverb (slightly modified) goes:

What I am told—I forget.
What I read—I recall.
What I see—I remember.
What I do—I understand.

If the group includes no critical reference group members, then a further range of 'touching base' questions can be asked, such as:

- How did your students/clients/patients/community members feel about that?
- What signs did you pick up of their reactions?
- Were they the reactions you'd hoped for?
- What do you think would have worked better for them?
- What do you think *they* are seeking?
- What have they said about it so far?

The group can vary in terms of the size, formality, number of times it meets, and so on. It might be three other like-minded souls you trust to reveal something you feel very vulnerable about, or it might be five people including an outsider with a fresh perspective, or it might be ten people who include some of your greatest critics! It might be a one-off, or you might 'contract' to meet once a month for six months, or once a week for four weeks, or on an *ad hoc* basis whenever a member would like it.

GSE examines 'circumstance, action and consequence' in an active **participatory** and organised learning process. It is more like **action research** when members work together on a particular shared interest, with strong action learning elements when members use the group as a crucible or catalyst for discussing and problem-solving regarding their own evaluand. While GSE has been developed for professionals working together in human services provision, there is no necessity for the approach to be limited in these ways. Service users, self-help groups or 'slices' of mixed **collaborative** groups made up of providers and users could use GSE, which in essence is 'learning by doing'. Even groups of managers could use GSE, perhaps involving service providers and end-users to get a fresh handle on their own practices. Groups operate as 'learning communities', united around shared interests, organising around joint tasks, and with a sense of solidarity around a desire to question, understand, learn and develop. Group processes do, however, need to overcome, or work hard at overcoming, the non-**democratic** effects of any power imbalances among members.

References

Brown, Lynton (1988) *Group Self-evaluation: Learning for Improvement*, Victorian Ministry of Education, Melbourne.

Brown, Lynton (1990) *Group Self-evaluation: A Collection of Readings*, Victorian Ministry of Education, Melbourne.

Wenger, E. (1998) *Communities of Practice: Learning, Meaning and Identity (Learning in Doing: Social, Cognitive and Computational Perspectives)*, Cambridge University Press: New York.

Guttman-type scale

The following example illustrates this kind of scale that has a set of items which increase on a scale along an attribute such as difficulty or favourableness. If a respondent ticks item three, it is assumed that items one and two also apply. It may be seen that this kind of data would leave an audit review-style of evaluation without much idea as to what to do to bring about change to the situation, and this formed the basis for critique in the 1970s of this kind of survey method as covertly 'preserving the status quo':

1   Would you object to a person with a mental disability living in your community?
2   Would you object to a person with a mental disability working where you work?
3   Would you object to having lunch with a person with a mental disability at work?
4   Would you object to a person with a mental disability coming to your home for dinner?

5   Would you object to a person with a mental disability marrying a member of your family?

Most of the problems with these kinds of scales come about from either the statement being badly worded (or conceptualised) and the responses being too closed, irrelevant or otherwise incurring unwanted resistance by the person who is meant to choose from among them. Another problem of this kind of survey approach is that it can contribute to reifying opinions, ideas or situations that are undesirable from the value standpoint of some disadvantaged group. Evaluation itself is not value-free, and asking particular questions in particular ways does not merely 'capture' truth-for-its-own-sake but can actually shape, influence and increase the strength with which people may believe things that may be damaging to themselves or to others. Conventional **positivist** approaches are unable to evaluate their own part in reifying both desirable and undesirable situations. **Interpretive**, **critical** and **constructivist** approaches can take these matters into account.

Reference

Gottman, John and Clasen, Robert (1977) 'Troubleshooting Guide for Research and Evaluation', in F. Cox et al., *Tactics and Techniques of Community Practice*, F.E. Peacock, Itasca, IL, p. 372.

Hermeneutic evaluation

The term 'hermeneutic' has traditionally been used to describe the practice of Biblical exegesis—that is, what scholars do when they are trying to understand and **interpret** the stories and material of scripture in terms of the wider social, political and economic context within which they were written. In social science, it has come to refer to the task of trying to put forward an understanding of a social message by grasping the context from which it was sent. It implies that one cannot know or interpret the particular without knowing the whole (just as the whole can only be hermeneutically grasped by reference to the particular). For example, the value of one self-help health group's efforts may only make sense by reference both to its own past history and to the current and past practices of other self-help health groups, all self-help groups, the medical profession and its institutional forms, and the nature and level of community support for self-help groups. In turn, each of these other contexts may better be understood by reference to the activities and existence of that one particular self-help group. The concept of 'hermeneutic' captures the popular idea of 'a grain of sand being a microcosm of the universe'—with it being impossible to understand the universe fully unless the grain of sand is included. When 'living' societies are studied, we can talk of a double hermeneutic, whereby the 'study matter' can be contextualised by an observer, who can then review and alter that contextualisation themself.

Reference

Bauman, Zygmunt (1978) *Hermeneutics and Social Science*, Hutchinson, London.

Illuminative evaluation

This is another approach concerned with description, **interpretation** and understanding rather than with measurement, **quantification** and prediction. Malcolm Parlett and David Hamilton coined the term 'illuminative' to describe evaluation that takes account of the wider contexts in which programs (in their case, education programs) take place. It draws on social anthropology traditions, and was developed in response to the dominance of what they call the 'agricultural-botany' experimental tradition. The 'context' element of **Context, Input**, **Process**, **Product (CIPP)** attempts a similar task.

Reference
Parlett, Malcolm and Hamilton, David (1977), 'Evaluation as Illumination: A New Approach to the Study of Innovatory Programs', in David Hamilton et al. (eds), *Beyond the Numbers Game: A Reader in Educational Evaluation*, Macmillan, London, pp. 6–22.

Impact evaluation

Impact evaluation is another **systems** theory approach, but one that concentrates on the immediate effects of services or programs, often in terms of operational aims and objectives and principles. It differs from **outputs** and **outcomes**. An impact evaluation of this book project would check to see whether the books had been read and considered to be readable, understandable and applicable to people's worlds. (Outcomes evaluation moves to the next logical step of seeing what effects reading the book had.) Impact evaluation might seek evidence that people reported feeling more confident and able to imagine evaluating their activities. A narrow systems theory view, however, limits us to examining an active element 'impacting' on a passive recipient. A fuller picture would include a more interactive picture of the person making active choices to receive some messages rather than others, and point towards a more **interpretative**, cultural and **constructivist** approach. As well, a more contextual analysis might avoid the difficulties associated with presuming that effects relate to the interventions made. That is, the 'black box' between input and output requires illumination of the context well beyond the boundaries of the service system.

Indicators (and performance indicators)

Indicators are generally thought of as the observable *signs* we accept as meaning that someone or some service has done what was expected in terms of objectives or goals. They are now most often linked to **standards** programs, **service agreements**, **program budgeting**, and audit review approaches.

The metaphor of machine performance—drawn from industry—has been applied to the human services sector since the extension of the contractual business exchange model to all kinds of human activity previously characterised as charitable, gift or love relationship-based. The machine metaphor generated indicators in terms of mechanistic arrows-and-boxes linear causal **systems** approaches—for example, performance indicators for service or program objectives, for inputs (resources), for throughputs, activities and outputs (workloads and efficiency), and for impacts and outcomes (effects and effectiveness). The pressure to quantify 'performance' in this way led to a lot of services being evaluated according to what could be objectified, commodified and counted, rather than what were humanly meaningful signs of effectiveness over time, allowing for responsive development.

PERFORMANCE INDICATORS

Better indicators or signs are those developed 'bottom up' by asking service-users and providers, 'How would you know if this was a good service?' or 'What would be the signs for you of getting/giving a good service?'. The value of this approach is twofold: users and providers reflect usefully on what they are experiencing, and managers get grounded indicators that are more likely to inform them and reduce their uncertainty. Some of the community well-being or community capacity-building indicators are of this nature. Such indicators may not be quantitative, or may involve only modest quantification. At the service level this will be even more so, while at the managerial level all descriptive material (numerical and verbal) will be in much more summarised form (although there are currently popular attempts to recapture meaning through the telling of 'performance stories' in methods such as **most significant change**). It is often the case that the more 'grounded', meaningful, negotiated and high the quality of indicators, the less likely it is that they can be mass standardised for application to a lot of different services. Centralised program managers will always have to tolerate some level of crudity and abstraction for the sake of some kind of comparability. They should strive to remember that the indicators or performance measures on which they rely are a lot like 'reading Braille through a doona', and thus be tolerant of a certain level of uncertainty!

'Indicators of performance' may differ from 'signs of achievement', remembering that current activity objectives may not turn out to be either the only or the best ways of meeting critical reference groups' needs and achieving the desired outcomes. Performance indicators sometimes suffer also from having been developed 'top down', and hence often are rather abstract and depersonalised or even misplaced and distorting.

Performance indicators are frequently confused with performance targets, with the terms being used interchangeably. A performance indicator for community participation may be that service-users elect a committee of management for the service. A performance target might be that all such services have elected committees by a certain time.

References

Community Services of Victoria (1990) 'Guidelines for Developing Performance Indicators', policy paper, Community Services of Victoria, Melbourne.

Guthrie, Hugh (1988) *Performance Indicators in TAFE*, TAFE National Centre for Research and Development, Adelaide.

Mayo, Toni (1990) *Performance of Community Organisations*, NCOSS, Sydney.

Social Justice Strategy Unit (1988) 'Performance Indicators and the Social Justice Strategy: A Discussion Paper', Department of Premier and Cabinet, Victoria, Melbourne.

Wyatt, T.J. and Hall, P. (1987) 'Some Limitations on the Application of Performance Indicators in Public Sector Organisations', paper presented to the National Evaluation Conference, Canberra.

Indigenous evaluation

With connections to **development evaluation**, **feminist**, **consumer** and other critical reference group-driven forms of evaluation, the methodologies of evaluation have slowly been taken up by Indigenous communities, mostly to try to adapt them to be more culturally sensitive and less exploitative or reabusive. Most incorporate **qualitative**, **narrative**, **participatory** and **action research** approaches; however, the work of Linda Tuhiwai Smith, a Maori woman from Aotearoa New Zealand, broke new ground in her book *Decolonising Methodologies*.

Reference

Tuhiwai Smith, L. (1999), *Decolonising Methodologies: Research and Indigenous Peoples*, Zed Books and University of Otago Press, London and Dunedin.

Input evaluation

This was once a routine form of evaluation in the balmy days before the end of the post-war economic boom. Input evaluation focuses on checking that a program or service commences, or is supplied with at the outset, grants, funds, staff and facilities. In the past, the mere supply of 'inputs' was deemed sufficient evidence that a program or service was operating effectively. Indeed, if adequate inquiry had been conducted beforehand, and there was little change or need to revise the purposes, theory and logic of goals, objectives and outcomes, then this may well have been enough.

Ironically, an input focus is having a curious *de facto* revival in some parts of the world where there is no evaluation of the *effect* of even radical human services reduction and restructuring. Instead, services are seemingly deemed 'appropriate' and 'in place' if, for example, three (even if ineffectual) phone calls are made in an attempt to place someone needing care.

Interpretive evaluation

'Interpretive' approaches rest on understanding that the nature of what we are evaluating is not in and of itself good or bad, valuable or unworthy—but that these are *judgements* that are entirely relative to the standpoints and contexts of the people making them. That is, we are faced with a task of interpreting the meaning of people's views in the context of the rest of their own lives, just as they are doing the same regarding us. To accomplish these acts of interpretation more accurately, we must become more like anthropologists who 'go native', or else risk missing grasping the true cultural meanings—'true' relative to those whose meanings they are. In the coffee mug example at the beginning of this book, the value and meaning of the ceramic mug changes radically if it is to be a gift, *or* used at a picnic, *or* is 'really' an artwork symbolising human caring. This is also sometimes referred to as a **hermeneutic** or **constructivist** task, and is a major focus of **qualitative** evaluation.

References

Denzin, Norman (1970) *The Research Act in Sociology*, Butterworths, London.

Rabinow, Paul and Sullivan, William (eds) (1979) *Interpretive Social Science: A Reader*, University of California Press, Berkeley, CA.

Judicial evaluation model (JEM)

This technique, like the **adversary** model (which emphasises the trial-by-jury element), draws on certain features of the legal system, such as:
- formal judgement by a panel of peers or judges
- presentation of evidence (or submissions) for or against fixed positions
- cross-examination of witnesses.

It can—if it can overcome everyone's fears and anxieties about 'kangaroo courts'*— sharpen people's arguments and evidence by exposing them to critical questioning, reassuring everyone they've been heard. Both techniques rely on there being opposing 'sides' to be argued. They can work a lot like debating teams. If they are to have value in everyday settings, they need to tone down the formality and narrow rules governing the operation of the legal system, and build in a dialogic element so questions (and decisions) can be revisited

---

*   A 'court' held outside the rules of law, often to more quickly and summarily administer 'bush justice' (originally in Australia used to judge strike-breakers by their peers who were seeking fairer working conditions).

if new evidence, information about context or ideas come forward, allowing fixed positions and decisions to change. Interestingly the legal system has been influenced by the constructivist research and evaluation paradigm to include such a responsive or dialogic element, notably in community justice, reconciliation, and joint custody matters.

Reference

Popham, W. Jones and Carson, Dale (1983) 'Deep Dark Defects of the Adversary Evaluation Model', in George F. Madaus, Michael Scriven and Daniel L. Stufflebeam (eds) *Evaluation Models: Viewpoints on Educational and Human Services Evaluation,* Kluwer-Nijhoff, The Hague, pp. 205–14.

Likert scales

Using Likert scales is a way of forcing evaluative responses into selecting from predetermined categories that represent varying degrees of discrepancy. They are typically composed of a series of statements, followed by a scale of five possible responses (note that the layout is usually horizontal), as shown in the diagram.

School is fun (tick)	*or*	*School is*: (circle)	
☐ Strongly agree		Fun:	1
☐ Agree		Some fun:	2
☐ Neutral		Neither fun nor dull:	3
☐ Disagree		Sometimes dull:	4
☐ Strongly disagree		Dull:	5

This kind of scale is sometimes termed a 'semantic differential item scale'. If the statements and wording of the possible responses are appropriate and meaningful, these kinds of scale can have some value. Most of the problems with scales come about from either the statement being badly worded or poorly conceptualised, or the responses being too closed (reductionist) or irrelevant, and incurring either resistance or unwanted compliance (without feedback) from the person who is meant to choose from among them. See **Guttman-type scale** for other drawbacks of written scale items.

Reference

Gottman, John and Clasen, Robert (1977) 'Troubleshooting Guide for Research and Evaluation', in F. Cox et al., *Tactics and Techniques of Community Practice,* F.E. Peacock, Itasca, IL, p. 371.

Logic models, logical frameworks/logframe

(*See* **Theory of change**)

Management by objectives (MBO)

This managerial technique, as its name implies, evaluates activities or programs against pre-established policy objectives (an audit review approach). See Diagrams 2 and 3 and the section on audit review in Chapter 3 for the major strengths and weaknesses of this. See also **goal-based evaluation**, **Financial Management Improvement Program**, **management for results**, **program budgeting**.

Reference

Carroll, S.J. and Tosi, H.L. (1973) *Management by Objectives: Applications and Research*, Macmillan, New York.

Management for excellence

This involved a valuable shift in the 1990s from closed linear approaches to more open complexity-based and systemic assumptions about the need for constant innovation, staff involvement in creative problem-solving and inspirational leadership to meet the imperative need for superior customer service. These assumptions contrasted with traditional management's need to control subordinates, give directions, motivate through rewards and punishments, and centrally determine goals and measures for their achievement. Management for excellence involved ideas about developing a culture of feedback and responsiveness, commitment, vision and openness throughout an organisation, not just focusing on the top. The popular instances of bosses 'doing time' as a worker or being on an inquiry counter reflects an element of this approach in 'touching base' and being open to new insights. It was a forerunner of strengths-based, capacity-building and **appreciative inquiry**, which looked more systematically at what was working *well* (rather than not), and on what that meant for the end beneficiaries.

Reference

Peters, Tom (1990) *In Search of Excellence: Lessons from America's Best-Run Companies*, Harper and Row, Sydney.

Management for results (MFR)

This technique represented the next step after **management by objectives**, using a linear **systems** approach. It rests on having:
- a formal statement of fixed objectives (corporate plan) for every aspect of activity
- a formal policy for evaluating performance in these activities against objectives

- performance indicators, identified for the program's efficiency and effectiveness
- management information systems (MIS) to monitor program resource inputs, through-puts, outputs and outcomes
- a set of procedures for deciding on evaluation recommendations
- mechanisms for linking evaluation to the budget process
- a calendar cycle to ensure all programs are reviewed regularly
- a unit that is responsible for these MFR evaluation processes.

This captures many of the elements described in this book; however, the distinguishing features of MFR are its 'top-down' managerialist nature and the corresponding invisibility of involvement by those who provide or use the services, its potential rigidity (shared with all fixed objectives-based approaches with no mechanism for open inquiry and hence the possibility of change, development and improvement), its decontextualised linear assumptions, and its emphasis on management information systems comprising statistical computerised databases (without explicative benefit of verbal descriptive, interpretive and narrative information).

Nevertheless, it has performed a useful function in making explicit some of the logical assumptions of programs and their evaluation, and program logic, systemic and narrative methodologies have subsequently 'filled' out more of the complexity involved in 'going full cycle' with evaluative inquiry.

Reference
Linard, Keith (1988) 'Program Evaluation and Resource Management Improvement in the Commonwealth Public Service', paper presented to National Evaluation Conference, Canberra.

Most significant change (MSC) technique

A British evaluator, Rick Davies, developed this **narrative** technique in Bangladesh to explicate what was not being **illuminated** in complex rural development programs by counting and measurement-type indicators. An Australian, Jess Dart, consequently worked on it with Rick and it has since been extended to use in urban areas and by Western countries, including by agricultural, environmental, health, community and human services. The authors have generously placed the guidelines on open access on the internet (see reference below).

There are ten key steps, of which 4, 5, and 6 are seen as central by its creators: 1. *Starting/ raising interest* by champions and small groups and among stakeholders of those interested; 2. *Defining 'domains' of change* to be storied; 3. *Identifying timelines and frequency* of monitoring the changes in the domains; 4. *Collecting the stories* from those field staff and participants most directly involved; 5. *Selection* of the most significant of the stories by regional or central committees; 6. *Feedback* about this selection process back to the field staff and participants; 7. *Verification* of the stories by site visits; 8. *Quantification* either within the story or across sites; 9. *Meta-analysis* across sites for recurrent themes; and 10. *Revising* the MSC process as a result of the learning that has emerged.

The characteristic MSC open inquiry question is of the nature: 'During the last month, in your opinion what was the most significant change that took place in … (domain)?' The characteristic filtering or selection question is: 'From among all these significant changes, what do you think was the most significant change of all?' People are encouraged to report the evidence or rationale for why they make their choices, and this effectively assists conversations about what is valued. Then the stories told are analysed (reflected on) and filtered up the organisational hierarchies by a sequence of selection.

It is seen as a supplementary technique to standard monitoring and evaluation (M&E) compliance methods such as **logframes**, with an ability to focus on learning about *noticeable* (valued or unvalued) effects rather than just general *descriptive* observation for accountability.

Reference

Davies, Rick and Dart, Jess (2005) *The Most Significant Change (MSC) Technique: A Guide to Its Use*, self-published, <www.clearhorizon.com>.

Multi-attribute utility measurement

This is a **quantitative** technique developed to try to deal with conflict over goals (and hopefully also between the differing interests and values of groups that lie behind this conflict). Translated, this extravagantly named technique means in part that the evaluator provides separate information to each competing grouping in terms of their own values. Decision-makers eventually have access to research data on issues that may not be consistent with their own values, but are consistent with those of the other relevant groups. This sophisticated kind of intelligence relies on everyone contributing so they can then know precisely where the differences and similarities in values between them lie. An adaptation of this technique to evaluation is called the **decision-theoretic** approach.

Reference

Gardiner, Peter C. and Edwards, Ward (1975) 'Public Values: Multi-Attribute Utility Measurement for Social Decision Making', in Martin F. Kaplin and Steven Schwartz (eds), *Human Judgement and Decision Processes*, Academic Press, New York, pp. 1–38.

Narrative evaluation

The use of narrative or 'storying' emerged originally as part of the qualitative movement, and particularly in women's services where feminist analysis focused on 'changing the story' (including domestic violence, prisons, homelessness, drugs and alcohol, etc.) It has now become a mainstream method, although central agencies have paradoxical responses to it—both *wanting* these 'rich thick' stories of actual on-the-ground practice that **illumin-ate** and interpret qualitatively what is actually going on, and particularly what changes are being achieved over time, and also still reverting to seeing mass quantitative statistics as the basic data and somehow more 'real', objective and reliable. Yet we see repeated failures of elegantly simple top-down public policy that lack sufficient 'up close and personal' field knowledge about the complex **systemic** detail of people's lives to which these program logics are to apply. Large-scale engineering, whether of environmental change or socially engineered change, is a high-risk endeavour without detailed observation-based reflective, meaningful narrative to inform the cycles in which 'bigger picture' planning, rational imple-mentation and practical action take place.

Narrative evaluation action research (NEAR) is a methodology using narrative to achieve international public health policy for integrated health promotion and **most significant change** (MSC) is another such narrative methodology being used in rural development, environmental, health, community and human services settings. Both are well-known Australian evaluation award-winning methodologies.

References

Davies, Rick and Dart, Jess (2005) *The Most Significant Change (MSC) Technique: A Guide to Its Use*, self-published, available at <www.clearhorizon.com>.

Riessman, C.K. (2008) *Narrative Methods for the Human Sciences*, Sage, Newbury Park, CA.

Wadsworth, Yoland, Wilson, Gai and Wierenga, Ani, *Writing Narrative Action Evaluation Reports in Health Promotion: Guidelines, Resource Kit and Case Studies,* Victorian Department of Human Services and the University of Melbourne, Melbourne, available at <www.health.vic.gov.au/healthpromotion/steps/evaluation.htm#narrative>.

White, Michael (2007) *Maps of Narrative Practice*, W.W. Norton, New York.

Naturalistic inquiry (NI)

The title of this technique picks up some of the meaning of the word 'natural' in the sense of inquiring into what is usual, customary and unaffected, and some sense of the old-fashioned 'naturalist' being someone who is skilled in the observation of nature as found in its ecological habitats. That is, NI uses **qualitative** or 'grounded' designs that try not to artificially manipulate the phenomenon or its environment in the way of traditional experimental designs (testing theory in practice), and that proceed more inductively from trial and error (developing theory *from* practice and then trying it further in close relation to complex systemic real-life practice). As a discovery-oriented approach, it has much in common with the open inquiry approach described in this book. Like many of the other evaluation techniques described, it arose in reaction to the more mechanistic engineering approach of laboratory-based science. Indeed, the late Egon Guba and Yvonna Lincoln—its most important exponents—note that it represents a paradigm shift from rationalist and positivist science, which they argued had generated many unused and unusable findings. The table illustrates its underlying axioms in contrast to those of conventional science.

Forms of Inquiry

	Conventional Inquiry	Naturalistic Inquiry
Philosophical base	Logical positivism	Phenomenology
Inquiry paradigm	Experimental physics	Ethnography; investigative journalism
Purpose	Verification	Discovery
Stance	Reductionist	Expansionist
Framework/design	Preordinate/fixed	Emergent variable
Style	Intervention	Selection
Reality manifold	Singular	Multiple
Value structure	Singular	Pluralistic
Setting	Laboratory	Nature
Contest	Unrelated	Relevant
Conditions	Controlled	Invited interference
Treatment	Stable	Variable
Scope	Molecular	Molar
Methods	Objective – in sense of factual/confirmable	Objective – in sense of inter-subjective agreement

Naturalistic Inquiry (Guba, Egon: 1978)

Guba and Lincoln also developed criteria to assist in what they call the 'assurance of trustworthiness' of findings (in contrast to conventional science's concern with reliability and validity). Thus, in contrast to rationalistic concerns about universal truth, validity, applicability, consistency and neutrality, NI's concerns are with credibility, transferability, dependability and confirmability. They suggest a number of techniques to ensure this. Guba and Lincoln carried their work a further step forward with the publication of their book on fourth-generation evaluation, or **constructivist** methodology.

References

Guba, Egon G. (1978) *Toward a Methodology for Naturalistic Inquiry in Educational Evaluation*, Centre for the Study of Evaluation (CSE), University of California, Berkeley, CA.

Guba, Egon and Lincoln, Yvonna S. (2000) 'Epistemological and Methodological Bases for Naturalistic Inquiry', in D.L. Stufflebeam, George F. Madaus and T. Kellaghan (eds), *Evaluation Models: Viewpoints on Educational and Human Services Evaluation*, 2nd ed., Kluwer-Nijhof, Dortrecht.

Neuro Linguistic Programming (NLP)

Developed by Richard Bandler and John Grinder, this approach to understanding the structure of human behaviour has been used as a training and development tool, as well as a therapeutic technique. It is based on the work of behaviourist Milton Erikson and the linguistic model of Noam Chomsky. Some of its basic assumptions, which make it relevant to the field of evaluation, are:

- People construct their responses to the world via mental models or 'maps' of the world.
- These models or 'maps' code or filter meanings (including matters of merit, worth, value and significance), and are grounded in people's neurological responses.
- In this way, the individual's mind and body work together in cybernetic (iterative energy feedback) loops—as, by extension, does the social 'mind' and body politic.
- Meaning and value therefore lie less in what people (or social organisations) say or mean than in the sense made of it by those who hear or receive the messages. Meaning is therefore not obvious and unproblematic, but must be discussed, clarified, negotiated and agreed.
- 'Good practice' or 'bad practice', 'success' and 'failure' therefore become 'mere' feedback for future action, behaviour and practice.
- Change takes place by the person (or social grouping) changing their own systemic behaviour to another pattern of action in the light of this feedback. One of the catch-phrases of NLP is 'Act as if . . .'
  See also **well-formed outcome model** and **constructivist evaluation**.

Reference
Bandler, R. and Grinder, J. (1975) *The Structure of Magic*, Science and Behaviour Books, Palo Alto, CA.

On-site analysis (OSA)

This was a technique developed by Bob Myers in the 1980s, drawing on business manage-ment approaches to personnel, resources, time management, budgets and organisational development, and assumptions about the unit measurability of human services perfor-mance. It involved an external paid consultant facilitator trained in the technique (developed by a Canadian fundraising organisation) coming into the service for one week and, via a thirteen-step process with management, staff and possibly volunteers, consumers and some other external peers:

- gathering participants' perceptions and looking at various statistical measurements (e.g. how many clients are being seen a day), which might be discrepant with expecta-tions or objectives (for example, social workers think they should be seeing more clients each day)
- identifying the 'problems' (e.g. clients' appointment cancellations)

- generating a solution (e.g. scheduling more appointments so social workers are seeing more clients after the cancellations), and
- making a public presentation to key outsiders of a final report at the end of the five-and-a-half day session.

There is a one day follow up after twelve months.

The two chief values of OSA lie firstly in it being conducted 'on site' in collaboration with staff (thus using some of the insights of **interpretive**, **hermeneutic**, **phenomenological**, **democratic**, **collaborative** or anthropological research), and secondly in it involving the fresh perception of a sympathetic outside consultant who might more quickly problematise and challenge a situation that has been more or less tolerated, perhaps for too long.

Its chief drawbacks are its reliance on:

- the outsider's selective interpretation of the statistical 'facts' (and particularly on that person's level of critical experience) to problematise what program participants had previously 'not noticed'—rather than, for example, training insiders to develop reflective skills about the meanings of their own records
- the apparent revelatory power of 'the numbers' (the technique privileges numerical 'facts' over verbal 'perceptions')
- its necessarily superficial approach to context and history, given its short timeframe.

For example, a consumer perspective, plus the depth of a more open inquiry approach, might provoke asking, in the example given above, *why* it was that clients broke their appointments. That is, pursue lines of inquiry that would lead to a different kind of service being seen as valuable rather than tinkering with more of the same, and risking doing so for a select group of clients (those who can tolerate a well-ordered professional appointment system). On-site analysis makes a laudable attempt to start by observing and gaining consensus around organisation values; however, in just one week, it is not clear how the limits to consensus (entrenched power and authority relations, etc.) can be overcome. Carried out in somewhat comparable ways are systematic review **standards program** techniques like CHASP and **PASSING**.

Reference

Myers, R.J., Ufford, Peter and Magill, M.S. (1988) *On Site Analysis: A Practical Approach to Organisational Change*, OSCA Ltd, Ontario, Canada.

Open space technology

This is a facilitated but otherwise largely self-organising conference about a main theme or topic in which all attendees have an interest. It operates a little like a marketplace, in which different people set up their 'stalls' or tables, with aids to help explain and share information about the sub-issue or sub-theme (e.g. whiteboard, poster-board, flip chart and circle of chairs for self-selecting participants). After an initial plenary briefing in which attendees who want to create sub-theme 'stalls' or workshops, discussion groups or task groups 'spruik' by speaking briefly to their theme or interests, the rest of the attendees are then free to assemble at the 'stall' about which they want to hear more to which they wish to contribute. All are encouraged in the first place to let go of outcomes, welcome the unexpected, and move freely between stalls once their interest is quenched at one. All continue to move around the stall sessions where they can actively learn or contribute until a point of saturation is reached and people may be ready to move to a now well-informed deliberation on either discerning overall conclusions, or pursuing a unified plan.

The method allows otherwise hidden issues or unknown information to emerge and be shared or dealt with, and also ensures that any topic raised will have someone to deal with it. It is not the best method for controlling or ensuring outcomes. However, for its high levels of involvement, shared exploration and self-organisation, it has become a runaway success and elements of it are now in use at many conferences or within evaluation processes.

There are now numerous variations—for example, a list of issues may be assembled in advance and then the assembly 'votes with its feet' as to whether any of them get spruiked or even attended/taken up. Or a list of names and contacts is taken in each sub-group and they remeet iteratively over subsequent days or weeks until there is an outcome or closure.

Reference
Owen, Harrison (1997) *Open Space: Open Space Technology: A User's Guide,* Berrett-Koehler, San Francisco.

Optional Proportional System

See Wadsworth, Yoland (2011) *Do It Yourself Social Research,* 3rd ed., Allen & Unwin, Sydney.

Organisational development (OD)/learning organisation (LO)

These are processes that, at their most enlightened, come very close to an **action research** evaluation model with both **reflexive** and **participatory**, or at the very least **collaborative**, elements, but on an organisation-wide scale. At their best, they involve staff development activities that are designed to enhance staff's self-awareness of what they are doing, and why they are doing it—in the context of consensus-building or generative thinking around forming organisational goals. However, in the current context, it often also refers to 'top-down' corporate restructuring of management into flatter but tighter structures, combined with program budgeting, implementation of corporate plans, computerisation and conventional staff retraining. Its corporate structural 'home' is usually nowadays the Human Resources Department rather than the Research and Development or Evaluation support unit.

Activities may be oriented towards increasing efficiency, and central command and control, rather than increasing 'grounded' quality and effectiveness and a diffused organisation of enthusiastic self-starters. Peter Senge has taken the concept further with the encouragement of 'systems thinking' (in the sense of interdependent feedback loops) in his 1990 book about learning organisations and its companion handbook.

References

Australian Taxation Office (1990) *People Action: A Plan for Human Resource Development*, The Human Resource Development Unit, Melbourne.

Senge, Peter (1990) *The Fifth Discipline: The Art and Practice of the Learning Organisation*, Doubleday Currency, New York.

Other government audit review mechanisms

Besides traditional internal accounting audits, governments use a range of evaluative mechanisms that are 'external' to the section of the government being reviewed. These include Royal Commissions, Committees of Inquiry, ministerial consultants, statutory inquiry bodies, management performance reviews (often investigated by Public Service Boards), the work of the Auditor-General's office, Parliamentary Committees of Inquiry and interdepartmental task forces. Some of these use quasi-judicial approaches; others might use approaches verging towards open inquiry. Primarily, though, they involve audit review methods.

Reference

Linard, Keith (1998) 'Program Evaluation and Resource Management Improvement in the Commonwealth Public Service' Paper to National Evaluation Conference, Canberra.

Outcomes evaluation

This **systems** theory element focuses on the longer-term effects of services or programs in terms of the broader goals or philosophical mission statements. Over the last few decades, we have seen service evaluation move from being **inputs-**based ('Did you receive the funding?') to **objectives-**based ('Do you know what you wanted to do with the funding?') to **process** (**formative** or throughputs)-based ('What did you do and how did you do it?') to **outputs-**based ('How many units of 'doing something' did you produce?') to **outcomes** ('Did it have the desired effects on or for people?'). An *audit review* outcomes evaluation of this book project would try to find evidence that the use of the book was related to an increase in people's own actual evaluative activity. Evidence and actual evaluation reports produced by groups that 'touched base' with critical reference groups would be sought. An *open inquiry* outcomes evaluation might ask 'What were the outcomes? (whether related to goals or not) and 'What was the value of these outcomes?' Asking questions about outcomes expands evaluation to examine matters that 'escape' being part of the 'system' under study. Jess Dart has developed a Participatory Performance Story Reporting (PPSR) technique for describing how a program has contributed to outcomes. A performance story report results from looking at written material, interviewing and consulting experts in a participatory dialogue that culminates in a decision-making 'summit' meeting. It includes a 'results' chart linking the program logic with evidence to tell the story of how activity has contributed to meeting long-term goals.

Output evaluation

This is another **systems** theory element that concentrates on the more immediate 'products' of services or programs. It identifies whether these intended or expected tangibles actually were forthcoming or produced. An audit review output evaluation of this book project, for example, would check to see whether the books were actually printed, delivered, published and available. An open inquiry evaluation might expand the evaluation by asking 'What were the outputs?' and 'What was the value of these outputs?', possibly beyond the written-down expectations or intentions.

Participatory evaluation

This again refers to the inclusion of some or all the parties to an evaluation (as does **collaborative** and **stakeholder evaluation**). Like collaborative evaluation, this can mean a pluralist kind of participation. Both these terms arose in reaction to the once-dominant form of evaluation that was conducted entirely by the external 'objective' expert using an old-paradigm form of objectifying science. The experience of being disempowered in the evaluation evidence-gathering process was felt by those most disempowered: service providers at the level closest to 'the ground', advocates of service-users and service-users themselves. The forms of participation were usefully conceptualised by Sherry Arnstein in a now-classical formulation involving a hierarchy of possibilities. I have matched these to a hierarchy of possible forms of participation in evaluation in the table below.

LEVEL OF POWER	MODELS OF COMMUNITY PARTICIPATION	RELEVANT MODELS OF EVALUATION
DEGREES OF CITIZEN POWER	CITIZEN CONTROL	Critical self-evaluation or action research, reflexive, self-organising
	DELEGATED POWER PARTNERSHIP	Responsive, participatory Collaborative, cooperative
DEGREES OF TOKENISM	PLACATION CONSULTATION INFORMING	Stakeholder (representative) Democratic Consultation, surveys Top-down feedback, Bureaucratic
NON-PARTICIPATION	THERAPY MANIPULATION	Depth interpretivism Controlled experimental, Autocratic

References

Arnstein, Sherry (1969) 'Ladder of Citizen Participation', *American Institute of Planners Journal*, July, pp. 216–24.

Whyte, William Foote (ed.) (1991) *Participatory Action Research*, Sage, London.

PASSING technique

'PASSING' is an acronym for Program Analysis of Service Systems' Implementation of Normalisation Goals. It is a sophisticated approach to evaluating services that are for people who have hitherto stigmatised characteristics but who are wanting to move (or are meant to be moving) towards integration and normalisation in mainstream community life. It became standard in the late 1970s and 1980s and then fell out of fashion; however, it is currently experiencing a resurgence after the institutionalisation of client-focused services in legislation and individualised funding have renewed interest in facilitating mainstream living for clients.

PASSING comprises a handbook, field manual and criteria ratings book, and involves a certified training program before it can be used (although the written materials are available in some libraries).

It is based on symbolic interactionism and role theory, and after 30 years of development, it represents a highly refined **standards program** audit review technique, but one which was built from the bottom up from very detailed consumer-perspective observation and judgement. It is designed to identify where services deviate from normal settings and normal interaction (in terms of 42 different characteristics) and to what extent (in terms of five different levels). It examines the physical settings of services, the nature of the relationships between staff and service-users, activities, language, symbols and images used. A residential service for the elderly would, for example, rate poorly if people were left wearing nightclothes all day, if it was named 'Sundowners' Home', if residents were called 'kids', carried around soft toys, were tied into chairs, or routinely had their first names only or children's cartoon images on their bedroom doors.

As in most **accreditation** programs, PASSING reviewers conduct tours of the facilities and neighbourhood, interview staff and clients, and draw on documentary materials. Like all highly refined audit review techniques, PASSING's strengths—such as the level and accuracy of meaningful detail, the rigour and discipline, the reliability of its items—and its sheer comprehensiveness—are the other side of the coin of its potential weaknesses—such as inflexibility (e.g. if an elderly individual chooses to have a children's toy) and contextually relative validity. The apparently objectivist nature of the ratings exercises may also disguise the subjectivism of the value-driven interpretation required to make the evaluative judgements on a five-point scale. As well, improvement still requires movement into an *open inquiry* evaluation mode if people are to understand why they are or are not doing the best thing, what to do instead, and how to get from where they are now to where they could be.

An open inquiry evaluation is also required if any of the PASSING ratings items themselves are to be subjected to critique or change. For example, if an element of normative mainstream life is sexist or ageist, should PASSING uncritically seek to reproduce such 'normality'? Or if the meaning of soft toys to adults turns out to be that they are a compensation for deprivation of physical intimacy, what is the value of merely removing them in order to rate well on a PASSING item, and in the absence of addressing the needs for loving intimacy? This raises the question of the needs assessment that lies at the core of each item. Within a purely audit review approach, such as PASSING, there is not always 'built in' a point of entry to re-evaluate the evaluation criteria against critical reference groups' own formulation and reformulation of their needs. However, PASSING remains a good model for this audit phase of the evaluation cycle, and new policies against social exclusion are revisiting the detail of what is excluded from people's lives, underpinning the revival of interests in PASSING.

Reference
Wolfensberger, Wolf and Thomas, Susan (1983) *PASSING Program Analysis of Service Systems' Implementation of Normalization Goals*: Normalization Criteria and Ratings Manual, 2nd ed. National Institute on Mental Retardation, Toronto.

Peer review

This is evaluation by peers—generally by and among fellow professionals. Peer review is a major ideological 'promise' by the professions. Professionals promise 'to do the right thing' and keep each other in line in exchange for autonomous control over their practices and rewards for service (such as high incomes). Negative peer review evaluations unfortunately can range from the career-ending (such as anonymous reviews for grant applications or journal publication) through to a barely audible 'tut tut' for malpractice. The strengths of peer review lie where there is genuine collaborative intention to raise standards or correct directions so as to better meet clients' needs (such as through **standards programs** like CHASP in community health, or **PASSING** in the disability area). The weaknesses lie where the separate class interests of professionals as professionals override these and lead to weak evaluative effort and a 'closing of ranks' against external criticism (well documented by Michael Scriven in his stinging description of the 'Country Club Model of Institutional Evaluation', reference cited below).

Reference
Scriven, Michael (1981) *The Logic of Evaluation*, Edgepress, Inverness, CA, pp. 105–13.

Performance indicators (PIs)

(*See* **Indicators**)

PERT (Program Evaluation and Review Technique)

(*See also* **Critical path analysis**)

PERT is a form of **critical path analysis** that introduced some useful features to the more traditional **GANTT** schedule. It comprises a timeline diagram of a network of activities and events that must occur before an end objective is reached. It is kind of like a roadmap between points A (start) and B (finish), which can be used so everyone knows who is to do what and when. This saves delays and confusions as people say 'I was waiting for you to . . .' PERT is systems thinking modelling, making connections between more or less sequential activities to aid foresightful planning, and hoping to bring order and clarity, as well as a reduction in uncertainty and complexity. This works exactly to the extent the world is also able to be more orderly, certain and simple! It is credited with shortening the US Polaris missile program by two years—so any of you designing the implementation of programs on this scale should find it particularly useful). Difficulties are in predicting, in advance, the time needed for each task, and also in ensuring flexibility if it turns out that some other tasks can best (and safely) be done before others, while it turns out others will have to be contingent on activities not previously thought to be so, or unexpected events or unknown contexts. A PERT chart might look like that illustrated below (Source: *Destination: Decisions*, 1985).

Program Evaluation and Review Technique (PERT)

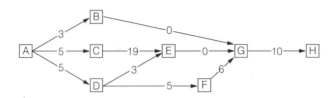

Critical path charts are presented according to the following simple rules:
• Work items or tasks are placed in boxes.
• Arrows show which tasks lead to or follow on from others.
• Numbers show how long each task is expected to take.
   Actual dates for beginning and completing a task can also be written in.
   In the example given in the diagram, task H cannot begin until task G is finished. Task G is expected to take ten days. Task G cannot begin until tasks B, E and F are completed, and so on. The longest path in terms of days is the A–C–E–G–H path, which will take 34 days. This is the *critical* path. No delays can be permitted if the project is to be completed on time. On the other hand, path A–B–G–H totals only thirteen days. Task B could begin as late as 21 days after work on task C has begun and still feed into task G on time.

References
Education Department of Victoria (1985) 'Critical Path' in *Destination: Decisions*, Curriculum Branch, Chapter 7, pp. 43–6.

Hoffer, Joe R. (1977) 'PERT: A Tool for Managers of Human Service Programs' in F. Cox et al., *Tactics and Techniques of Community Practice*, F.E. Peacock, Itasca, pp. 287–98.

Phenomenology

Phenomenology, like **naturalistic**, Verstehen or **interpretive** approaches, refers to a methodology (originally developed by Edmund Hussel and popularised by Alfred Schutz) for grasping the meaning of everyday social life by studying events, activities and practice as they are experienced and perceived. It focuses on the business of interpreting individuals' meanings as well as the intersubjective construction of those meanings through their relationships and reactions to life.

Reference
Schutz, Alfred (1972) *The Phenomenology of the Social World*, Heinemann, London.

Positive evaluation

This was a new non-patented, non-copyrighted technique that anyone could practise that I invented in the late 1980s as a result of observing countless instances of evaluations that produced reports concentrating on All The Things That Are A Problem! You know the sort of thing—page after page of negative conclusions about what is wrong—then at the end, either a conclusion that 'more research is needed', or a giant leap to recommendations that appear to have little to do with the rest of the report but seem like good ways to go, and which are rarely enacted! Now, negative evaluation conclusions may be a necessary stage in realistic evaluation, as they are a critical way people are alerted to inquire to improve Things Going Wrong. However, this humble new approach (which shouldn't really be graced with the title of a model or technique, although it subsequently has been—and to great effect as **appreciative inquiry** and strengths-based approaches), is more of a plea that we spend some time examining the Things That Have Gone Right as a source of ideas and visions for other Things That Might Also Go Right in future. Whenever we look at recommendations for new practice, they pretty much always stem from the evaluator making a theoretical leap from 'how things are now' to imagining ways (or remembering instances) that might theoretically address the conditions *missing* in the current worlds-before-our-noses. **Brainstorming** solutions or desirable **scenarios**, or creative visualisation, might give some leads out of negative evaluation. The knack is to shift from a picture of 'what is' to a picture of 'what is the best that could be'. Positive evaluation can contribute to this.

Positivist evaluation

'Positivist' is a term that is now often used in a pejorative sense to describe the fundamental philosophy of once hegemonic conventional or traditional science. This conventional view of science rests on two key assumptions.

Positivist philosophy firstly holds that the subject-matter of science (or research or evaluation) is independent of the observer (or the researcher or evaluator). That is, that there is a single, real, true, factual world 'out there' that is knowable separately from the knower. Hence the observer (or scientist) should strive to capture this truth objectively without bias or contamination, and this should be achieved by remaining separate, impersonal and uninvolved. (The observed person or people can also be seen as biased and contaminated in their own opinions or views, and thus these should be avoided. Unobtrusive or laboratory research is seen as exemplary, so the researched are either not even aware of the study or the researcher's hypotheses or are held at a cool arm's length to enable manipulation of the variables.)

The **interpretive**, **naturalistic**, **qualitative** or **constructivist** critique says that this is a largely inappropriate, distorting, unachievable or unhelpful science for the human world, in which subjective *and* objective meanings are socially constructed and negotiated, and multiple realities are characteristic of all human societies. To try to avoid this is to risk missing out on deeply understanding human phenomena. (Interestingly, modern physics makes the same arguments about the natural world—for example, relativity theory, the uncertainty principle, etc.)

The second assumption of positivist philosophy, is closely related to the first. It holds that the reasons for pursuing science (or research or evaluation) reflect no particular valued purposes but ideally derive from mere curiosity for its own sake. Indeed, to admit to reasons or purposes other than intellectual disinterested curiosity is, in this view, to risk biasing and contaminating inquiry with values or interests. Inquiry seeks only to know the truth of 'what is'. Values about 'oughts' are supplied later by users of the otherwise neutral information. (Hence scientific researchers or evaluators have no logical responsibility for the use of their work—nor need to select morally defensible topics in the first place.)

The critical interpretive or value-interested critique says that the purposes of science, research or evaluation *always* derive in some way from the values and interests of those whose situation gives rise to the inquiry in the first place. Even 'idle curiosity' is curious about some things and not others (interestingly, most science is conducted for military purposes), and all inquiry is necessarily impactful in the world, even if the observer has a sense or feeling of being detached. That is, all inquiry is inspired by some discrepancy between an experienced and an expected state, and this sense of discrepancy is always charged with a 'valuation', whether small or large, conscious or not conscious. Hence, all knowledge is in some way 'interested'. Far from being value laden, all research, science or evaluation is essentially *value driven*, and the best way to avoid error or 'getting it wrong' for the purposes at hand is to be critically questioning or sceptical about one's own reasons and thus questions, answers, conclusions and grounds for knowing until competing explanations can be answered, or refuting evidence explained. Hence researchers and evaluators, once aware that their work will be in 'some interests and not in others', must choose as best they can 'whose side (or sides) they are on'—or what the purposes of the domains they want to study might be, and consciously and self-sceptically focus attention on developing the best and best-evidenced theory possible. Got that? Sorry—it's a bit hard getting 400 years of philosophy of science into a couple of paragraphs!

References

Bryman, Alan (1988) *Quantity and Quality in Social Research*, Unwin Hyman, London.

Fay, Brian (1975) *Social Theory and Political Practice*, George Allen & Unwin, London.

Process evaluation, process indicators

Sometimes mistakenly called 'performance evaluation' or 'performance assessment', this is evaluation that concentrates on what is done 'within' a service or program: the activities, who does what with whom, and other matters of implementation. It is the often-unexplained 'black box' in a **systems** theory approach to evaluation. An audit review process evaluation of this book project would check to see whether the management committee met, whether the writer produced drafts, whether discussions were held about the ideas and content, whether files of material were collected, and so on. An open inquiry process evaluation may ask 'What happened?' and 'How did things unfold?' 'What was done?' and 'Why?' and 'What was its value?' This may take the evaluation beyond a systems approach into considering a range of unintended and unexpected events, contexts, needs, conflicts, negotiations, and so on that, for example, could call into question the original goals or objectives intended to determine the process. This more dynamic feedback approach would begin to break down the artificiality of separating systems components. For example, early feedback regarding effects (or even imagined effects) could alter 'inputs' and other 'processes'. Cybernetic feedback to 'steer' more effectively towards valued points on the horizon may be a better way to conceptualise this.

Program budgeting (PPBS)

Program budgeting and its more ambitious version, the Planning Programming Budgeting System (developed in the US Department of Defence), are variants of cost-effectiveness analysis and performance budgeting, and hence are approaches to evaluating the spending of money in relation to objectives. This continues to be a major passion of Western governments—and it has been ever since the late 1970s and late 1980s recessions. It is a management tool designed to both contain spending within boundaries and tighten awareness of spending relative to other spending within a department. Relativities are able to be identified by linking budgets to goals and objectives in a hierarchy of programs that are broken down into sub-programs and components. (Previously, budgeting had been by line item spending categories such as recurrent costs, salaries, capital costs, equipment, and so on). Program budgeting enables some crude but useful descriptions of the world to become more obvious. For example, if objectives are related to the provision of more health promotion or prevention services, it could easily be seen that there is a huge imbalance in spending, with the vast majority of money going to ill-health hospital treatment. Or if policy wished to devote more attention to women's and child-care services, the evidence from program budgeting could indicate where a shift in resources was needed. On the other hand, the approach breaks down when objectives start to be altered to match the budget reality (for example, implementation of policy may now be 'over time'; or when waiting list reduction policy gets converted into more-money-for-hospitals instead of, for example, more-money-to-retrain doctors to work in community-based preventive practice). The technique uses an audit review approach.

Reference
Victorian Government (1984) *Program Budgeting 1983–1984*, Victorian Government Printer, Melbourne.

Program logic, logical frameworks/logframes

(*See* **Theory of change**)

Qualitative evaluation

This term has come to be applied to various streams of evaluation that otherwise might be called **interpretive, phenomenological, naturalistic, hermeneutic**, grounded, anthropological, inductive, experiential, symbolic interactionist, emergent, field-based or responsive. The naming of all these meaning-making methods as 'qualitative' has much more to do with a reaction to the historic dominance of measurement-oriented **quantitative evaluation**, and a kind of multi-methods truce to the 'paradigm wars' has been reached in a current insistence that you must always have both. The primary flaw in calling some material or evaluation 'qualitative' (or quantitative) is that the unhelpful split between words and numbers is perpetuated. Many research and evaluation reports are actually being written up under the headings of 'quantitative' and 'qualitative', rather than under headings that relate to the questions and their content in relation to *the purposes* of the study. In practice, all verbal or observed matters could be counted and all numbers could be 'unpacked' to show how they are really composed of a lot of words. It is perhaps more important to ask, 'What are the questions for *this* study?'. 'How many' or 'How much' type questions will need numbers as an answer. 'Who', 'which', 'what', 'when', 'why' and 'how' type questions may need words. Features of 'qualitative' methodology include those in the box (Patton, 1989). One of the most powerful achievements of the 'qualitative turn' has been the renewed respect for the facticity of people's experiences (particularly given that they are real in their consequences).

Reference
Patton, Michael Quinn (1989) 'Qualitative Methods in Health Care Evaluation', in *Health Care Evaluation*, Public Health Association of Australia, Canberra.

Quality assurance (QA)/quality control/quality improvement (QI)

Quality control is a process that has been widely used for more than a century in manufacturing industry. It typically involves periodic checking of a product to ensure it conforms to a pre-existing example, benchmark (originally this was literally) or standard. It involves the idea of feedback—theoretically from supervisor to the production worker. *Quality assurance* emerged in the mid-1900s as the analogue for professional and human services where, instead of bosses or inspectors correcting workers' outputs, the professionals examined their own or each other's work (more often the processes), to check that they were 'up to standard'—either via **peer review** or by specially designated peer quality assurance officers, the use of small-scale surveys, formal benchmarking, and so on.

THEMES OF QUALITATIVE INQUIRY

1 *Naturalistic inquiry.* Studying real-world situations as they unfold naturally; non-manipulative, unobtrusive, and non-controlling; openness to whatever emerges—lack of predetermined constraints on outcomes.

2 *Inductive analysis.* Immersion in the details and specifics of the data to discover important categories, dimensions and interrelationships; begin by exploring genuinely open questions rather than testing theoretically derived (deductive) hypotheses.

3 *Holistic perspective.* The whole phenomenon under study is understood as a complex system that is more than the sum of its parts; focus on complex interdependencies not meaningfully reduced to a few discrete variables and linear cause–effect relationships.

4 *Qualitative data.* Detailed, thick description; inquiry in depth; direct quotations capturing people's personal perspectives and experiences.

5 *Personal contact and insight.* The researcher has direct contact with and gets close to the people, situation and phenomenon under study; researcher's personal experiences and insights are an important part of the inquiry and critical to understanding the phenomenon.

6 *Dynamic system.* Attention to process; assumes change is constant and ongoing, whether the focus is on an individual or an entire culture.

7 *Unique case orientation.* Assumes each case is special and unique; the first level of inquiry is being true to, respecting and capturing the details of the individual cases being studied; cross-case analysis follows from and depends on the quality of the individual case studies.

8 *Context sensitivity.* Places findings in a social historical and temporal context; dubious about the possibility or meaningfulness of generalisations across time and space.

9 *Empathetic neutrality.* Complete objectivity is impossible; pure subjectivity undermines credibility. The researcher's passion is understanding the world in all its complexity, not proving something; not advocating; not advancing personal agendas, but understanding. The researcher includes personal experience and empathetic insight as part of the relevant data, while taking a neutral stance towards whatever the specific findings are which may emerge.

10 *Design flexibility.* Open to adapting inquiry as understanding deepens and/or situations change; avoids getting locked into rigid designs that eliminate responsiveness; pursues new paths of discovery as they emerge.

Source: (Patton, Michael Quinn: 1989 *Qualitative Evaluation*, Sage, CA.)

Accreditation and **standards programs** are closely related mechanisms. *Quality improvement* emerged in the 1990s when it was found that quality assurance—if it reached its basic targets—had no internal method for moving beyond the limits of its audit review questions into open inquiry and wider contextual valuation. QI focuses on continuous cycles of improvement, using an **action research** model—for example, the PDCA business cycle (Plan–Do–Check–Act). Like organisational development, even QI is beginning to become excessively proceduralised to the point where it will need a new way of getting 'outside the box' again.

Quality circles

As a contribution to **quality** and **organisational development**, Japanese companies established small voluntary teams of management and workers (usually six to twelve people) who **collaborate** to solve a quality or performance-related problem by the contribution of ideas to assist production, product quality, output and innovation. This approach recognises that shop-floor workers have practical experience and problem-solving capacities if given a rewarding environment in which to contribute them. While the end-purpose of quality circles in industry is to increase profits, everyday evaluators could use quality circles to increase the meeting of human needs. British post-war industrial democracy **action 'learning** circles' developed by Reg Revans have much in common with this idea, and the monthly meetings described in Chapter 4 of this book are a practical example of some of the principles in practice.

There has, however, been a critique of the use of quality circles to defeat union organising by a labour researcher's inside account of Johnson and Johnson's use of quality circles for team development.

References

Hutchins, David C. (1985) *The Quality Circles Handbook,* Pitman, New York.

Grenier, Guillermo (1989) *Inhuman Relations: Quality Circles and Anti-Unionism in American Industry*, Temple University Press, Philadelphia, PA.

Quality of life indicators (QUALYS)

These are intended as ways of escaping from the messy uncertainty of real-life ethical value judgements (e.g. about whether to think that people's lives have different value) into apparently more reassuring 'objective scientific' quantifying ones, which permit—given the rationalistic logic of finite economic resources and infinite medical capacity to prolong life at a cost—judgements regarding whose life is worth saving or prolonging and whose isn't. They attempt to answer the coolly and narrow utilitarian question, 'To whom can we do the most good per unit of resource used?' Efforts to date have been conceptualised in terms of length of life and quality of life—with these two concepts being united in the measure called QUALYS (Quality Adjusted Life Years). At its simplest formulation, this involves saying that if we can do something that gives a person an extra year of healthy life expectancy, that is one QUALY. If we can only offer an extra year of disabled or distressed life, it would be rated as less than one. From then on, the researchers in this area construct classifications of multiple levels of cross-tabulated distress or disability, calculate statistics for each, argue over whether others should have any say in which levels apply to which outcomes of any particular medical interven-tion (doctors? nurses? managers? politicians?), and whether people's valued and unvalued states can be standardised and how the benefits can be costed (direct costs—equipment, staff; indirect costs—lost earning power of caring relatives, etc.). Some urge that there should be participative decision-making, as to date the accountants and economists have dominated the area, and patients, citizens and communities don't usually get much of a look in here. Accountants and economists have not traditionally been noted for their interpretive sensitivity, but then on the other hand doctors and scientists are rarely encour-aged to stop and consider the deeply personal human, moral, ecological or even economic costs of their new technology either. In practice, it has been price, market and health insurance that increasingly have been left to shape who can afford to live and who can't.

Reference
Williams, Alan (1989) *200 Years is Not Enough!* Australian Hospital Association, Canberra.

Quantitative evaluation

Quantitative evaluation is really a term that has gained currency as part of a debate about whether numbers or words are better as sources of meaning when attempting to judge the discrepancy between valued or unvalued descriptions of the world. Quantitative material is assembled to answer questions about 'how many', 'how often' or 'how much' (while **qualitative** material addresses questions like how? why? when? who? where? which? whose? and what? and **appreciative** and **critical** questions ask what would be good or better and what would not—and why). It is important to ask the right questions to get the relevant answers. As noted earlier, describing Beethoven's 5th symphony in C Minor as 22 minutes and nineteen seconds may be the right description if it is being evaluated as a contribution to a carefully timed radio program, but this method leaves something to be desired if it is used as a description in response to the question 'What does it provide of value to the audience?'

Just as all qualitative material *could* be quantified, so all numbers comprise meanings that can be expressed in words. While expressing numbers in words may often increase their meaningfulness, reducing words to numbers seems to reduce complexity and result in more apparent certainty. If we say the service is a seven out of ten, this somehow seems to crystalise matters in a way that makes us more confident of saying, 'Oh, so it is OK then'. If we say we have determined it is a 7.48 compared with another service that is a 7.2, this seems to give a more detailed sense of reassurance. However, when we 'unpack' the wordy rationales, things may seem even more uncertain! Where uncertainty is intolerable, then exact measurement may be sought even if the sacrifice of meaning is great. If there can only be one winner of a race, then it is this context that determines that a photo-finish discrepancy can be detected to hundredths of a second! Or if a local council is near bankruptcy, it may want to count every leaf before declaring it is autumn—and then subcontract the street-sweeping service! It is not surprising that the most avid of quantitative evaluation is to be found in central 'command and control' agencies where budgetary considerations and competing claims for funding are a major concern, or in educational agencies where children must be sorted, graded, rated and ranked to determine place-getters in the life stakes, or in health agencies where the capacity to show the precise cost per output will ensure funding (regardless of broader value questions about the values of such 'performance').

Nevertheless, everyday evaluators may use quantification in sensible ways to try to 'firm up' some daily impressions or to give new leads on hitherto undetected discrepant patterns. For example, the keeping of simple records about numbers of phone calls or emails, volume of demand, amounts of time spent on tasks, and degree of value placed on activities or services by consumers has time-honoured value. Such records may not need to be kept continuously. Or time-series samples may suffice so

as not too much time is spent on them. The main thing is to ensure that people together determine their meaning and value. For example, if 30 emails take two hours, is that the best use of your time? For this you will need to return to your more deeply valued purposes and reassess whether they are being met (perhaps in new ways by email) or not (thus needing further research on how to resolve the issue).

Reference
Bryman, Alan (1988) *Quantity and Quality in Social Research*, Unwin Hyman, London.

Realist/realistic evaluation

Not to be confused with Roy Bhaskar's 'critical realism' with its roots in emancipatory critical theory (although Baskar also produced a defence of the potential of rational scientific and philosophical enquiry against both positivist and post-modern challenges)—the realistic approach to evaluation is most strongly associated with Ray Pawson and Nick Tilley's 1997 manifesto and Ray Pawson's later critique of the meta-analyses of the Cochrane collaboration evidence-based empiricism. Embedding ideas about the empirically *real*, the philosophically *realist* and the practically *realistic*, the 1997 book mounted a spirited attack on constructivist evaluation (notably Egon Guba and Yvonna Lincoln's fourth generation evaluation). The up side of this work was its contribution to thinking about how to combine a range of more qualitative literature and evidence about complex 'interventions', particularly policy initiatives by governments, and how to develop, refine and test theories about how, for whom and in what contexts policies and programs might be effective.

Unfortunately the realistic polemic also rests on quoting constructivism's claims somewhat out of context just as Ray Pawson and Nick Tilley seem to have laid themselves open to the same form of narrow quotation, for example about their seeking the elimination of constructivism from Eliot Stern's *Evaluation* journal (or claiming Norman Blaikie as a 'closet realist' when I personally learned a great deal about interpretivist, inductivist theory-building from Norman Blaikie!) This rather spoils their otherwise embracing of constructivist insights about the wisdom of their 'subjects' (although they *are* 'subjects' as the researcher sits firmly at the top of the evaluation division of labour hierarchy, including on top of policy-makers and practitioners as well). In this way of seeing, subjects only know what they've received, practitioners only know what they've done, and only evaluation researchers know why. But are professional researchers the only theorists, while everyone else only has 'ideas' that are grist to the researcher's mill? Isn't there any big picture thinking and theorising going on among 'subjects'? Could researchers' 'ideas' instead be grist for the theories of critical inquirers (i.e. those ultimately intended to benefit from the evaluand by it being of value to them) or even to those trying to assist them? Aren't there any up close and personal policy-makers interested in theory that helps people? Or small picture literal thinking researchers struggling to develop theory? Pawson and Tilley's own favoured inquiry preferences mean their key questions start from the hypothetico-deductive causal explanation experimental observational part of the research cycle (p. 220), and asking for example who knows what? and who to ask? rather than also-important driving questions from any other part (e.g. for who?/for what?)

In a way realistic evaluation is an elaborated and sophisticated restatement of **program theory** evaluation and the testing of **program logic**, acknowledging but perhaps greatly underplaying how that theory is developed from the lived experience of those with whom the dreaded constructivists may be much more comfortably at home. But between theory-laden inductive observation and theory-driven deduction-testing there is still a critical gap in the research cycle about how or why new theory comes into abductive being. In the absence of this missing and philosophically idealist link, evaluation can usually not do a lot more other than after-the-event auditing and before-the-next-events tinkering within the terms of the dominant theory or logic. But as 'piecemeal social reform' is what Pawson and Tilley claim to aspire to (p. xiv), perhaps that does not seem to be such a problem.

References
Bhaskar, R.A. (1975), *A Realist Theory of Science*, London, Verso.
Pawson, R. (2006) *Evidence-Based Policy: A Realist Perspective*, Sage, London.
Pawson, R. and Tilley, N. (1997) *Realistic Evaluation*, Sage, London.

Reflexive evaluation

This systemic thinking term means that, whether **self-evaluation** or **group self-evaluation**, **action research** or **organisational development**, the evaluation is able to refer back to its own grounds for knowing, and in this way can be change orientated. The important meaning of this term is that we are not only being *reflective* about what we are observing and experiencing (looking at ourselves in a mirror is a useful metaphor), but also that this feedback effort will assist us to *act back on ourselves* (and our world) in ways that change both ourselves and what is around us. In this way, there is more likely to be a closing of the gap between what we do and what we intended to do, or between what we *say* we do and what we *actually* do.

References
Freire, Paulo (1972a) *Cultural Action for Freedom*, Penguin, Harmondsworth.

Freire, Paulo (1972b) *Pedagogy of the Oppressed*, Penguin, Harmondsworth.

Responsive evaluation

Developed particularly in the evaluation context by Robert Stake, this also was a systemic thinking reaction to the dominance of the laboratory science-based experimental approach. He saw it is as based on what people do naturally when they evaluate—that is, they observe, evaluate and respond to the valuation. He advocated steps to bolster reliability of observation and opinion-gathering without sacrificing relevance. His view was that the tradeoff of some measurement precision was compensated for by the increase in meaning and usefulness of the findings. An earlier version of this was called the Countenance Model. Like all early systems thinking, this has received renewed attention as the need for change has become more of an imperative.

References
Greene, Jennifer and Abema, Tineke (eds) (2001) 'Responsive Evaluation', special edition of *New Directions for Evaluation*, no. 92, pp. 1–105.

Stake, Robert (1975) *Evaluating the Arts in Education: A Responsive Approach*, Charles Merrill, Columbus, OH.

Wadsworth, Yoland (2001) 'Becoming Responsive—and Some Consequences for Evaluation as Dialogue Across Distance', in J. Greene, and Tineke Abema (eds), special edition of *New Directions for Evaluation*, no. 92, pp. 45–58.

Scenarios, foresight

A scenario is a detailed description of a possible service or program, projected into the future. It can be an optimistic, negative or most-likely projection, depending on the factors used to generate it. It can be a most helpful way of describing the 'template descriptions in our heads' by allowing them to unfold unencumbered by reality. Nevertheless, they are usually an attempt to be foresightful about the systemic unfolding of already-existing factors. Thus they are of most value in helping to guide future actions when creative visions are firmly grounded in understanding the 'rich thick' world as it is now. In this way, scenarios can have a better chance of coming to fruition without sacrificing the ideals that have emerged from the same realities. Like **search conferences**, **brainstorming** and **Delphis**, a scenario can be of use at the point in an evaluation research cycle when creativity and imagination are needed to leap from reflection on observation to planning implementation (or 'real-isation') in action.

References
Ackoff, Russ (1970) *A Concept of Corporate Planning*, Wiley-Interscience, New York.

Ramos, Jose (2002) 'Action Research as Foresight Methodology', *Journal of Futures Studies*, vol. 7, no. 1, pp. 1–24.

Search conferences

A search conference is future-orientated like a **Delphi**, **scenario**, **brainstorming** or nominal group technique; however, unlike a **Delphi**, it is face to face and participative. Developed by Fred and Merrilyn Emery in the late 1960s, it is typically held over two to three days, often in a remote residential setting, and for around fifteen to twenty people. It requires a facilitator skilled in large-group processes, and enables sharing of values and different viewpoints and searching for common ground.

References
Emery, Fred and Emery, Merrilyn (1976) *A Choice of Futures*, Martinus-Nijhoff, Leiden.

Emery, Merrilyn (1976) *Searching: for New Directions—in New Ways—for New Times*, Centre for Continuing Education, ANU, Canberra.

Self-evaluation

The whole of this *Everyday Evaluation on the Run* book is essentially about the process of self-evaluation—that process of thinking about what we are doing, why we are doing it, and what is its value, whether in comparison to things already designated 'of value' or 'not of value', or in prospectively reviewing what might be of more value for the future. To call it 'self'-evaluation is to imply that we can engage in this critical inquiring process within ourselves as individuals; however, this is not the same as thinking we are necessarily being individualistic about this. What we are doing, even in the apparent privacy of our own minds, is inevitably socially contextualised, socially constructed and socially systemic. All the ways in which we think and feel are derived from verbal or non-verbal forms of communication or 'languaging' with the outer worlds of people and things, whereby the meanings of experiences are socially coconstructed, learned, affirmed, challenged or modified. Even the most introspective and self-contained self-evaluator 'touches base' in this social sense—whether with friends, peers, fellow workers or critical reference group members—to share observations and reflections, calibrate, critique or check that we are on the right track *or* to resist this. The growth in self-evaluation reflects the realisation that it has strengths which can address the limitations of 'external' evaluation (just as internal evaluation has flaws addressed by interaction with external or other viewpoints), as explored in Chapter 2. Self-evaluation is also potentially **reflexive** self-managing or autopoetic. *See also* **Group self-evaluation**.

Reference

Brinkerhoff, Robert O. (1983) *Self-evaluation: A Key to Effective Social Programs*, Phillip Institute of Technology, Bundoora, Vic.

Service agreements (or funding and service agreements)

Service (and funding) agreements are tools of *audit review*, which these days evaluate against **outcomes**. Service agreements state what a funder will fund and what a funded organisation will do, generally for a period of a year, in relation to objectives or goals (although program agreements may be over three or even five years). Sets of **performance indicators** are generated so that a detailed contract can be operationally specified in terms of performance or impact or outcome targets. An assumption underpins service agreements that achievement of performance this year will be a condition for seeking continued funding for the next year. This supplies a rough outline of an action–feedback–planning evaluation cycle (though often missing time spent in deeper reflection on the meaning and relevance of wider contexts). Service agreements make several further important assumptions: that objectives or goals are for desirable states of affairs; that the performance indicators, if met, will mean the activities have been carried out and the goals will also have been met; and that if goals are met then outcomes will also be achieved. Each of these logically sequential assumptions—which together comprise the program's logic model or 'theory of change'—can only be tested by moving from an internally referential audit review approach ('Did we do what we said we'd do?') to an *open inquiry* approach that 'joins up the cycle' by re-touching base with the end-beneficiaries' experience ('Were the outcomes still of benefit for them?'). As there is no provision for this in most service agreements, organisations often find that service agreements lose their critical edge after two or three years without a means of re-touching base with community needs to regenerate visions for improvement. The more funding and service agreements are used only for reporting and accountability (for justificatory reasons), the less risk will be taken in proposing innovative indicators or targets. Some service agreements are becoming more sophisticated and focusing on areas that will change, although services need to move to an open inquiry approach to learn what to change and how. Others are using **narrative evaluation** to provide more holistic 'performance stories' of what has actually happened and to what effect.

Reference

Community Services Victoria (1990) *Framework for Service Agreements: A Coordinated Approach*, Government of Victoria, Melbourne.

Skill review/skill audit

These techniques enable a kind of 'census' to be done, usually by a central authority such as an employer or a trade union, to ascertain the current skills range and levels of skill proficiency in the industry or enterprise. The census may be of a population sample in order to establish a profile of an industry or enterprise, or it may be of individuals in order to establish personal plans. There are two kinds of evaluation associated with these. First there is the valuation of the different tasks and skills needed to accomplish the tasks that go to make up the job positions. Second, there is the evaluation of the industries and workers using this skill profile to ascertain whether change has occurred or the training program has been effective. In the first census stage, the process uses more of an open inquiry approach, while the second stage uses more of an audit review approach. In skill reviews, it is critical both *who* decides both what is done and how it is valued. Two examples, each using different techniques for determining both what is done and the relative values of the components, are CODAP (Comprehensive Occupational Data Analysis Programs)—which leaves the decisions largely in the hands of the researchers—and DACUM (Design and Curriculum)—which builds in decision-making by those who do the work and who are seen as best understanding the skills they need and use.

References

Byrne, Ann (1989) 'Skills Reviews', *Labour Resourcer*, no. 6, pp. 20–2.

Kokkinos, Anna (1989) 'Gender Bias in Job Evaluation Schemes', *Labour Resourcer*, no. 5, pp. 11–14.

Social impact assessment

Conventionally, this is an attempt at before-the-event prediction of what effects an event or service might have on various groups or populations—taking into account the bigger picture, just as environmental impact assessments do for natural habitats and flora and fauna populations. Generally, they try to identify longer term results or effects (rather than immediate outcomes). They might use resident consultation methods or stakeholder scenario groups. They typically examine alternatives, various future projections, and who will lose and who will gain. They are mostly carried out by external evaluators, but increasingly utilise **democratic** and **participatory** approaches.

Reference

Meidinger, E. and Schadiberg, A. (1980) 'Social Impact Assessment as Evaluation Research', *Evaluation Review*, vol. 4, no. 4, pp. 507–35.

Stakeholder evaluation

Stakeholder evaluation draws on the assumptions that all those with an interest in the evaluation will, if involved, be more likely to contribute vital knowledge to it, learn from it, make sure it can get done, draw conclusions together from it, and then make decisions to plan and implement it or otherwise act on the results. In this way, it draws on similar assumptions to **client-centred**, **collaborative**, **participatory** and **democratic** evaluation. These assumptions can hold up provided there is enough sharing of the relevant data, observations, experiences and dialogue about it to establish common ground. The less common ground is achieved, the more risk there is that the negotiations at the point of taking action might get into trouble or 'paper over' important differences. Categories of stakeholders are generally described in terms of their relationship to a program rather than their relationship to the evaluation, and the evaluation is more often of a program rather than at the service level (and hence of most interest to managers and policy-makers). Stakeholders may be, for example:

- community or consumers (clients, citizen organisations, service-users, students, parents, self-help groups, local civic bodies, service clubs, etc.) who comprise the primary stakeowners
- policy-makers (parliamentarians, government officers, funding bodies, etc.)
- program managers (at the national, state or local level)
- service practitioners (service providers, professionals, non-professional staff)
- larger audiences or the general public.

As noted before, the greatest strength of attempts like stakeholder evaluation is that they are **utilisation focused**. Their deepest potential flaw can be when the common ground is inadequate and the separate value-interests lead to it falling apart or glossing over real differences that mean the evaluation is not heeded. From both an evaluation and a social justice point of view, the greatest risk of all is when the common ground does not centre on stakeowners'—or critical reference groups'—needs and interests: those who the evaluand is intended to benefit.

References

Bryk, A. (ed.) (1983) *Stakeholder-based Evaluation*, Jossey-Bass, San Francisco.

Lawrence, John E.S. (1989) 'Engaging Recipients in Development Evaluation: The "Stakeholder" approach', *Evaluation Review*, vol. 13, no. 3, pp. 243–56.

Standards programs

(*See also* **Accreditation**)

Standards programs often develop in the first place after years of open inquiry have yielded more and more refined understandings about what is of merit or worth. They can be rather overwhelmingly comprehensive, and comprise reams and reams of detailed questions in sections and sub-sections relating to objectives and aims or activities (see the community health example accompanying **accreditation**.) The answers to the questions indicate that the practices are or are not meeting (pre-valued) standards. Standards programs generally comprise the use of benchmark standard manuals, an on-site study visit for a few days by a team that possibly includes some outside peers, a written report, and the award of a certificate of accreditation that typically might last for three years. These programs are most effective when dealing with services or activities that are relatively unchanging or stable, and where there is enough homogeneity to allow generalised descriptions of 'what ought to be'. CHASP in community health, and **PASSING** in the disability area, are good examples. In their early days, they generally did not contain inbuilt mechanisms for changing or improving items, but most have since added open inquiry questions as part of the exercise, or this is built into a one-, two- or three-yearly cycle of reviewing particular items designated for compliance or improvement.

The major problems (besides those inherent in **peer review** evaluations conducted without the presence of independent end-users among the reviewers) are that, like all audit review approaches, there is the risk of ossification of items and the difficulty of altering expected practices once they are set in people's minds, or where the conventions become routine and the rationales are forgotten so that it becomes a ritual for its own sake. They may be good conventions, but without regular open inquiry-type evaluation that can admit new evidence or information about changed contexts or perceptions, we won't know for sure. Their greatest value is, however, to make intentions explicit, identifiable and accountable. They often rely on statistical measures, but not necessarily so. Both CHASP and **PASSING** have non-quantitative questions, and in the case of CHASP, the quantification of ratings is not extensive. Listed in the references below are the program standards for evaluation *per se*.

References

Commonwealth State Working Party on Nursing Home Standards (1987) *Living in a Nursing Home: Outcome Standards for Australian Nursing Homes*, AGPS, Canberra.

Community Services Victoria (1989) *Standards for Residential Services*, Office of Intellectual Disability Services, Melbourne.

Department of Health (1989) *Sexual Assault Services Standards Manual*, NSW Department of Health, Sydney.

Fry, Denise and King, Lesley (1985) *A Manual of Standards for Community Health*, AGPS, Canberra.

Sanders, James R. with the Joint Committee on Standards for Educational Evaluation (1994) *The Program Evaluation Standards: How to Assess Evaluations of Educational Programs*, 2nd ed., Sage, Newbury Park, CA.

Scriven, Michael (1981) *The Logic of Evaluation*, Edgepress, Inverness, CA, pp. 105–13.

Victorian Accident Rehabilitation Council (VARC) (1989) *Standards for Providers of Occupational Rehabilitation Under Workcare* (VARC), Melbourne.

Strengths-based evaluation

(*See* **Appreciative inquiry**)

Summative evaluation

This is Michael Scriven's term to describe evaluation that is done periodically (or at 'ends' of periods of time or cycles of development of a service program or activity), usually for management purposes of making decisions about the funding, refunding, completion, continuation, etc. of that service, program or activity. Scriven gets impatient with people if they point out that, in a continuous cycle, summative purposes might also be seen as formative in the context of the *next* phase of that continuous cycle (and that **formative evaluation** might even be seen as consisting of lots and lots of micro summative evaluations—and summative evaluations as made up of lots of formative ones!).

Nevertheless, the point may usefully be made that Scriven never intended the interpretation that has been so widely made of his two terms as being *forms* of evaluation. To meet his original purpose for coining the terms, we should not use them as terms describing kinds of evaluation but rather as terms describing two of the possible *purposes* of evaluation—namely, for improvement purposes (formative), and for reporting and decision-making purposes (summative). This book has used the terms *open inquiry* and *audit review* to try to refer to the purposes of evaluation as for improvement (inquiry) and checking (audit), while noting that *both* these kinds of evaluation might be drawn on for *both* reporting and accountability purposes in a way comparable to Scriven's original intentions—and *both* for continuous improvement. That is, inquiry and audit approaches might both be used during both formative and summative purposes, despite a preponderance of audit review in summative evaluation for accountability and open inquiry in formative evaluation for continuous improvement. It may be that this curious preponderance has more to say about the typical 'reach' of inquiry preferences for central planners compared with those of 'up close and personal' service-users and practitioners on the ground (see Yoland Wadsworth, *Building in Research and Evaluation: Human Inquiry for Living Systems*, 2010). A 'whole-cycle' collaborative living systems epistemology closes the gaps between these bifurcations (see Chapter 3).

Reference

Scriven, Michael (1981) 'Summative Teacher Evaluation', in J. Millman (ed.), *Handbook of Teacher Evaluation*, Sage, Beverly Hills, CA.

Systems analysis, systems theory

A systems approach to evaluation has in the past typically utilised a more linear boxes-and-arrows and machine metaphor drawn from manufacturing industry (as illustrated).

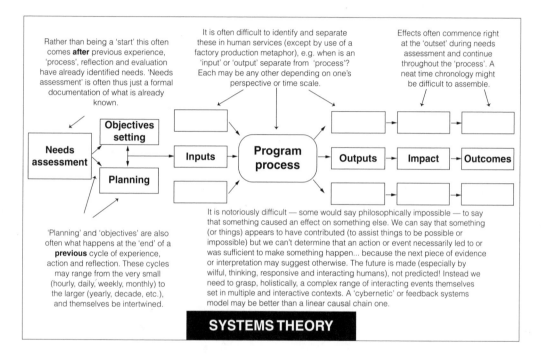

The attraction of this continues to lie in its apparent neatness, and in the plausibility of its logical and sequential chronology. It seems like what we *should* have done! And often it is—particularly with the commencement of new projects that have a start and a finish, although even these always have pre-existing histories and will go on to have 'futures' in some shape or form. However, for most of the time we are 'in process'—or in a process of perpetual incremental development. 'Starts' and 'finishes' may be imposed arbitrarily, such as according to calendar or financial years, yet *in practice* all the components of the systems model are coexisting. That is, we are more or less all constantly observing action, assessing needs, constantly forming and reforming values, purposes and intentions, constantly reflecting and deciding on then planning new actions, constantly trying new things and constantly assessing effects. As suggested throughout this book, these constant feedback loops operate on a very small scale right through to a very large scale, with small loops 'nesting' within larger ones, which in turn 'nest' within even larger ones.

Perhaps a better metaphor is that of a developing 'living' organism, where the inter-action with multiple environments and contexts and history means that our activities or services grow (or atrophy) through constant feedback loops. A more dynamic approach—for example, to the evaluation of this book project—would have seen much more scope for change and adjustment to the agreed 'inputs, process and outputs' in the light of engaging with the critical reference groups in the field (for example, to timelines, to extend the project over a longer period of time, to enable reworking of content, more contemplation, feedback, honing of concepts, etc.). Thus, where creativity, change and improvement are characteristic of the service or program, then a systems-based evaluation may feel somewhat mechanistic, constraining and even distorting.

Other and more recent formulations of systems theory and analysis have concentrated on 'soft systems', cybernetic or organic ecological metaphors and the matching human cognitive and social co-constructions of these. Reflecting these insights, some have preferred the use of the word 'systemic' as an adjective to describe the 'fifth discipline' of management of complex human endeavours rather than 'a' system as a stand-alone noun (Flood, 1999; Senge, 1990). I myself have used the term 'systemicity' as an attempt to acknowledge the apparent 'structural form' of repeated and reliable process at the same time as the necessity for dynamic movement (See Chapter 2 of *Building in Research and Evaluation: Human Inquiry for Living Systems*).

References

Flood, Robert L. (1999) *Rethinking the Fifth Discipline: Learning Within the Unknowable*, Routledge, London.

Hawe, Penelope, Degeling, Deirdre and Hall, Jane (1990) *Evaluating Health Promotion: A Health Worker's Guide*, Maclennan and Petty, Sydney.

Rossi, P.H., Freeman, H.E. and Wright, J.R. (1979) *Evaluation: A Systematic Approach*, Sage, Beverly Hills, CA.

Senge, Peter (1990) *The Fifth Discipline: The Art and Practice of the Learning Organization*, Doubleday Currency, New York.

Wadsworth, Y. (2008a) 'Is it safe to talk about systems again yet? Self organising processes for complex living systems and the dynamics of human inquiry; *Systemic Practice and Action Research*, Springer, NY, vol. 21, no. 2, pp. 153–70.

Wadsworth, Y. (2010) *Building in Research and Evaluation: Human Inquiry for Living Systems*, Action Research Press, Hawthorn, and Allen & Unwin, Sydney.

Theory of change (program logic, logical frameworks/logframe)

Over the past few years, *program logic* (also sometimes called *program theory*) has become a preoccupation of most human services programs' and funders' evaluation accountability requirements. In a nutshell, these are the *logical rationales* we give for what we are doing. It is how we *think* the program works or should work, not how the program may *actually work* or have worked, or how others perceive it working. Later we look for signs (using indicators) to see whether we got this logic right. But it is very helpful to be aware of what we are *trying* to achieve and *why*—particularly what you *expect* to see in your theory-driven 'experiment' in order to notice or know if you *are* seeing it (or aren't). The question '*Why are we doing this?*' is useful to keep checking back on whether you are 'holding your course' for what you purposefully intended for your client groups or community. While you may need to change your purposes, actions and their underlying theory in future, when you're in the *action* part of the action research cycle, you *do* need to be trying to actually do what you intended to do as a result of your last cycle of evaluative research. Otherwise, you will not be able to learn from your practice.

The use of the word 'program' means it is usually asking for a 'tree-and-branch' (or hierarchy) of logical inferences, assumptions or theories that underpin *a whole program* of sub-programs, where each is in turn made up of clusters of micro actions, activities, projects or processes. You can apply it to every element of this 'tree'.

Historically, the current program logic/program theory focus is coming after an era of preoccupation with tree-and-branch hierarchies that have established mission, goals, objectives and aims. Program logic/program theory goes back a step to spell out the theoretical inferences or assumptions about *why* we would have that mission and those goals, objectives and aims, and choose the inputs, actions, activities, projects or processes to achieve them.

In turn, historically the goals-and-aims focus (plan) came after the needs assessment (observe, reflect) era that led us to form those theories, goals and plans in the first place.

In terms of the familiar action research cycle, program logic/program theory therefore spells out what observing and reflecting concluded or 'discovered' (or 'found out', generated or constructed) that led to planning the new action.

A program theory and the program logic it contains constitute an 'if this, then that' kind of causal thinking, and represent our theory of how change takes place—or should or will take place. That is, 'if we do x, then y will result', and 'the reason we are doing x is because of *abc*', and '*abc* happen because of *opq*', and so on.

Some users of program logic take the next step to say, 'and we will know x is taking place because we will observe there is no *abc*, or the *opq* has changed into whatever was wanted instead …', and have included constructing *indicators* that will show logical anticipated signs of the desired changes as evidence of impacts or outcomes of the inputs and processes resulting from the theorised planning.

There are various critiques of program logic/program theory, one important issue being the observed potential for simplistic inferences of linear causality—for example, 'this leads to that'—when for the most part we are dealing (particularly in human services and community health) with much more complex, cybernetic (feedback based) and changing causation—for example, 'this and this and this lead to that, which in turn causes this and that, and this event affects the original "cause"'. To add further complexity, the multiple changes—even to the original 'causes' themselves—may only be observable if one is deeply engaged 'up close and personally' in the middle of such highly symbolic interactions in order to be able to make attributions about effects. At a distance, we may see broad changes, but were they due to what we did? Or were they due to other things, perhaps that we can't even know about? This is called the risk of false attribution or false inference. Ahhh! The joys of evaluative research within complex changing living systems contexts! (Enter **narrative**, as an evaluation method that can manage this kind of complexity without sacrificing meaning.) But we *can and do* more or less effectively do this kind of theorising, and get by well enough, and ideally use of program logic should just help spell out some of these assumptions in a way that is not so detailed as to become unmanageable.

The simplest sequence of program logic questions might be something like:
- What is the/a single main assumption lying behind this program? ('If we … then …')
- List more assumptions about what you believe will or should happen as a result of this program/intervention. ('If we … then …')

Take each of these and ask: 'What would count as a sign or evidence that my logic was right—or wrong?' ('If they were … or we observed … then that would mean …' or 'If they weren't …or we observed … then that would mean instead …')

You can try to specify this further stipulating, for example, 'In one year (or three years), I would expect to see … Or I would expect they could/or will be ….'

You can even try to put a percentage on how many will change in the theorised direction, or a measured extent to which change will have taken place.

A simple sequence to develop new program theory questions might be something like:
- What could or should we be doing? And why do you think this?
- Now take time to brainstorm some alternatives (this is tricky, as usually you would ask the client group or community to do this, so be aware you are second-guessing here).
- For each suggestion, say why you think it would be better.

Utilisation-focused evaluation

This is a fancy title for saying that this kind of evaluation derives its questions from, and orients its answers towards, those who will make use of the evaluation. While all evaluation arguably does this implicitly or covertly (and either well or badly), this approach does so explicitly and overtly, and finds it is then more likely to do its job well. Michael Patton wrote a whole book on it that has been so useful worldwide it has recently gone into its fourth edition. Where users of evaluation conflict in terms of values or goals, Patton discusses conflict-resolution techniques like **multi-attribute utility measurement, decision-theoretic** approaches, **fuzzy set theory** and **goal-free evaluation**. Utilisation-focused evaluation, like **participatory** and **democratic evaluation**, involves users and decision-makers in question-framing (to ensure relevance), methods-selection, design decisions, possibly data-collection, but certainly data analysis and interpretation. Keeping the whole exercise closely in touch with users' needs ensures it is **responsive**. A social constructivist and justice perspective would add critical reference groups as the most important participants or 'utilisatory agents'.

Reference
Patton, Michael (1997) *Utilization-Focused Evaluation: The New Century Text*, 3rd ed., Sage, Thousand Oaks, CA.

Well-formed outcome model

This is a goal-setting tool used by the psychotherapeutic communication science called **Neuro Linguistic Programming**. Drawing on the idea that you need to be more aware of where you value going before you can get there, it assists people to state their desired positive outcomes in advance in terms of:

- positive solutions, rather than staying only with a focus on the problem
- identifying images of what the outcome will look like in behavioural terms
- working out what effects it will have on others around oneself—for example, family, work group, and so on.

Its strength is that it helps make explicit one's valued intentions. Drawbacks are that you may not need (or be able) to know precisely where you are going before you begin to try to get there. That is, life objectives may be more emergent and contingent on other events and feedback than the method might allow.

Reference
Mitchell, Frank (1987) 'Behind the Painted Smile', *Nursing Times*, vol. 83, no. 33, pp. 34–5.

World café

This is a process in which a large group potentially has the intimacy and engagement of small-group dialogue without losing the broader understandings and connections possible in the full group. It evolved in 1995 out of conversations and experimentation by consultants Juanita Brown and David Isaacs with their friend Nancy Margulies. There are seven design principles: (1) set the context; (2) create hospitable space; (3) explore questions that matter; (4) encourage everyone's contribution; (5) connect diverse perspectives; (6) listen together and notice patterns; and (7) share collective discoveries.

A World Café is set up with space for groups of four to eight people to sit in circles, preferably around circular tables (although you can do it with no tables at all) and ideally— to enhance a relaxed and creative frame of mind—with flowers, candles, paper tablecloth and marking pens (for writing notes on the tablecloth). A host welcomes participants and tells (or reminds) them of the topic, which is a question worth asking or statement worth exploring and something of real interest to those present. He or she explains that, after a set period of time (usually 30 to 45 minutes), people will be asked to bring the conversation to a close and move to a new table. The host encourages them to record on the tablecloth (or note paper) any ideas, insights or questions that emerge.

When the first round is up, the host rings a bell and asks each table to decide who will be its host. That person will remain at the table for the whole session. Then the rest of the people move to different tables. When everyone is seated in their new places, then the home table host welcomes the new people and shares with them the key ideas and questions that emerged from their table's earlier discussion. Then the others share what occurred at their original tables.

At the end of the second round, the presiding host asks everyone to return to their home tables to compare notes with their original companions. At the end of this third round, most people in the room will have heard the ideas generated by all the others in the café. In longer cafés, people can just keep moving from table to table.

The method is not completely systematic, and cannot be used as a quantitative survey. Its value is to allow more insights to emerge and be shared than is possible in normal life—and to do so in an interesting and pleasurable way. It is easily dismissed as 'just impressionistic'; however, as a method of sharing observations and experiences and reflecting on them, it can catalyse further action by those who have learned from the experience. It does not itself organise the next step to calculating implications for action (remaining more like a crucible for others to do this), although if table companions form ongoing groups, it could. The other drawback is its fleeting nature, so participants have not necessarily formed a group that could take forward the insights (which may get lost, abstracted or otherwise dismissed). On the other hand, they may fuel later action in surprising, untraceable and unpredictable ways.

References

Brown, Juanita, Isaacs, David and the World Cafe Community, (2005) *The World Cafe: Shaping Our Futures Through Conversations That Matter*, Berrett-Koehler, San Francisco.

The official World Cafe website: <www.theworldcafe.com>.

Zero-based budgeting (ZBB)

Developed as a sequel to **Management by Objectives** (which was in turn a sequel to **program budgeting**), this technique tried to overcome the drawbacks of agencies simply resubmitting the same old budgets each year (plus increments for growth) to funding bodies who just checked that the cost amounts were similar to the previous year's and then rubber-stamped them (I'm simplifying here!). Instead, agencies were asked every year to start with a clean slate and show every item requiring funding, plus their rationale (related to agency purposes or objectives), and build up a 'new' budget with complete new justifications for each item. Like all rationalistic techniques, the novelty (and value) of 'problematising' everything wears off unless the technique is used sparingly, and people will default to 'business as usual'.

Reference

Parliament of the Commonwealth of Australia (1979) *Through a Glass Darkly: Evaluation in Australian Health and Welfare Services*, vol. 1, AGPS, Canberra, pp. 44–5.

FURTHER USEFUL READING

A voluminous literature has grown in evaluation accompanying 30 years of professionalisation of the field. Little guides and manuals produced by government departments, often for particular service programs from the 1980s, have largely given way to three forms of literature.

First and most recently, a number of sometimes elaborate 'evaluation frameworks' have been produced by external consultants as well as internal evaluation units (e.g. UNICEF's is at <www.unicef.org/evaluation/files/RBM_Guide_20September2003.pdf>. The World Bank's advice is at <www.worldbank.org/ieg/ecd/better_government.html>.)

Second, there are several still-existing small guides by people who are 'having to do some evaluation', maybe as a small or one-off activity—a need that has been embraced by the internet, including by some public-spirited consultants who have placed collections of short definitions of various methods on their home pages (see list below).

Third, there is a proliferation of relatively dense (for everyday evaluators on the run!) academic textbooks and journals, most of which have been written more for professional and managerial evaluators. Of these, only a small literature has been produced (following the initial publishing of this book) with more of an 'everyday' applied perspective (e.g. for the developed nations, such as Haillie Preskill's work in the United States, and for developing nations, such as Daniel Selener's in Ecuador).

Very few books map all the methods and approaches so that the interrelationships can be seen between this often rather bewildering array (e.g. Wadsworth 2010), or give guidance about the differing settings or purposes that might call forth one method rather than another—for example, quantitative outcome evaluation or narrative evaluation. Many texts still opt for just one approach in the belief that it is the only or best approach—

for example, all those that start off with the statement 'To do an evaluation you must firstly have clear measurable objectives . . .'! There are some excellent journals—such as *Evaluation*, produced by Sage out of Tavistock in London; the *American Journal of Evaluation*, Jossey-Bass's *New Directions for Evaluation*; and the *Evaluation Journal of Australasia* (which is a particularly high-quality periodical packed with news, reviews and short technical notes on a range of methods and approaches, and well-subscribed internationally).

For this brief bibliography, I have thus chosen a small number of accessible resources that cover a range of methods in a range of health, education and community services settings. Some small guides may now only be available through individual organisations or skulking at the back of small library collections in services or departments, but which foreshadowed the significant changes at the paradigm level towards more holistic epistemologies that emerged over the past decade (e.g. Wadsworth 2008b, 2010). I have also added some website examples that may be fairly stable, demonstrating an array of methods. In addition, I have retained a small number of classic textbooks that are more accessible as well as being theoretically sound and practice-informed.

REFERENCES FOR THIS INTRODUCTION

Russ-Eft, Darlene and Hallie Preskill (2009) *Evaluation in Organizations: A Systematic Approach to Enhancing Learning, Performance, and Change*, 2nd ed., Basic Books, New York.

Selener, Daniel, with Purdy, Christopher and Zapata, Gabriela (1996) *Documenting, Evaluating and Learning from Our Development Projects: A Systematization Workbook*, IIRR, New York.

Wadsworth, Y. (2008b) 'Systemic Human Relations in Dynamic Equilibrium', *Systemic Practice and Action Research*, vol. 21, no. 1, pp. 15–34.

Wadsworth, Y. (2010) Chapter 3, *Building in Research and Evaluation: Human Inquiry for Living Systems*, Action Research Press, Hawthorn, and Allen & Unwin, Sydney.

SMALL GUIDES AND ARTICLES

Barton, J. et al. (2009) 'Action Research: Its Foundations in Open Systems Thinking and Relationship to the Scientific Method', *Systemic Practice and Action Research*, 22, pp. 475–88.

British Journal of Social Work (1987) vol. 17.
- The whole volume of this early and influential journal issue was devoted to evaluation, and contains several good articles including those by Stuart Rees and Eric Sainsbury; Sonya Hunt (pp. 661–7), in which she raises some fundamental questions about how 'outcomes' are better understood as value-driven decisions and not as matters of 'scientific' judgement, and concludes that judging value requires us to ask 'Whose perspective?' and 'For whose benefit?'; and by Bob Holman (pp. 669–83), in which he

makes a powerful argument for the investigated doing the investigating and involving the poor in research into the conditions of their own poverty—defining the issues to be researched, deciding on how it is researched, and participating in both collecting the material and the interpretation of findings. It uses five case research projects as illustrations.

Education Department of Victoria (1985) *Destination: Decisions—Decision-making Strategies for School Communities,* Curriculum Branch, Education Department of Victoria, Melbourne.
*   Extremely readable collection of techniques and models including action research, advocate teams, brainstorming, Commission of Inquiry, consensus 1–3–6, content analysis, critical path, Delphi, force-field analysis, goal-free evaluation, interviews, nominal group technique, observation, the possible school, questionnaires, scenario, a second opinion, fishbowl, transactional evaluation, trial by jury.

Guthrie, Hugh et al. (1985) *Making Changes: Evaluation and Validation of TAFE Programs,* TAFE National Centre for Research and Development, Adelaide.
*   This is a set of 21 generally applicable discussion papers, including definitions of evaluation, issues and problems, techniques, critical assessment of various evaluation methods, etc. The cartoon below is from one of these papers.

Guthrie, Hugh et al.: 1985

McDermott, Fiona and Pyett, Priscilla (1990) *The Meaning of Treatment: An Evaluation Handbook for Alcohol and other Drug Treatment Agencies,* University of Melbourne, Melbourne.
*   An interpretive explication approach that concentrates less on identifying the worth/merit of, and more on practitioners' understanding their actions in relation to, planned activities.

Reeve, Pat et al. (1987) *Lessons from Victoria's School Improvement Plan for the Practice of Self Evaluation,* SIP Clearinghouse, Victorian Education Department, Melbourne.

- This short and readable booklet describes the practical steps and tasks involved in implementing the government mandated program of school self-evaluation, focusing on the education needs of students while firmly in the context of a 'school community' comprising students, teachers, parents, administrators and a school council.

Wilson, Gai (1989) *Self-evaluation Kit*, Victorian Association of Citizens' Advice Bureaus, Melbourne.

- A simple and accessible guidebook with exercise sheets and questions. The cartoons below are taken from the Kit.

SOME WEBSITES

Evaluation Methods and Tools for the Voluntary Sector from a UK philanthropic called the Evaluation Trust: <www.evaluationtrust.org/tools/introduction>.

Long lists of management methods for valuation, etc.: <www.valuebasedmanagement.net/index.html>.

Paul Bullen's Management Alternatives for Human Services: <www.mapl.com.au/evaluation/eval2.htm>.

143 methods!: <http://en.wikipedia.org/wiki/Category:Evaluation_methods>.

Carter McNamara's methods, adapted from his *Field Guide to Nonprofit Program Design, Marketing and Evaluation* (itself a well-known resource in the 1970s, now in its fourth edition): <http://managementhelp.org/evaluatn/fnl_eval.htm>.

Gene Shackman, an applied sociologist's methods home page: <http://gsociology.icaap.org/methods/>.

And for a final bit of informative fun, check the list down the left-hand side of the site!: <www.businessballs.com/trainingprogramevaluation.htm>.

Wilson, Gai: 1989

BOOKS

Brinkerhoff, Robert O. et al. (1983) *Program Evaluation: A Practitioner's Guide for Trainers and Educators*, Kluwer-Nijhoff, The Hague.
*   This is an epic 'package' of several volumes—a sourcebook of guidelines, questions and resources, a casebook of 12 real cases of evaluation, and a design manual of directions, worksheets, examples, checklists. It commences with the 'open-inquiry' directive:

If it works . . .
Notice and nurture.
If it doesn't work . . .
Notice and change. (1983: i)

Brown, Lynton (1988) *Group Self-Evaluation: Learning for Improvement*, School Improvement Plan Secretariat, Victorian Ministry of Education, Melbourne.
*   This remains one of the most detailed, sophisticated and readable accounts and definitions of group self-evaluation, enabling conditions, practicalities, etc. Lynton was part of the highly influential Deakin University School of Education action research group. Highly recommended.

Fetterman, D., Kaftarian, S. and Wandersman, A. (1996) *Empowerment Evaluation: Knowledge and Tools for Self-Assessment and Accountability*, Sage, Thousand Oaks, CA.
*   This is a comprehensive set of case stories and theory pieces for those using more participatory and action-oriented approaches to evaluation—particularly in areas of social justice and disadvantage, such as human services. It has been followed by a practice-based book—*Foundations of Empowerment Evaluation* (Sage, 2000)— and a more philosophical text—*Empowerment Evaluation Principles in Practice* (Guilford Press, 2004).

Feuerstein, Marie-Therese (1986) *Partners in Evaluation: Evaluating Development and Community Programs with Participants*, Macmillan, London.
*   This is a particularly comprehensive but highly accessible text which, while oriented to developing countries, has a lot to say to any audience. Its Freirean approach is applied to some more conventional survey and quasi-experimental techniques, and makes it an excellent primer on these.

Guba, Egon G. and Lincoln, Yvonna S. (1989) *Fourth Generation Evaluation*, Sage, Newbury Park, CA.
*   This was a path-breaking text on new paradigm science as it applied to evaluation. Having rejected their own term 'naturalistic' as less useful than the term 'constructivist', Guba and Lincoln make a compelling case for replacing old-paradigm positivist science with a constructivist methodology. First-generation evaluation measured variables; second-generation evaluation was objectives-based; third-generation evaluation was decision

and judgement oriented; fourth-generation evaluation is value driven and collaborative. It is a rather dense and hard work to read, but it represents a significant step forward.

Some of us subsequently made a case for a fifth generation of evaluation, which was internal evaluation (Ernie House) or based on the self-organising properties of living systems using 'full cycle' evaluative research from inductive, to new theory-building, to field-based experimental, and passing through all the 'generations' of evaluation as process moments (Wadsworth 2010).

Hamilton, David et al. (eds) (1977) *Beyond The Numbers Game*, Macmillan, London.

- This is a textbook of classic readings in educational evaluation arranged around the objectives versus alternative approaches debate. It includes articles by most of the major thinkers—for example, Tyler, Glaser, Scriven, Stenhouse, Eisner, Stake, Parlett and Hamilton, Barry McDonald and Rob Walker, and Ernest House.

House, Ernest R. (1977) *The Logic of Evaluative Argument*, Centre for the Study of Evaluation, University of California, Los Angeles.

- A useful book out of the CSE stable, this one illuminated the view that evaluation consists of the act of persuasion on the basis of arguments about evidence—plausibility and credibility rather than Cartesian certainty. House grounds his logic in the perceptions of the evaluation's 'audience'. Nevertheless, like most other evaluation textbooks, it is not light reading over a coffee break! More head-down-in-a-quiet-library.

Kemmis, Stephen and McTaggart, Robin (eds) (1988) *The Action Research Planner*, 3rd ed., Deakin University, Melbourne.

- The 1982 version of this was a more popularised 44 page format, while this is 154 pages of more detail. Pages 22–25 of the third edition contain an excellent short description of seventeen key points of definition. An important piece of reading.

Patton, Michael Quinn (1986) *Utilization-Focused Evaluation*, 2nd ed., Sage, Beverly Hills, CA (1st ed. 1978, 2nd ed. 1986, 3rd ed. 1997, 4th ed. 2008).

- This review that follows applies to the classic second edition which is smaller and more accessible, but possibly still beyond some everyday evaluators—hence the detailed review. The subsequent third and fourth editions are spectacularly expanded revisions, with some considering the fourth edition to be the single most comprehensive evaluation text in the world. The fourth edition gives greater emphasis to mixed methods; analyses the pluses and minuses of the increased emphasis on accountability and performance measurement in government at all levels, details the explosion of international evaluation and provides a full chapter detailing numerous evaluation methods.

Michael Patton has had an illustrious career as practitioner, theorist, profession leader and best-selling author. He is from Saint Paul, Minnesota in the United States and has a creative and metaphoric turn of speech that makes his books a pleasure to read. His books are packed with more advanced material largely consistent with the approach of *Everyday Evaluation on the Run*.

This was the first of four books. It starts with an account of the history of evaluation research as emerging from science offering to come to the rescue of policy-makers and government-funders, particularly when post-war human service expansion collided with late 1970s economic rationalism. It goes on to describe the political process of deciding on focus and content of evaluation by identifying and organising specific relevant decision-makers and information-users around a user focus. Design, techniques and impact then follow (Chapters 1–3). He argues also for the value of evolutionary and incremental evaluation (for the reduction of uncertainty), which enables increased confidence and a speeding up of change. There is a humorous but important treatment of goals-clarification as a game.

There are also discussions of Delphi, multi-attribute utility measurement, decision-theoretic approach, fuzzy sets theory, social judgement theory, goal-free evaluation (Chapter 6); goal attainment model, systems model, open systems perspective, active-reactive-adaptive decision-making evaluation, and the construction of goals-objectives distinctions (Chapter 7); outcome evaluation versus implementation, effort, process evaluation (Chapter 8); causation and theory construction (Chapter 9); and science and methodology—quantitative/qualitative, objective/subjective, distance/closeness, induction/ deduction, uniformity/diversity, reliability/validity, fixed/dynamic, holistic/componential, traditional science/Verstehen (Chapter 10).

It describes some now folkloric metaphors (the man looking for the key he lost in the nearby 'dark pasture' under the light pole because that was where the light was, and the saying 'when you're up to your ass in alligators, it is difficult to remind yourself that your initial objective was to drain the swamp'). And Nasrudin the Sufi evaluator finds his way through many philosophical thickets!

Patton, Michael Quinn (1980) *Qualitative Evaluation Methods*, Sage, Beverly Hills, CA; (1990) expanded 2nd ed., *Qualitative Evaluation and Research Methods*; and (2001) 3rd ed., *Qualitative Research & Evaluation Methods*, Sage, Newbury Park, CA.

• The second of Patton's four books, this makes detailed arguments for, and suggestions about how to do, non-standardised, open-ended evaluations (while not being a 'how to', recipe book). We have the reappearance of the philosopher Halcolm the Wise (who scores his own place in the Author index!)—for example, point 4 of Halcolm's Evaluation Law states: 'Evaluation is too serious a matter to be done by someone who has never been a client in a program.' [1980: 15]; or, 'Evaluation results always make clear to people what they had really wanted to know but forgot to ask.' (1980: 90). The first four chapters of the book present material that demonstrates effectively not only the differences between quantitative data and qualitative information, but also the reason why quantitative data without qualitative meaningfulness will, in practice, be unusable or damaging. Incompatible models such as systems analysis and behavioural performance evaluation are contrasted with compatible models such as transaction or responsive and illuminative goal-free and decision-making models.

Patton's 'respect for people' approach generally mitigates any tendency to voyeurism, or what Rob Watts has called 'social ventriloquism' ('To ask is a grave responsibility [it] ... is to seek entry into another's world. Therefore ask respectfully and with sincerity' [1980: 254]). References in earlier editions to descriptions of the world being seen as factual or not (rather than that factuality or objectivity being value-guided, relative and mutually subjectively constructed), like many other matters are resolved in the later editions. Patton's key contribution is to insist on the necessity of entering the field, staying in the field and engaging with the field—and of making notes that are detailed and meaning-revealing. The material on wording of questions is excellent (pp. 211–43). His Chapters 8 and 9 on analysis helpfully identify 'relatively useful perspectives'—albeit accurate, valid, reliable, etc. ones—as the end-point (rather than positivist 'Truth'), and give concrete illustrations of how to conceptualise field material.

Patton, Michael Quinn (1987) *Creative Evaluation,* 2nd ed., Sage, Beverly Hills, CA.
- This third Patton volume gives special attention to a range of creative techniques, drawing on arts and media professions, metaphor, etc. It describes what Patton calls an 'eolithic' approach (goals emergent), comparable to an iterative open inquiry approach.

Patton, Michael Quinn (1982) *Practical Evaluation*, Sage, Beverly Hills, CA.
- This book is the last of the quadrella.* Chapter 2 is on definitions and models; there are also chapters on utilisation-focused, collaborative, goals-based (he talks of goal-clarification) and goal-free evaluation, thoughtful questionnaires, thoughtful interviews, and management systems methodologies.

Preskill, Hallie and Catsambas, Tessie Tzavaras (2006) *Reframing Evaluation Through Appreciative Inquiry,* Sage, Newbury Park, CA.
- This book lays out an accessible step-by-step description of what appreciative inquiry means in practice, and ends with a focus on building evaluation capacity and evaluation systems using this approach for organisational learning.

Rees, Stuart and Wallace, A. (1982) *Verdicts on Social Work*, Edward Arnold, London.
- A well-known study of research on the efficacy of social work. It includes a chapter that reviews research done on clients' evaluations of the services they received and their experiences of these, and some very interesting side-by-side comparisons of these with social workers' evaluations of their own casework (there are some illuminating examples of clients and social workers evaluating the same encounters!).

---

* Australian horse-racing slang, meaning one of four (horse races).

Schön, Donald (1983) *The Reflective Practitioner*, Basic Books, New York.

- This hugely influential classic is about how professionals think in practice; however, its observations apply equally to any everyday evaluator, including the professionals' clients! It covers tacit knowing and contrasts reflection-in-action (where cumulative knowledge comes from lengthy modifications by trial and error) with technical rationality (where research is separated from practice, and knowing is separated from doing). It amplifies the nature of positivism, and talks about problem-setting rather than the predetermination of means–ends.

Wadsworth, Yoland (2011) *Do It Yourself Social Research*, 3rd ed., Allen & Unwin, Sydney.

- Beautifully cartooned by Simon Kneebone, this introductory text became Australia's best-selling social research text, and has been in continuous print since it was first published in 1984. It covers where to start; how to manage a research project; methods, techniques and resources; and interpretation, analysis and communication. It is the first volume in the trilogy of which *Everyday Evaluation on the Run* is the second, and *Building in Research and Evaluation: Human Inquiry for Living Systems* is the third and final volume.

Wadsworth, Yoland (2010) *Building in Research and Evaluation: Human Inquiry for Living Systems*, Action Research Press, Hawthorn, and Allen & Unwin, Sydney.

- This is the third volume in the trilogy with *Do It Yourself Social Research* and *Everyday Evaluation on the Run*, and takes up the matter of a 'joined up' cyclic epistemology of retrospective interpretive inductive evaluation, prospective abductive evaluation, and naturalistic (field-based) experimental deductive evaluation. It matches these moments around the cycle with ten sets of questions, methodologies and techniques (Chapter 3). The exploration of 'inquiry preferences' associated with each of these illuminates the different approaches to evaluation in greater detail.